Becoming
INTERCULTURAL

*To my family, the source of my strength
to look far and beyond*

Becoming INTERCULTURAL

An Integrative

Theory

of

Communication

and

Cross-Cultural

Adaptation

YOUNG YUN KIM

Sage Publications, Inc.
International Educational and Professional Publisher
Thousand Oaks ▪ London ▪ New Delhi

For information:

Sage Publications, Inc.
2455 Teller Road
Thousand Oaks, California 91320
E-mail: order@sagepub.com

Sage Publications Ltd.
6 Bonhill Street
London EC2A 4PU
United Kingdom

Sage Publications India Pvt. Ltd.
M-32 Market
Greater Kailash I
New Delhi 110 048 India

Printed in the United States of America

Library of Congress Cataloging-in-Publication Data

Kim, Young Yun.
  Becoming intercultural: An integrative theory of communication and cross-cultural adaptation / by Young Yun Kim.
       p. cm.
Includes bibliographical references and index.
  ISBN 0-8039-4487-X (cloth: alk. paper)
  ISBN 0-8039-4488-8 (pbk.: alk. paper)
  1. Intercultural communication. 2. Assimilation (Sociology).
  3. Emigration and immigration—Psychological aspects. I. Title.
  HM1211 IK55 2000
  303.48′2—dc21   00-010052

01   02   03   04   05   10   9   8   7   6   5   4   3   2   1

Acquiring Editor:	Margaret H. Seawell
Editorial Assistant:	Heidi Van Middlesworth
Production Editor:	Denise Santoyo
Editorial Assistant:	Victoria Cheng
Typesetter/Designer:	Susan Selmer
Indexer:	Teri Greenberg
Cover Designer:	Michelle Lee

Contents

Part III. Elaboration of the Theory

Part IV. The Theory and the Reality

List of Figures and Tables

Figures

Tables

Preface

Millions of people change homes each year, crossing cultural boundaries. Immigrants and refugees resettle in search of new lives, side by side with a variety of temporary sojourners—from artists and construction workers seeking employment overseas to diplomats and journalists on foreign assignments for extended periods. In this increasingly integrated world, cross-cultural adaptation is a central and defining theme: The multicultural world is enhanced by the experiences of sojourners, immigrants, and others who successfully make the transition from one culture to another. What challenges do such individuals undergo? How do they overcome those challenges? What internal changes are these individuals likely to experience over time? Why are some more successful than others in attaining a level of "goodness-of-fit" in a new environment? This book, as well as its predecessor, *Communication and Cross-Cultural Adaptation: An Integrative Theory* (Kim, 1988), addresses these and related issues of cross-cultural adaptation.

One of the motivations behind this work has been a keen recognition that the field of cross-cultural adaptation continues to be in need of interdisciplinary integration. Couched in various terms, such as *acculturation, cross-cultural adjustment, international migration and resettlement,* and *interethnic/intergroup relations,* studies of cross-cultural adaptation have been enriched but fractioned by differing perspectives and foci. Researchers examine segments of the adaptation phenomenon specific to their disciplinary and individual interests pertaining to psychological realms on the one hand and to group and societal realms on the other. What is needed is a continuing effort to see cross-cultural adaptation in its entirety, with all its richness and complexity—a dedicated search for a way to connect various probes of limited conceptual domains with one another and to gain some coherent insight into what it means for an individual to adapt to a new and unfamiliar cultural milieu. Such an effort would counterbalance the atomistic method of compartmentalized specialization and would allow a meaningful cross-pollination across disciplines to occur. Indeed, a number of investigators have argued for conceptualizing certain facets of cross-cultural adaptation as a multivariate phenomenon in which societal, community, interpersonal, and intrapersonal levels of factors operate simultaneously. Some notable integrative efforts have been made by social psychologists such as John W. Berry, Richard Y. Bourhis, Richard Clément, Ronald Taft, and Henri Tajfel. Their works are cited throughout this book.

The present work echoes their concerns and ideas as it moves forward to broaden, refine, and integrate existing models associated with the phenomenon of cross-cultural adaptation. In this volume, I seek to build a system of understanding and explanation at a new height, a "big picture." This theorizing effort takes a communication approach that links the individual and the surrounding environment in a single, large frame. It is predicated on a set of "open-systems" assumptions, based on which cross-cultural adaptation is conceived of as a case of "organized complexity" and the unfolding of the natural human tendency to struggle for internal equilibrium in the face of often adversarial environmental conditions. Conjoining the individual (the central "figure") and the environment (the "ground"), this systems-communication approach is a consolidation of previously separate theoretical foci, such as the person, the group, and the society. This approach moves beyond the linear-reductionist assumption underlying most existing models and treats cross-cultural adaptation as neither a "dependent" variable nor an "independent" variable of something. I view the conventional cause-and-effect notion as at least partly responsible for many fragmented and often conflicting knowledge claims that cannot tell us how a number of different factors act together when exposed to a number of different influences at the same time.

The present approach addresses this problem by elevating the status of cross-cultural adaptation to the level of a universal human phenomenon. The term *cross-cultural adaptation* is treated not as a specific analytic unit (or variable), but as a complex, dynamic, and evolutionary process an individual undergoes vis-à-vis a new and unfamiliar environment—a process that "moves" with a structure of multidimensional and multifaceted forces operating simultaneously and interactively. Although I do not claim that the theory presented in these pages is either complete or final, I offer it as by far the most broad-based theoretical account of cross-cultural adaptation, bringing together many existing conceptions and clarifying the interrelationships among them.

My work on this volume has involved a complete rewrite, refinement, and expansion of my 1988 book. I have streamlined and elaborated the theoretical structure and elements so as to achieve a sharper focus, a greater coherence, and an increased depth in the theory's presentation. I have updated the examination and analysis of the pertinent literature to present a wide range of existing approaches to cross-cultural adaptation, and I have documented an extensive array of relevant research findings in the theorizing process. I have made a special effort to bring this theoretical rendition closer to the everyday realities of people through stories made readily available in popular media sources. The stories, testimonials, and insights offered here add to the accessibility of this book for a broader readership.

I am indebted and thankful to Professor Howard Giles, who originally welcomed my 1988 volume into the Intercommunication Series, which he edited for Multilingual Matters in England. He offered many encouragements and helpful suggestions for that volume as well as for the present one. My own cross-cultural journey in the United States, which began in 1970, when I was a graduate student from South Korea, gives this work a special sense of gratitude and assurance.

Young Yun Kim

Part I

The Background

Introduction

*You could not step twice into the same river; for other waters are
ever flowing on to you.*

Heracleitus, *On the Universe*

We live in a world of "simultaneous events and overall awareness"
(McLuhan, 1962, p. 40). In the dizzying interface of national,
cultural, linguistic, and religious traditions, the once-clear definitions
of "us" and "them" are being blurred. We are challenged to face one
another's numerous cultural differences and search for profound
human similarities. The business-as-usual ways of doing things are
fast losing their relevance. The swirling global transformation spins
off problems that necessitate new learning and new solutions to new
problems, compelling us to stretch the limits of our customary imagi-
nation and creativity.

At the forefront of this new reality are numerous people who are on
the move across cultural boundaries. Think of the millions of immigrants and refugees who change homes each year. Finding themselves
driven by natural disasters, political oppression, economic need, or
hopes of social and economic betterment, people uproot themselves
from their familiar homes and embark on journeys of building new
lives in alien and possibly even hostile milieus. Among the 249 million
Americans recorded by the 1990 census, about 21 million, or 1 in 12,
were foreign-born (Roberts, 1993, p. 64). About one-fourth of the populations of New York, San Francisco, and Los Angeles is made up of

3

immigrants and their children. Some native-born Americans have moved elsewhere: About a third of those who once migrated to the United States have returned to their countries of origin, primarily Canada and Mexico, but also European countries such as the United Kingdom and West Germany. Settlements of immigrants and refugees have been also on the rise in many other Western countries, notably in Australia, Canada, Germany, England, France, and Sweden (see Castles, 1986; Foster & Stockley, 1988; Meznaric, 1984; Penninx, 1986; Phizacklea, 1984; Warren & Kraly, 1985).

In addition, millions of people cross cultural boundaries under various arrangements on a temporary basis. Workers—from artists, musicians, and writers to construction workers and nurses—leave home for employment in other countries. More than 120,000 Peace Corps volunteers have worked in nearly 100 nations since President John F. Kennedy initiated the program in 1960. They have lived and worked in countries in Africa, Latin America, the South Pacific, and Eastern Europe (Bryce, 1995). Also crossing cultures are diplomats and other government agency employees; researchers working in cultures other than their own; professors and students visiting, working, and studying at foreign academic institutions; military personnel on foreign duty; missionaries carrying out their religious service; and journalists on prolonged overseas assignments. Unlike immigrants, most short-term sojourners tend to limit their contacts with their host cultures to peripheral areas—they have crossed cultures primarily to pursue a vocation, obtain a degree, or enhance their prestige in the eyes of the folks at home. Their reasons for sojourning are specific and narrowly defined, requiring less commitment to the host environment (Ady, 1995; Taft, 1977).[1]

Common Experiences of Crossing Cultures

Despite the variations described above, and related circumstantial differences, all individuals crossing cultures face some common challenges as they pioneer lives of uprootedness and gradually establish working relationships with their new milieus. The gap between the familiar and comfortable surroundings of home and the unfamiliarity of the host environment limits their ability to function effectively. Many of the behavioral modes useful in the old setting may prove maladaptive in the new setting. Recognition of verbal and nonverbal codes and interpretation of the hidden assumptions underlying them are likely to be difficult. As Schuetz (1944/1963) notes, "The cultural pattern of the approached group is to the stranger not a shelter but a field of adventure, not a matter of course but a questionable topic of investigation, not an instrument for disentangling problematic situations but a problematic situation itself and one hard to master" (p. 108).

To a degree, the same cross-cultural predicaments are repeated when sojourners return home. A course of readaptation takes place as they find themselves strangers in their home environments. Marcia Miller (1988), an American woman who taught for a year in the isolated town of Daqing in northeast China and later returned to New York, has written about her homecoming experience:

> I felt different in my own home. It all seemed so strange. . . . Walking on Broadway, I thought I was walking through a corridor in an insane asylum. . . . In north China, people stared at me wherever I went. Here, at home, my role was reversed. Now, I was the one who did the staring. . . . I had been isolated in Daqing, but I felt just as isolated here with the additional component of depression. (pp. 13-14)

In a way, individuals crossing cultures can be described as experiencing a degree of existential alertness. Many people struggle to cope with feelings of inadequacy and frustration in their changed environments: Some resist change and fight for their old ways, whereas others desperately try to "go native" and live with an acute sense of failure and despair. The degree to which people undergo such cross-cultural challenges varies widely, depending on their situations involving international migration and their motives for relocating in another culture. Different reasons for crossing cultures accompany different degrees of commitment that individuals feel toward their new environments. Refugees, for instance, typically experience abrupt and involuntary moves. Owing to the sudden nature of their departure from their home countries, most refugees have little chance to prepare themselves for life in their host countries. At least during the initial phase of the change, they tend to suffer from severe psychological dislocation and sense of loss (Chan & Lam, 1987b; David, 1969).

Regardless of resettlement circumstances, all newcomers are compelled to make adjustments in their habitual ways of carrying out their life activities. Those who fail to do so may have to return home prematurely or find themselves staying on yet experiencing emotional and social isolation from the new environment. Most people, however, learn to detect similarities and differences between their new surroundings and their home cultures, and they become increasingly proficient in handling situations they encounter. Each adaptive challenge, in turn, offers them an opportunity to grow beyond the perimeters of the original culture. With physical and psychological distance from familiar milieus, strangers are awakened from their taken-for-granted assumptions with a heightened sense of self. Such adaptive change can be seen in the following excerpts from the diary of Vicki Holmsten (1978), a Peace Corps volunteer. Holmsten graduated from Macalester College in St. Paul, Minnesota, in the spring of 1975. Upon completion of her Peace Corps training, she was assigned with 55 other trainees to teach in secondary schools and universities in Liberia. She was sent to the small town of Foequellie, where for 2 years she taught language arts and some math to elementary and junior high school students. During her stay in Liberia, she kept a diary in which she reflected on her cross-cultural experiences; many of the entries reveal the human adaptability that enabled her to overcome the challenges of cultural differences and intergroup posturing. Holmsten's diary also demonstrates that, after a relatively short period of cross-cultural adaptation, she returned home a changed person.

December 12, 1975—I am visiting the town that I have been assigned to—it's in the bush! A small town called Foequellie, it's about 27 miles and an hour of dirt roads out of Gbarnga, the Bong County capital. Here I am to spend the next two years. To be honest, I have a bad case of culture shock. Not much English spoken in town—the language is Kpelle, the people here mostly of the tribe of the same name. No electricity. Kerosene lamps and battery-run radios seem to be modern touches. The running water is provided by the houseboy who brings the buckets from the well.

December 14, 1975—I am still positive. I want to succeed and will do whatever I can to do my best. This is perhaps the most determined I have ever been. I feel that I am testing myself to the utmost—pushing my limits. Everything is reduced to a matter of survival. Can I do it?

January 5, 1976—Why am I doing this? Why, why, why? We stayed in Monrovia long enough to shop for household necessities, then the members of our group took off for various parts of the country. . . . I move into a house in Foequellie and wait for school to begin. We are objects of great curiosity in the town, and are visited almost constantly during these first few weeks. It is not easy to feel as if we are on permanent display.

February 19, 1976—Rice, rice, rice. If I see another bowl of rice. . . . We eat rice every day. Our houseboy cooks a big pot along with a pot of "soup" to pour over it. More like a stew, soup can be any kind of greens, vegetables, sometimes even peanut paste, cooked with fish or meat, onions, hot peppers, and various flavorings to taste. It's usually quite good, it's just this day-in, day-out routine that is getting to me.

March 17, 1976—When you're sick you want to go home because there's nothing worse than being in a steamy jungle clearing when your entire body is hurting—your head pounding, sweat pouring down, your insides gushing out of both ends until you think there must be nothing left. But still it comes, and you lie there waiting for death or some form of relief from this wretched torture. So you travel to the hospital where you will be shuffled through lines with crying babies, weary-eyed children, and puffy-faced old ladies. Hours of waiting, waiting in lines that couldn't possibly make sense or lead to anything.

April 6, 1976—School is going well. The students are trying hard even though some are far below grade level. No books, no paper, not much of anything. On good days it is challenging, on bad days it is impossible.

May 11, 1976—What is it all for? I don't know. One of my students is dying. Life and death, the essence here. It's getting enough food to keep going and watching people die because there's no way to prevent it. I'm hurting very badly. Am I doing the right thing by being here? I know I'm not doing my best, I'm not even sure what that is anymore.

August 26, 1976—Malaria, slight case of anemia. Don't worry, Mom, I'll be fine. Got all the right medicine, be just like new in no time. No big deal—who, in Liberia, doesn't already suffer both ailments?

October 17, 1976—I think I am only just now coming to terms with Africa. It is a very alive place. Life-giving and deadly at the same time. Life and death all out in the open, nothing muted or subtle. I am excited to be a part of it. I will never be African, but I am a part of it because I am investing myself in the future of the continent. One small part of Africa is mine, I am in one small part African.

January 16, 1977—Eleven months to go. I'm sure now that I can do it. Positive feelings about being here. Good ideas about what to do in my teaching, the ability and self-confidence to implement them that are gradually coming with experience.

March 25, 1977—Today I ate roasted termites. Not bad.

May 17, 1977—I'm sitting under the giant cotton tree. . . . Next door neighbors cooking and hollering at the children. The ladies across the way are closing the house against the coming weather. . . . This is a feeling of fitting in, of belonging to a point in space and time and putting my own marks on it.

> *September 10, 1977*—I'm enjoying life here now. I finally belong, I'm accepted. I am at last Vicki Holmsten to the people of Foequellie, not the "Peace Corps volunteer." It's almost time for me to leave. I'm not sure I really want to.
>
> *September 25, 1977*—When I go to Monrovia, the first stop is always for hamburgers and ice cream. But if I'm there for more than two days, I get really hungry for my accustomed daily bowl of rice, and end up in a chop shop with an enormous serving of rice in front of me.
>
> *December 6, 1977*—I'm sad to be going home but nevertheless feel that the time is ripe. The school had a going away party for me Saturday night. It was absurdly perfect. People all over the house, palm wine, tear-jerking farewell speeches, appropriate exits and entrances at calculated moments. I was presented with a beautiful African country cloth robe—it is probably the most precious thing I will ever own. It's over now, time to pack up and go.

Holmsten's adaptation experience has been shared by many other Peace Corps volunteers who have been changed by their experiences. In presenting some of their stories in her edited book *From the Center of the Earth*, Geraldine Kennedy (1991a) describes the essential change shared by her fellow Peace Corps volunteers:

> We are born at the center of the earth, into the insular and complete given of an infant's domain. All assumptions about who we are and how things work are reflections of the context of family, community, and culture which surround us. Most of the important assumptions are rarely stated and almost never questioned. . . . The returned Volunteers know—in some deep place in their consciousness—that there is another center, another definition of life, another way. Much like immigrants, they live with the complexity and the richness of another vision, and know they will never again see with only one. (pp. 10-11)

Testimonials such as these have been made by countless others around the world. Mostly they have discussed their experiences among their families and friends, but many have also told their stories publicly, in books, newspapers, and magazines. Japanese American Lydia Minatoya, in her book *Talking to High Monks in the Snow* (1992), tells about her visit to her "mother" country of Japan, where she was considered a stranger, an outsider. Leila Philip, who grew up on an apple farm in upstate New York, apprenticed at the pottery workshop of Kazu Nagayoshi in Japan between 1983 and 1985. In her book *The Road Through Miyama* (1989), Philip shares many of the insights she gained from her 2-year sojourn in Japan—insights into cultural differences between Americans and Japanese and into the reverence of the Japanese for uniformity and convention as well as their deep distrust of individuality. Stories such as those related by Minatoya and Philip bear witness to the fact that every traumatic experience changes us. They reveal the remarkable capacity of human beings to face challenges when estranged from home, from the familiar—to repair themselves and, in doing so, transform themselves. In Arthur Koestler's (1967) words: "There is no sharp dividing line between self-repair and self-realization. All creative activity is a kind of do-it-yourself therapy, an attempt to come to terms with traumatising challenges" (p. 177).

Indeed, the process of crossing cultures challenges the very basis of who we are as cultural beings. It offers opportunities for new learning and growth. Being "uprooted" from our home brings us understanding not only of the people and their culture in our new environment, but of ourselves and our home culture. Although the tribulations that can arise from crossing cultures are often staggering, success stories are everywhere. Despite, or rather because of, the hardship and ambivalence we undergo when we cross cultures, we gradually find ourselves uniquely privileged to define ourselves and others anew with clarity and insight that we could not have cultivated without leaving home. Adapting to a new and unfamiliar culture, then, is more than survival. It is a life-changing journey. It is a process of "becoming"—personal reinvention, transformation, growth, reaching out beyond the boundaries of our own existence. The process does not require that we abandon our former personalities and the cultures into which we were born. Rather, it compels us to find ourselves as if for the first time, particularly those "cultural invariants" within us—facets that we hold dear and refuse to compromise (Neumann, 1992). Author Salman Rushdie has reflected on this process of self-discovery as he has experienced it in his own life as an immigrant. First as a Muslim in predominantly Hindu India, next as an Indian migrant to Pakistan, and then as an Indian-Pakistani living in Britain, Rushdie has faced firsthand some drastic and all-encompassing cross-cultural experiences. In *Imaginary Homelands* (1992), Rushdie writes about the tug between the old and new, the familiar comfort of home and the freedom of the unknown:

> Our identity is at once plural and partial. Sometimes we fall between two stools. But however ambiguous and shifting this ground may be, it is not an infertile territory for a writer to occupy. If literature is in part the business of finding new angles at which to enter reality, then once again our distance, our long geographical perspective, may provide us with such angles. (p. 15)

Theorizing About Cross-Cultural Adaptation

Insights such as Rushdie's inform my effort in this volume to theorize about the phenomenon of cross-cultural adaptation. Along with a body of empirical research evidence, such personal and unsolicited insights serve as the grounding for my attempt to offer a systematic and comprehensive theoretical account of cross-cultural adaptation. The theory articulates how resettlers change from being cultural outsiders to increasingly active and effective cultural insiders. It describes what adapting to a new culture entails and what it takes to prevail in that process. The main concern here is not *whether* individuals adapt, but *how* and *why*. It is my aim to discern those consistent patterns that are universally present among varied and unique individual experiences and to organize them into a set of interrelated and generalizable theoretical principles. Guiding this effort are several broad questions:

1. What is the meaning of cross-cultural adaptation? What does it mean to be "successfully adapted" or "poorly adapted"?

2. How do individuals adapt to a new and unfamiliar culture? What are the common adaptive experiences that people share beyond those that are unique to their differing situations and personal idiosyncrasies?

3. What is the common trajectory of the cross-cultural adaptation process that unfolds over time? How does the trajectory begin and move in the direction of intercultural transformation?

4. Why are certain individuals more successful than others in moving along the adaptive trajectory? What internal and external factors help explain their successes or lack thereof?

5. How do individuals change as they undergo a prolonged cross-cultural adaptation process? What kinds of internal transformation commonly take place among those who have undergone extensive cross-cultural experiences?

Even though I address these issues in this volume primarily in the context of immigrants, refugees, and other long-term settlers as well as temporary sojourners, these same issues also apply to individuals who relocate across subcultures within a given society and face significant adaptive pressures from the new subcultural milieu, as well as to those who find themselves confronted with similar adaptive pressures as their own "home" milieus undergo cultural shifts due to rapid changes in ethnic composition.

Existing Approaches to Cross-Cultural Adaptation

The principal cause of stagnation and extinction is over-specialisation.

Arthur Koestler,
The Ghost in the Machine, 1967

Since the beginning of the 20th century, the phenomenon of cross-cultural adaptation has been investigated extensively in the United States, a nation that throughout its history has dealt with a large and continuous influx of immigrants and sojourners. Significant academic attention has also been given to the phenomenon in other countries, including Australia, Canada, England, Germany, Israel, and Sweden (see Abbink, 1984; Berry, U. Kim, Minde, & Mok, 1987; Coleman, 1987; Noels, Pon, & Clément, 1996; Wilpert, 1984). Today, investigators of cross-cultural adaptation must examine a vast array of books and articles to gain a thorough understanding of the field. These works are, however, far from intellectually cohesive. The complex nature of the phenomenon manifests itself in the variety of existing conceptions, making it difficult for individual investigators to gain a clear picture of the body of knowledge accumulated over the decades. Although the field has benefited from rich information and insights, it suffers from increased disconnectedness and confusion as well.

11

This chapter presents an overview of this extensive and complex field and identifies issues that emerge as major hurdles that need to be addressed. A close examination of these issues serves as a rationale for an interdisciplinary integration and the development of a more general theory into which many of the existing conceptions of cross-cultural adaptation can be incorporated.

Macro-Level and Micro-Level Perspectives

Most of the existing conceptions of cross-cultural adaptation can be grouped in two categories: macro-level and micro-level. Macro-level inquiries have traditionally been common among anthropologists, going back more than 50 years. During the 1930s, the Social Science Research Council created a Subcommittee on Acculturation composed of three anthropologists (Redfield, Linton, and Herskovits) and charged the subcommittee with the task of defining the parameters for inquiry into acculturation within the domain of cultural anthropology. Acculturation was formally adopted as a legitimate new area of study dealing with "those phenomena which result when *groups* of individuals have different cultures and come into first-hand contact with subsequent changes in the original pattern of either or both *groups*" (Redfield, Linton, & Herskovits, 1936, p. 149; emphasis added). In this tradition, Spicer (1968) later defined acculturation as "those changes set in motion by the coming together of *societies* with different cultural traditions" (p. 21; emphasis added).

By viewing acculturation primarily as a group phenomenon, anthropological researchers traditionally observed the dynamics of change in "primitive" cultures (e.g., Herskovits, 1947/1966, 1958; Mead, 1964) and the presence of kin, friends, and ethnic community organizations in supporting immigrants' adaptation (e.g., Banton, 1961; Eames & Schwab, 1964; Southall, 1961). Anthropologists have also approached cross-cultural adaptation by examining the "ideal type" of personality or "dominant" values and life patterns of a cultural group, with primary emphasis placed on the internalization of new personality traits or new values by a society as a replacement for those of the original culture. For example, Spindler (1955), in studying the acculturation patterns of Ojibwa and Menomini Native American cultures, focused on the change in the tribes' personality type characteristics as a result of contact with the dominant American culture.

From this study, Spindler concluded that there was a definable "personality type characteristic" of the old culture and that significant breakdown of the "native-oriented personality structure" had occurred in the transitional segments of the tribes (p. 2).

The anthropological emphasis on the acculturative change in cultural personality has not produced a consistent and concrete picture of a new personality. Hsu (1981), an anthropologist, succinctly points out this problem:

> What do we mean when we say of an immigrant, "He is Americanized"? It seems clear that we do not have a precise idea as to what we mean by "Americanization," nor have anthropologists who deal with culture contact and culture change helped in this regard. . . . How can we gauge the extent of acculturation without a precise notion about the culture to which the acculturated have supposedly acculturated themselves? We cannot but agree that the picture is by no means clear. We must develop a more precise idea on the notion of Americanization to answer the question at all. (p. 111)

The expressed difficulty of establishing an "ideal type" in anthropological studies of acculturation is echoed in the empirical data from sociological studies on American value systems. In the area of marriage and family life, for example, considerable variability exists among different subgroups distinct in socioeconomic status, ethnic traditions, religious preferences, and racial ascriptions (e.g., Adams, 1971; Winch & Spanier, 1974). Even when one accepts the general notion that *the* American culture is represented by those who are White, Anglo-Saxon, and Protestant, differences in attitudes and values still exist among different age groups and socioeconomic groups.

Whereas the majority of anthropological studies have observed changes in the target culture as a whole, sociological studies have focused primarily on issues pertaining to "stratification," that is, the hierarchical classification of the members of society based on the unequal distribution of resources, power, and prestige (Parrillo, 1966, p. 80). Many sociological studies have investigated minority-majority relations in which minority groups are structurally integrated into the political, social, and economic systems of the host environment (e.g., Amersfoort, 1972/1984; Marrett & Leggon, 1982; Spiro, 1955, 1987). Like anthropologists, sociologists generally have treated individuals as abstract entities forming social categories, classes, or strata and have focused on such adaptation phenomena as "assimilation" and "marginality" of immigrants or racial hybrids (e.g., Ansari, 1988; Gordon,

1964, 1973, 1981; Schuetz, 1944/1963; Simmel, 1908/1950, 1921, 1955; Stonequist, 1935, 1937, 1964; Wood, 1934). In one edited volume, for example, the contributing authors address the structural assimilation of Japanese Americans as an ethnic group by focusing on the peculiar economic and social success and generational differences among first-, second-, and third-generation groups (Conroy & Miyakawa, 1972). More recently, Anderson and Saenz (1994) investigated the intermarriage of Mexican Americans with Anglos and identified variations in opportunities for contact, levels of Spanish-language maintenance, and socioeconomic mobility.

Relatedly, Glazer and Moynihan (1963, 1975) have analyzed the positions of ethnic groups in the United States in such areas as political salience, religion, community structure, and group identities. In a more comprehensive approach, Blalock (1982) has presented a theory of race and ethnic relations by focusing on social class conflicts, inequities, labor arrangements, power conflicts and minority reactions, competition, discrimination, and segregation. Blalock's approach combined attitudinal factors (such as hostility and intergroup tension) that have been investigated extensively in social psychological studies of prejudice (e.g., Levine & Campbell, 1972) with factors found in macrosocial studies of ethnic group discrimination.[1] Other researchers have conducted ethnographic studies of immigrant communities. Gallo (1974), for example, conducted a participant observation study of the political alienation of Italian Americans from the American political system. Similarly, Gans (1962) applied qualitative, ethnographic methods in his study of the community life patterns of Italian Americans. More recently, ethnographic studies (e.g., Lamphere, 1992) have described institutional barriers and resulting incidents of conflict in the interaction of newcomers with established residents.

Sociological researchers have studied immigrant groups in various societies outside the United States as well. Bharati (1972), for example, investigated demographic patterns, caste and marriage patterns, entrepreneurship, interpersonal relations, interethnic images, and the maintenance of beliefs and religious practices by Asians in East Africa. In Europe, "race" has emerged as a political issue in recent nationalist campaigns, and the sociology of race relations has received increasing academic interest. A body of literature that constitutes a British sociology of immigration has placed central attention on the negative significance attached by the indigenous population to certain migrant groups from former British colonies and their offspring (see Phizacklea, 1984). British scholars have investigated the conflict relationships between classes and races, and the extent to which the colonial "immigrants" are incorporated into the British class structure (e.g., Amersfoort, 1972/ 1984; Krau, 1991; Suárez-Orozco, 1990).

In the macro-level sociological and anthropological studies described above, emphasis has been placed almost exclusively on structural issues involving immigrant groups; few researchers have taken into account the experiences of individuals. Conversely, social psychological studies (examined in the next section) have dealt primarily with the intrapersonal and interpersonal experiences of newcomers in unfamiliar environments. In these micro-level studies, however, important structural conditions of the receiving environment, such as the status of the newcomer's ethnic group and the native members' attitudes toward that group, have not been considered in the examination of the individual's adaptation process. Given the differing foci across social science disciplines, little attention has been paid to the *interface* of macro- and micro-level factors. To the extent that the individual and the environment codefine the adaptation process, we must integrate the two research perspectives in order to explain the adaptation experience of an individual.[2]

Long-Term and Short-Term Adaptation

Among the micro-level cross-cultural adaptation studies of individuals, there is a division between studies of immigrants and refugees living in a new culture more or less permanently and studies of the short-term adaptation of temporary sojourners. These two groups of studies have been carried out largely independent of each other, with few cross-citations. On the one hand, long-term adaptation has been investigated over the past several decades mainly in social psychology and, more recently, in communication. These studies have employed anthropological and sociological concepts such as acculturation, assimilation, and marginality to analyze individual adaptation experiences, along with newer concepts such as "psychological acculturation" (Berry, 1970, 1975, 1980, 1990). In such micro-level analyses, *acculturation* has been commonly defined as "the change in individuals whose primary learning has been in one culture and who take over traits from another culture" (Marden & Meyer, 1968, p. 36). The term *assimilation*, on the other hand, has been used by many to emphasize the process of a more comprehensive change whereby immigrants become "absorbed" into the native population through convergence in cultural values and personal traits as well as economic and occupational "mainstreaming."

For instance, Taft (1957) identified concepts such as attitudes, frames of reference, social motivation, ego involvement, beliefs, reference groups, role expectations, and role behavior as key aspects of immigrants' assimilation in the new culture. Based on these variables, Taft delineated seven stages of assimilation, moving progressively from "cultural learning" to "congruence." Taft conceptualized each of these stages as having two dimensions: internal and external. He further presented a schema in which assimilation is viewed as consisting of four major facets: cultural adjustment, national and ethnic identity, cultural competence, and role acculturation (Taft, 1977). The main premise behind Taft's and various other researchers' long-term adaptation studies is that adaptive change naturally occurs over time in individuals whose primary socialization has been in one culture and who subsequently move to another culture.

The substantial history of academic interest in long-term adaptation of immigrants and ethnic communities has been followed by more recent studies of short-term adaptation. Studies of temporary sojourners began increasing in number during the 1960s, stimulated by the founding of the Peace Corps as well as by the increase in both international student exchange programs and multinational trade during the postwar reconstruction period. Companies found that their overseas operations were being hampered because their employees were not effective in coping with unfamiliar social and business practices. Military personnel and experts engaged in technical assistance experienced similar problems when sent overseas. Accordingly, short-term adaptation studies have been influenced predominantly by practical (and less theoretical) concerns with "easing" individuals' temporary but often bewildering transition into new environments.

Extensive studies in this area have addressed the psychological problems that arise when individuals encounter unfamiliar environmental demands during overseas sojourns (e.g., Ward, Okura, Kennedy, & Kojima, 1998). Many researchers have focused on "culture shock," or the psychological (and sometimes physical) responses of sojourners to an unfamiliar culture. Others have examined factors associated with sojourner effectiveness and adaptive changes over time (e.g., Kealey, 1989; Ruben, 1989; Ruben & Kealey, 1979). Some of the key variables discussed in these studies are related to (a) perception of and attitude toward the host society, (b) satisfaction and psychological adjustment, (c) patterns of interpersonal relationships, and (d) linguistic and other elements of intercultural competence.[3] The concept of culture shock has been extended to include "reentry shock"—that is, the emotional and physiological difficulties an individual may experience on returning home after a sojourn in another culture (e.g., Adler, 1981; Austin, 1983, 1986; Brabant, Palmer, & Gramling, 1990; Brein & David, 1971; Enloe & Lewin, 1987; Gullahorn & Gullahorn, 1963; Hansel, 1993; Martin, 1984; Uehara, 1986; Wilson, 1993).

The apparent divergence between the research foci of long-term and short-term adaptation studies is clearly due to the relative isolation in which such studies have been carried out over the years. This divergence, of course, reflects the fact that the adaptive experiences of long-term and short-term settlers are different in many significant ways. Immigrants who reside in a new culture for a long, indefinite period are likely to be more committed to adapting than are temporary sojourners. Also, hosts may not expect culturally appropriate behavior from short-term sojourners in all situations; mistakes are often forgiven as long as the sojourners appear interested in or respectful of the host culture. Hosts tend to expect greater cultural conformity and proficiency from sojourners staying for longer periods, especially immigrants, and may react negatively when their expectations are not met. When closely examined, however, the two areas of adaptation studies reveal much in common. Regardless of the length of the sojourn, certain experiences of cross-cultural adaptation are shared by everyone involved in a new and unfamiliar milieu. Everyone is challenged by the unfamiliar milieu to engage in at least some degree of new cultural learning and modification in old cultural habits. To the extent that there are commonalities, short-term and long-term adaptation phenomena can be identified in a broader, more parsimonious theory.

Adaptation as Problem and Adaptation as Learning/Growth

In both short- and long-term adaptation studies, the main emphasis has been the problematic nature of cross-cultural experience. Most investigators have tended to view the intercultural experiences of sojourners mainly as undesirable, justifying their studies as scientific efforts to find ways to help ease such predicaments. This problem-based view of cross-cultural adaptation is most apparent in studies of culture shock that focus almost exclusively on individual sojourners' frustration reactions to their new environments (Anderson, 1994) or on the lack of such reactions measured using global psychological indicators such as satisfaction and happiness (Ady, 1995). Because encounters with alien cultural environments present surprises and uncertainties (depending on the severity of cultural dislocation), the idea that entering a new culture is potentially a confusing and disorienting experience has been amply investigated.

Oberg (1960) first defined culture shock as the "anxiety that results from losing all of our familiar signs and symbols of social intercourse" (p. 177). Since then, researchers have employed the concept of culture shock in various ways. Taft (1977), for instance, has identified a number of common reactions to cultural dislocation: (a) "cultural fatigue" as manifested by irritability, insomnia, and other psychosomatic disorders; (b) a sense of loss arising from being uprooted from one's familiar surroundings; (c) rejection by the individual of members of the new society; and (d) a feeling of impotence stemming from being unable to deal with an unfamiliar environment. Bennett (1977) has expanded the meaning of this term and regards it as part of the general "transition shock," a natural consequence of the individual's inability to interact with the new environment effectively. According to Bennett, transition shock occurs when an individual encounters "the loss of a partner in death or divorce; change of life-style related to passages; loss of a familiar frame of reference in an intercultural encounter; or, change of values associated with rapid social innovation" (p. 45). Zaharna (1989) adds to the discussion of culture shock the notion of "self-shock," emphasizing "the double-binding challenge of identity" (p. 501). Zaharna delineates three dimensions of self-shock: (a) loss of communication competence vis-à-vis the self, (b) distorted self-reflections in the responses of others, and (c) the challenge of changing identity-bound behavior.[4]

Concern regarding the problematic nature of cross-cultural adaptation has also been a force behind many long-term adaptation studies of immigrants. Park (1928) and Stonequist (1935, 1937, 1964), for instance, examined the strain of isolation called *marginality*. Similarly, Berry and his associates have emphasized "acculturative stress" in the adaptation process of immigrants (see, e.g., Berry, 1970, 1990; Berry & Annis, 1974; Berry & Sam, 1997; Mishra, Sinha, & Berry, 1996). Many researchers in the fields of psychology and psychiatry have dealt with immigrants' mental health–related issues, looking for clinical implications of the cross-cultural experience and the extent to which the experience challenges the individual's mental health. The central research interest in this approach has involved the assessment of immigrants' mental health status or the presentation of specific clinical cases of mental illness (e.g.,

Dyal & Dyal, 1981; Fabrega, 1969; Kinzie, Tran, Breckenridge, & Bloom, 1980; Williams & Westermeyer, 1986).

From the perspective of "critical" (or "postcolonial") analysts, the challenging nature of cross-cultural adaptation has recently been reinterpreted as a form of "cultural oppression." Critical analysts focus on the fundamental power inequality that exists between the dominant group in a given society and that society's ethnic minorities, and place a spotlight on the politics of identity and the perpetual struggle on the part of nondominant group members as "victims." Based on interviews with 10 Asian Indian immigrant women in the United States, for example, Hegde (1998) characterizes the experiences of these women using terms such as "displacement"; she emphasizes the "struggle" they face in having to deal with the "contradictions" between their internal identity and external "world in which hegemonic structures systematically marginalize certain types of difference" (p. 36).

In sharp contrast to these articulations of the problematic nature of the adaptation process is the work of researchers who emphasize the learning and growth-facilitating nature of the same process. Adler (1972/1987) asserts that the culture-shock experience should be viewed in a broader context of "transition shock," a phenomenon that leads to profound learning, growth, and self-awareness. To Adler, culture shock is not a "disease for which adaptation is the cure, but is at the very heart of the cross-cultural learning experience, self-understanding, and change" (p. 29). Similarly, Ruben (1983) questions the problem-oriented perspective in his discussion of a study of Canadian technical advisers and their spouses on 2-year assignments in Kenya (Ruben & Kealey, 1979). In this study, the intensity and directionality of culture shock was found to be unrelated to patterns of psychological adjustment at the end of the first year in the alien land. Of particular interest is the finding that, in some instances, the magnitude of culture shock was positively related to the individuals' social and professional effectiveness within the new environment. Based on this finding, Ruben (1983) speculates that, rather than impeding adaptation, culture-shock experiences might, in fact, encourage effective adaptation. Adler (1975) echoes this point when he states that culture shock is a transitional learning experience reflecting a "movement from a state of low self- and cultural awareness to a state of high self- and cultural awareness" (p. 15).

Evidence for the learning and growth-facilitating function of culture shock has been indirectly supported by other sojourner studies that have attempted to describe the "stages" of the adaptation process. Oberg (1960, 1979), for instance, describes four stages: (a) a "honeymoon" stage characterized by fascination, elation, and optimism; (b) a stage of hostility and emotionally stereotyped attitudes toward the host society and increased association with fellow sojourners; (c) a recovery stage characterized by increased language knowledge and ability to get around in the new cultural environment; and (d) a final stage in which adjustment is about as complete as possible, anxiety is largely gone, and new customs are accepted and enjoyed. Closely related to efforts to identify adaptation stages has been work aimed at tracing adaptive changes over time. Focusing on the degree of satisfaction in or positive attitude toward the host society as a frequent indicator of adaptation, some investigators have gathered evidence for what is commonly called the "U-curve hypothesis" (e.g., Brein & David, 1971; Church, 1982; Furnham, 1988). According to this hypothesis, sojourners typically begin their cross-cultural adaptation process with optimism and elation in the host culture, followed by a subsequent dip or "trough" in satisfaction and a recovery. The U-curve hypothesis has been further extended to a "W-curve," which adds the reentry (or return-home) phase during which the sojourner once again goes through a similar process (Brein & David, 1971; Gullahorn & Gullahorn, 1963; Trifonovitch, 1977).

Research findings on the U-curve process have been mixed. In a study of groups of Swedes who had returned from sojourns in foreign countries, Torbiorn (1982) found that the subjects' satisfaction levels followed a pattern similar to the U-curve. After the sojourners had spent about 6 months in the host country, their satisfaction was significantly lower than it had been at arrival. Toward the end of that year, their satisfaction slowly started to increase. Other researchers have reported, however, that sojourners do not always begin their lives in new cultural environments with elation and optimism as described by the U-curve. A longitudinal study of psychological and sociocultural adaptation of Japanese students in New Zealand found a more or less linear, progressive process of psychological adaptation—that is, adjustment problems were greatest at the entry point and decreased over time (Ward et al., 1998).[5]

The process of adaptive change has been further investigated in studies of long-term adaptation. In one of the earlier such studies, Nagata (1969) demonstrated a trend toward increasing levels of social and cultural integration of Japanese Americans across three successive generations. Others have documented a "cumulative-progressive" adaptation process that is generally upward moving and linear (e.g., Hurh & K. C. Kim, 1990; Kim, 1976, 1978a, 1978b, 1978c, 1979a, 1980, 1989, 1990; van Oudenhoven & Eisses, 1998).[6] Based on cross-sectional comparisons according to the length of residence, these studies have shown a gradual and incremental trend in psychological and social adaptation.

What needs to be clarified between the problem-oriented and learning/growth-oriented approaches is the fact that all individual experiences of cross-cultural adaptation, long-term or short-term, are both problematic and growth producing. As people experience difficulties in an alien environment, they also acquire new cultural learning and growth. Cross-cultural adaptation is thus a double-edged process, one that is simultaneously troublesome and enriching. Despite, or rather because of, the difficulties crossing cultures entails, people do and must change some of their old ways so as to carry out their daily activities and achieve improved quality of life in the new environment.

Varying Theoretical Accounts and Empirical Assessments

As investigators have searched for generalizable patterns of adaptive change, they have also been concerned with the fact that no two individuals adapt identically. Questions have been raised as to what factors help explain individual differences in adaptation and how we can best assess different levels of individual adaptation. A variety of theoretical models have been proposed to address the issue of differential adaptation. Factors included in these models range widely, from psychological/personality characteristics (e.g., patience, empathy, and flexibility) and communication patterns/skills (e.g., language competence/preference, listening skills, interpersonal relationship development/preference, mass-media behaviors, and job-related technical skills), to demographic characteristics (e.g., age, age at the time of resettlement, socioeconomic status, length of residence, and marital status). For example, Epstein, Botvin, Dusenberry, Diaz, and Kerner (1996) have defined and assessed cross-cultural adaptation narrowly in terms of "linguistic acculturation." Gudykunst and his associates, on the other hand, have focused on two psychological factors, uncertainty reduction and anxiety reduction, as central to explaining individual differences in adaptation (see, e.g., Gao & Gudykunst, 1990; Gudykunst, 1995). Others, such as Coelho (1958), Selltiz, Christ, Havel, and Cook (1963), and Barona and Miller (1994), have focused on the complexity of the perceptions of Americans held by sojourners in the United States.

Hawes and Kealey (1981) have assessed multiple psychological/ behavioral variables, including interpersonal skills, cultural identity, and realistic predeparture expectations, as the best "predictors" of "overseas effectiveness" of temporary sojourners. Still other researchers have focused on patterns of mass-media usage (Kapoor & Williams, 1979; J. Kim, 1980; Stilling, 1997) and on socioeconomic status (Cuéllar & Roberts, 1997).[7]

More broad-based multivariate models have been proposed by investigators who have argued that adaptation rates should be assessed and/or explained based on combinations of psychological, social, demographic, and cultural factors. Weinstock (1964), a sociologist, focused on an "occupational prestige scale" in the country of origin and "the transferability of skills" in explaining differential rates of acculturation in the country where an individual settles. Silvers (1965) added to Weinstock's proposition another variable, the "positive value upon ethnic identity" by members of the host society, seen as contributing to higher rates of acculturation. Others have included an even wider range of factors—from demographic factors (such as age and sex) and psychological factors (such as knowledge of the host language, motivation for adaptation, and positive attitude toward the host society) to factors of social integration (including interpersonal relationships with the natives). Shuval (1963), for example, examined the nature of settlers in Israel in their early phase (first 2 years) by using three key variables: (a) acceptance of certain norms that immigrants perceived as representative of Israel, (b) seeking old-timers (rather than other immigrants) as sources of information and advice, and (c) general attitude toward the host population.

Berry and his associates have also offered comprehensive explanatory systems (see, e.g., Berry, 1975, 1980, 1990; Berry & Annis, 1974; Berry & U. Kim, 1987; Berry & Sam, 1997). In attempting to explain the "acculturative stress" among immigrants in Canada, Berry and U. Kim (1987) identified several groups of factors: (a) the nature of the host society, (b) the type of adapting group, (c) the type of adaptation being experienced (i.e., integration, assimilation, separation, or marginalization), (d) demographic factors, (e) psychological factors, and (f) social characteristics of individual immigrants.[8] Similarly, Hurh and K. C. Kim (1990) have explained the mental health of immigrants (measured by their overall "life satisfaction") in terms of psychological, social, and economic adaptation indicators. Attempting to develop a reliable scale of acculturation (broadly defined as "the process by which an individual becomes socialized into an unfamiliar culture"), Dawson, Crano, and Burgoon (1996) have utilized a wide range of background/

demographic, psychological, and social indicators, from "where raised," "generation," "self-identity," "mother's identity," and "language spoken" to "associate with now," "friends 6-18 years," "TV," and "movies." [9]

Revealed in these existing models is a lack of consensus. Different models are based on different conceptions of what constitutes the domain of cross-cultural adaptation in varying foci and levels of comprehensiveness. Disagreements abound as to whether a given set of factors should be regarded as constituent elements of the phenomenon or as "causal" (or "independent") variables that help explain (and predict) it. Indeed, the problem of varying and divergent conceptions has been repeatedly pointed out as a major impediment to continuing theoretical development in the field (e.g., De Vos, 1990c; Kim, 1988; Padilla, 1980a; Taft, 1986, 1988).

Divergent Value Premises: Assimilationism and Pluralism

Traditionally, studies of cross-cultural adaptation have been largely predicated on the assumption that cross-cultural adaptation is a natural phenomenon and that successful adaptation is a desirable goal. Most theories and empirical studies, of both short- and long-term adaptation, have been framed in such a way that the models and findings would be useful in helping to ease the transition and facilitate individuals' eventual functioning in the new environment. This affirmative view of cross-cultural adaptation reflects the widely accepted "assimilationist" or "melting-pot" social ideology. Originally popularized by Jewish immigrant Israel Zangwill's interpretation of it in his 1908 play *The Melting Pot*, this vision accepts and calls for the convergence of alien cultures into a mainstream cultural tradition and the accompanying fusion of diverse elements into a coherent system of ideas and practices (Postiglione, 1983). Reflecting the melting-pot view, Gordon (1964) broadly conceptualizes assimilation in terms of seven subprocesses: cultural or behavioral, structural, material, identificational, attitude receptional, behavior receptional, and civic.

The assimilationist view and its expectation of cultural convergence, however, has been questioned since the 1970s, when the "new ethnicity" movement began, prompted by the civil rights movement in the United States. In *The Rise of the Unmeltable Ethnics*, published in 1971,

Michael Novak argued against cultural assimilation and advocated equal ethnicity for all. He described the feelings of alienation held by one large ethnic group, Poles, who were drawn to ethnic power movements in the competition for jobs, respect, and attention. In a subsequent article, Novak (1973) contended:

> There is no such thing as *homo Americanus*. There is no single culture here. We do not, in fact, have a culture at all—at least, not a highly developed one, whose symbols, images, and ideals all of us work out of and constantly mind afresh; such "common culture" as even intellectuals have is more an ideal aspired to than a task accomplished. (p. 18)

Social scientists have not been immune to the ideological debates that have taken place for the past several decades. As suggested by the selective ways in which cross-cultural adaptation has been defined and theorized, the trend in the academic discourse has been one toward an increasing "pluralism," emphasizing the importance of ethnicity maintenance (Billig et al., 1988; Diesing, 1991; Thornton, 1996). Teske and Nelson (1974), for instance, suggested a pluralist position when they argued that assimilation is only a special case of changes involved in the acculturation process, and that acculturation should be seen as a bidirectional process that does not require changes in values within the acculturating group. Likewise, Stonequist (1964) viewed the adaptation process as following one of three distinct paths: (a) assimilation into the dominant group, (b) assimilation into the subordinate group, or (c) some form of accommodation and reconciliation of the two societies.

Research along pluralist lines has documented a continued structure of ethnic group characteristics from one generation to another. Glazer and Moynihan (1963) noted in their sociological analysis that ethnicity pervades all spheres of life among ethnic individuals and groups; they concluded, "The point about the melting pot is that it did not happen" (p. 290). Greeley (1974), Parenti (1967), and Wolfinger (1965) all found that "ethnic" Americans possess political orientations different from those of "nonethnic" Americans as shown by respective voting patterns that persist for many generations. Along this line, based on a study of Korean immigrants in Los Angeles, Chang (1972) differentiated the adaptation of three types of groups: a "cultural assimilation group," a "nativistic group," and a "bicultural group."

The pluralist view of cross-cultural adaptation has been further suggested in the work of Berry and his associates (Berry, 1980, 1990;

Berry, U. Kim, & Boski, 1988; Berry & Sam, 1997). In characterizing different "acculturation modes," Berry and his colleagues rely on two key questions concerning the subjective identity orientation: "Are [ethnic] cultural identity and customs of value to be retained?" and "Are positive relations with the larger society of value and to be sought?" By combining the response types (yes, no) to these two questions, Berry and his associates identify four modes of adaptation: "integration" (yes, yes), "assimilation" (no, yes), "separation" (yes, no), and "marginality" (no, no). A modified version of this model has been offered recently by Bourhis, Moiese, Perreault, and Senecal (1997), who replace "marginality" with "anomie" and "individualism." Pluralist models such as these share an emphasis on the significance of an individual's acceptance (or rejection) of the host culture and of his or her own cultural heritage.[10]

What distinguishes these pluralist models from traditional models of cross-cultural adaptation is the implicit assumption that adaptation is a matter of conscious (or unconscious) *choice* on the part of individuals, depending on the sense of group identity they hold in relation to the dominant group in the receiving society. In Berry's and others' conceptions, an individual can make one of several choices: to identify with the mainstream society, to identify with the ethnic group, to identify with both groups, or to identify with neither group. In contrast, the traditional melting-pot view emphasizes that adaptive change in individuals is not a matter of identity choice so much as a matter of necessity if they are to survive and function in an unfamiliar cultural milieu. According to this view, few individuals would choose not to become better able to function in the new environment. That is, most people who live and work in a new environment are assumed to *need* and *want* to be better adapted to the local culture, so as to achieve some level of functional proficiency in their daily lives.

We must be cautious, however, in automatically denying either the assimilative or the pluralist tendencies of minorities. No immigrant or sojourner can completely escape adaptation as long as he or she remains in, and is functionally dependent on, the mainstream culture. Conversely, no immigrant or sojourner can attain complete assimilation, no matter how hard or how long he or she tries. Regardless of differing ideological views, ample evidence exists to demonstrate that individuals of minority cultural backgrounds do undergo adaptive change over time and across generations. Some form of new learning, accommodation, and internalization occurs among those who undergo, willingly or not, some degree of adaptive change over time.

Toward Integration

The field of cross-cultural adaptation remains far from cohesive. The various disciplinary and individual interests and emphases, as well as implicit value assumptions, have contributed to the unwarrantedly dichotomous distinction drawn between macro- and micro-level processes, between short- and long-term adaptation, between stress response and learning, and between assimilation and ethnic plurality. A realistic understanding of cross-cultural adaptation has been further frustrated by narrowly based variable-analytic conceptualizations. Many existing models, indices, and scales offer varied conceptualizations leading to often inconsistent depictions and explanations of cross-cultural adaptation. Proponents of differing perspectives and models often argue past one another, with little mention of the relations that exist between them.

The fragmentation of knowledge regarding cross-cultural adaptation reflects the intense specialization in the field (see Easton, 1991). One way to counter this trend is to work toward a theory within which many of the existing approaches and models can be housed, with their interrelationships clarified. Such a theory needs to transcend particular disciplinary and ideological viewpoints so as to link them into a coherent system of description and explanation—one that offers a fuller and thus more realistic understanding of what happens when someone crosses cultural boundaries.

Part II

The Theory

Organizing Principles

If all of human knowledge, everything that's known, is believed to be an enormous hierarchic structure, then the high country of the mind is found at the uppermost reaches of this structure in the most general, the most abstract considerations of all.

Robert M. Pirsig, *Zen and the Art of Motorcycle Maintenance*, 1974

A theory is a system of interconnected and generalizable statements that, taken together, increase our understanding of a given phenomenon. It does so by highlighting the elements that are deemed essential to the phenomenon and articulating more or less consistent patterns of interrelationships among them. The "goodness" of a theory is to be determined ultimately when isomorphism is established between the logical system and empirical reality. Just as a good map must accurately correspond to the physical territory, a good theoretical account must fit the reality it purports to help understand. The present effort is in concert with this principle. The theory described in this volume seeks to achieve a close correspondence with the reality of cross-cultural adaptation and to offer a broad understanding of what cross-cultural adaptation entails, how it occurs, and what factors make a difference in the process.

Given this general goal, the theory I am proposing represents an attempt to bridge the existing divisions in the field by addressing the following five areas in which the existing approaches have shortcomings, as identified in Chapter 2:

1. In investigating the cross-cultural adaptation of individuals, researchers have paid little attention to macro-level factors such as the cultural and institutional patterns of the host environment and the ethnic community within it, or to micro-level factors such as the backgrounds and psychological characteristics of individuals. Both macro- and micro-level factors need to be taken into account if we are to gain a fuller understanding of the cross-cultural adaptation process.

2. The two traditionally separate areas of investigation of long-term and short-term adaptation need to be integrated. These two areas have common conceptual issues that inform each other.

3. The problematic nature of cross-cultural adaptation must be viewed in the context of new learning and psychological growth. Taking both of these aspects of adaptation together will allow us to arrive at a more balanced and complete interpretation of the experiences of individuals in an unfamiliar environment.

4. Divergent sets of factors have been identified as constituting and/or explaining (influencing) the cross-cultural adaptation processes that individuals go through. Researchers must make an effort to sort and consolidate these factors so as to achieve greater coherence in describing and explaining differing levels or rates of adaptive change in individuals.

5. Two ideological views, assimilationist and pluralist, have influenced the way cross-cultural adaptation has been conceptualized and researched. The traditional assimilationist view has influenced investigators to place their research emphasis on adaptive changes, whereas the pluralist view has tended to tilt attention toward the maintenance of ethnicity and ethnic identity. Both views need to be recognized and incorporated into a clearer and more complete depiction of how individuals change in the process of cross-cultural adaptation.

The Domain and Boundary Conditions

To integrate the various existing approaches to cross-cultural adaptation, we must elevate the status of cross-cultural adaptation to the level of a universal human phenomenon. This requires that we treat the phenomenon as a higher-order concept that is sufficiently broad and flexible that it can bring together many of the existing conceptions and clarify the interrelationships among them.

Key Terms and Definitions

Many different terms have been used to refer to what is essentially the same process undergone by immigrants and sojourners in unfamiliar cultures. As previously noted, the term *assimilation* (or *amalgamation*) has often been employed to emphasize acceptance and internalization of the host culture by the individual. *Acculturation* has been defined as the process by which individuals acquire some (but not all) aspects of the host culture. In a more limited sense, *coping* and *adjustment* have been employed to refer to psychological responses to cross-cultural challenges, whereas *integration* has been defined as social participation in the host environment.[1] The terminological usage becomes more complex when we consider the variations in the operational definitions (or indicators) of these terms. In assessing acculturation levels, for example, many psychological researchers have focused on their respondents' own subjective accounts of feelings of satisfaction or difficulties they have experienced. Others have employed more objective indicators, such as interpersonal relationships with native members of the new environment, language competence as assessed by observers, and other demographic information, such as occupational status, income, and housing.

In the present approach, all of these terms are embraced and incorporated into the more generic and overarching concept of *cross-cultural adaptation*, which is defined as *the dynamic process by which individuals, upon relocating to new, unfamiliar, or changed cultural environments, establish (or reestablish) and maintain relatively stable, reciprocal, and functional relationships with those environments.* This definition follows the open-systems perspective, in which human adaptation is viewed as "the process by which organisms or groups of organisms, through responsive changes in their states, structures, or compositions, maintain homeostasis in and among themselves in the face of both short-term environmental fluctuations and long-term changes in the composition or structure of their environments" (Rappaport, 1971, p. 60). At the core of this view of adaptation is the individual goal of achieving an overall "fit" between the individual and the environment (Mechanic, 1974; Moos, 1976, 1986) to maximize the individual's social life chances. Adaptation, thus, is an activity that is "almost always a compromise, a vector in the internal structure of culture and the external pressure of environment" (Sahlins, 1964, p. 136).

By placing adaptation at the intersection of the person and the environment, the present approach views cross-cultural adaptation essentially as a communication process—the process that makes the intersection possible through the exchange of messages. As such, the present definition underscores *the necessary condition of communication between the individual and the host environment for the occurrence of adaptation.* Cross-cultural adaptation is viewed as occurring as long as the individual remains in interaction with the host environment. The only situation in which adaptation cannot and does not take place, then, would be under the condition of complete insularity from the host environment (Lum, 1991). This interactive, communication-based conception moves beyond the linear-reductionist assumption underlying most existing models and conceptualizes cross-cultural adaptation not as an independent or dependent variable, but as the *totality* of an individual's personal and social experiences vis-à-vis the host environment in and through a complex system of communicative interfaces.

The term *communication* is defined broadly to include all activities of message exchange between an individual and the environment. All actions and events are communicative messages as soon as they are perceived by a human being. Messages are more than explicit, verbal, and intentionally transmitted messages. They include all those implicit, nonverbal, and unintentional messages by which people influence one another. This broad conception echoes Ruben's (1988) view of communication as "a basic life process," as well as the view of Ruesch and Bateson (1951/1968), who regard communication to be the very substance of all things social and who note that "all actions and events have communicative aspects, as soon as they are perceived by a human being. . . . Where the relatedness of entities is considered, we deal with problems of communication" (pp. 5-6). This emphasis on person-environment interface allows an integration of the more conventional disciplinary foci in the field of cross-cultural adaptation—the person, the group, and the society, all of which operate in the communication activities of processing and generating messages. It helps to bring together the studies of subjective responses to crossing cultures (dominant in social psychological research) and the studies of group-level phenomena (dominant in sociology and anthropology), such as structural changes in ethnic/cultural communities in relation to the larger society.

The term *stranger* is employed here to consolidate and represent a wide range of individuals crossing cultures and resettling in alien cultural environments. The term is derived from Simmel's (1921, 1908/1950, 1955) early conception of the stranger as someone possessing the contradictory qualities of being both "near and far":

The unity of nearness and remoteness in every human relation is organized, in the phenomenon of the stranger, in a way which may be most briefly formulated by saying that in the relationship to him, distance means that he, who is also far, is actually near. . . . The stranger . . . is an element of the group itself. His position as a full-fledged member involves being both outside it and confronting it. (Simmel, 1908/1950, p. 402)

Along this line, many others have elaborated on the concept with somewhat differing emphases and interpretations in studying the social behaviors of individuals who are relatively unknown and unfamiliar to the natives of a given society. Wood (1934) and Schuetz (1944/1963), for example, have described the stranger as one who has come into face-to-face contact with a group for the first time and who lacks intersubjective understanding. Herman and Schield (1960) emphasize the stranger's lack of the security and knowledge necessary to understand the new environment fully. All of these characteristics of the stranger are embraced in the present theory, in which the concept serves as an inclusive one, taking in various types of resettlers, from long-term immigrants to short-term sojourners. All strangers begin their cross-cultural journey as "outsiders" and move in the direction of "insiders" as they go through the stresses of daily interactions with the new environment.[2]

The primary focus of the present theory is on those strangers who cross societal boundaries, as well as those who cross subcultural boundaries within societies and face significant adaptive pressures from their new subcultural milieus. Such would be the case, for example, for a Native American leaving an Indian reservation to find employment in a predominantly Anglo urban environment, for a farmer migrating to an industrial work situation in a metropolitan area, and for an individual who decides to leave an urban area, with all its conveniences, to start a quiet new life in a remote rural town. Strangers can also include those who face dramatic demographic changes in their social milieus due to incoming and outgoing population movements. For example, among longtime inner-city residents, Whites may find themselves changing from being members of the majority to rapidly becoming a minority group due to a significant influx of Asian and Hispanic immigrants and a corresponding movement of the White population to the suburbs.

Also included in this conception of strangers are those who return "home" after sojourns in foreign cultures or subcultures. Generally, readapting to one's original culture is a less demanding and prolonged process than is adapting to a foreign culture. Yet, to the extent that the returnee has been changed by the sojourn experience, and to the extent that the original cultural (or subcultural) milieu has changed during the sojourn, the individual must once again go through a process of adaptation.

Boundary Conditions

The three core concepts described above—cross-cultural adaptation, communication, and the stranger—set broad conceptual perimeters for cross-cultural adaptation. As "master concepts" or "superordinate categories" (White, 1976, p. 18), these core concepts bring a variety of cross-cultural adaptation situations into the present theoretical domain delimited only by the following three boundary conditions:

1. The strangers have had a primary socialization in one culture (or subculture) and have moved into a different and unfamiliar culture (or subculture).

2. The strangers are at least minimally dependent on the host environment for meeting their personal and social needs.

3. The strangers are at least minimally engaged in firsthand communication experiences with that environment.

Given these boundary conditions, the present theoretical domain does not directly address the situations of young children who accompany their parents to a new culture (or subculture). Having been brought into the host environment by their parents during the formative years of childhood, or having been born after their parents have relocated, these children's adaptation in the host environment is uniquely influenced by forces of both the receiving culture and the subculture of the parents at home early on in the children's socialization process. A more appropriate approach to understanding the adaptation processes of young children may be found in the psychological and sociolinguistic literature on bilingual and bicultural socialization (e.g., Arnberg, 1987; Durgunoglu & Verhoeven, 1998; Fantini, 1985; Igoa, 1995; Lvovich, 1997). Similarly, the present theoretical domain addresses only indirectly the situation of native members of the host environment who may experience limited adaptive change through contacts with individuals from different cultures or subcultures. The fact that they remain in their own "home territory" keeps the adaptive pressure on them to a minimum.

Assumptions:
Strangers as Open Systems

Given the focus on individual strangers and the broad domain of cross-cultural adaptation, the present theory is predicated on three basic assumptions about the nature of human adaptation grounded in the general systems perspective, particularly of "open systems." Open-systems theory "presents a way of thinking about living things—as living systems—and focuses attention on the fundamental life processes that all living things have in common: the metabolism of matter-energy and the metabolism of information" (Ruben, 1972, p. 120). Each person is seen not as a rather static package of more or less stable internal structure, but as a dynamic and self-reflexive system that observes itself and renews itself as it continuously interacts with the environment (a suprasystem made up of many person-systems).[3]

Assumption 1:
Humans have an innate self-organizing drive and a capacity to adapt to environmental challenges.

Adaptation is a fundamental life goal for all humans, something that all of us share and do naturally and continually as we face challenges from our environment (De Vos, 1993; Slavin & Kriegman, 1992). As Cohen (1968) puts it, "The purpose of life is to maintain life; adaptation is life" (p. 8). The introduction of new experiences, particularly those that are most drastic and disorienting, challenges this basic life force, leading to individuals' struggle to maintain themselves (White, 1976, p. 23). From the first frustrations of early childhood to later changes in life circumstances, people go through a series of graduated "sink-or-swim" situations. For the most part, individuals handle challenges successfully, without the complete breakdown of their internal systems. The natural adaptive drive is reflected in an instinctive curiosity and the power of initiative in pursuit of "efficacy," a sense of being an agent in the living of one's life.

Adaptation as a fundamental life-sustaining and life-enhancing activity of humans is rooted in the self-organizing, self-regulating, and integrative capacity in all living systems, particularly humans (Dobuzinskis, 1987; Jantsch, 1980; Kauffman, 1995). The degree of self-organization a given person achieves reflects the quality of his or her adaptive behavior. As Heath (1965) notes, "Adaptation and self-organization are reciprocal terms" (p. 37). This basic adaptive capacity is a built-in biological feature of the human mind; it is manifested in the plasticity humans enjoy in the form of relative freedom from prepro-grammed reflexive patterns—we can free ourselves from archaic and unnecessary constraints, we can use culture to construct ourselves socially, and we can negotiate the complexities of the human social environment. Humans are "active, if not always successful, strategists of their own development and synthesizers of their own 'inclusive self-interest' in a world of deceptively competing and overlapping interests" (Slavin & Kriegman, 1992, pp. 11-12).

Assumption 2:
Adaptation of an individual to a given cultural environment occurs in and through communication.

Humans continually exchange information with the environment through communication activities. Adaptive change takes place as long as individuals are engaged in a given sociocultural environment through the two basic communication activities, the encoding and decoding of messages (see Figure 3.1). In this interactive process, indi-viduals generate information output to the environment as well as internally generate meaning for information input or feedback. Posi-tive feedback increases the discrepancy between desired and current states, resulting in internal change, whereas negative feedback reduces the discrepancy and serves to maintain stability (Ford & Lerner, 1992; Geyer, 1980).

These input and output messages are not limited to linguistic or other explicitly coded symbols, such as traffic signs, mathematical symbols, and computer languages. The messages also include more spontaneous and expressive nonverbal messages that are often unin-tentional and implied—that is, all actions and events (as well as nonactions and nonevents). As Watzlawick, Beavin, and Jackson (1967) have pointed out, "One cannot not communicate." This means that adaptation occurs in individuals as long as they live in and remain in contact with a given environment. As communicators, individuals "record, monitor, and promote a dialectical process in which the ambig-uous, deception-filled web of competing and overlapping interests in the relational world is continuously negotiated and renegotiated" (Slavin & Kriegman, 1992, p. 12).

✦ **Figure 3.1.** Communication as a Person-Environment Interaction Process

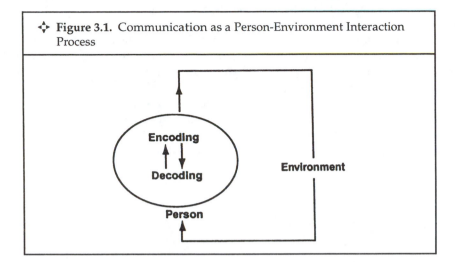

Assumption 3:
Adaptation is a complex and dynamic process that brings about a qualitative transformation of the individual.

Because adaptation occurs through the continual give-and-take of communication, it is a phenomenon of multiple dimensions. In the person-environment communication interface, both internal (intrapersonal) and external (social/environmental) conditions play roles in shaping the course of adaptation. The adaptation process is also multifaceted, in that various parts of the individual's internal system and the environment are engaged simultaneously and interactively, mutually influencing one another. Change in one part has functional consequences in many other parts; change does not take place in a linear, unidirectional manner, as has been commonly assumed in many empirical studies.

In this complex adaptation process, humans strive to meet environmental challenges and to maintain themselves; they are thereby continually organizing and reorganizing their relatively enduring internal conditions. In Heath's (1965) words: "The organization of the self guides adaptation by determining what is perceived, how it is assimilated, and what actions are available for accommodating to the information. Adaptation produces changes in the organization of the self by opening it to a different range of environmental requirements" (p. 37). As such, to adapt means to so regulate behavior as to optimize both the stability of the internal structure and its accommodation to external conditions. Adaptive changes occur in the direction of increase in the complexity of the person's structural and functional characteristics while maintaining the inner coherence and unity of the person as a whole (Ford & Lerner, 1992). In this view, a person is never a finished product; rather, he or she is always in the business of "growing" or "maturing." Although the present is shaped by the past, "personality" changes are possible, as individuals continually refine and revise themselves.

Mechanics of Theorizing

Given the fundamental conditions of human adaptation noted above, the main concern for the present theorizing effort is not *whether* individuals adapt, but *how* and *why* they adapt. Given this focus, the theory seeks to resolve the shortcomings in the existing approaches identified earlier and to present a comprehensive description and explanation of the process through which individual strangers gradually transform themselves from "outsiders" ultimately to fully functioning "insiders."

In this approach, cross-cultural adaptation is conceptualized in terms of the "whole" (the structure of the environment) and of "parts" (the behaviors of the individual). The relationships between and among the elements of the host environment are regarded as setting limits on the adaptive behavior of the stranger. This integrative systems logic counters the atomistic, reductionist strategies of explanation commonly employed in most of the existing theoretical models in the field. Instead, it emphasizes the unitary nature of psychosocial processes and, hence, the mutual interdependence of systems, subsystems, and elements. This approach is guided by the idea that we need to move beyond the practice of applying linear causality between independent and dependent variables. Instead, cross-cultural adaptation is viewed in terms of its multidimensional structure, in which social and individual facets of adaptation are treated as *layers* that interact with one another in complex ways. Instead of assuming simple dichotomies between levels, this approach regards the boundaries that mark these layers and the dynamics of the processes going on within and between them as co-constituting the totality of the cross-cultural adaptation phenomenon.

Accordingly, the micropsychological and macrosocial factors are taken together into a theoretical "fusion" (Berkowitz, 1982, pp. 12-13; Fielding & Fielding, 1986, p. 83). In this way, we can achieve a "vertical integration" by grounding the micro-observational level of adaptation in an intermediate milieu as well as in macro-level factors of the environment, including its historical and cultural context. This systemic approach is consistent with the perspective taken in the philosophical tradition of pragmatism (see Givón, 1989; Joas, 1993; Langsdorf & Smith, 1995), which has variously influenced such methodological schools as "contextualism" and "ecological psychology" as reflected in the works of Ruesch and Bateson (1951/1968) and Watzlawick et al. (1967).

Underlying the present approach is the systems-theoretic view of the fundamental goal of science as "pattern recognizing" (Monge, 1973, 1977, 1990). The theory attempts to identify the patterns that are commonly present among a clearly defined set of varied individual cases and to translate these patterns into a set of *generalizable and interrelated principles* that maximally reflect the evolutionary process of cross-cultural adaptation. It is built on the view that the preeminent scientific activity is model building based on such principles. Models act as maps or templates for complex physical, natural, and social phenomena that can then be observed in the real world. Ideally, these analogues should be isomorphic or homomorphic to the phenomena they are seeking to capture (Berkowitz, 1982, p. 7).

The present methodological stance is not intended to replace previous approaches; rather, it is intended to represent the multidimensional, multifaceted, and dynamic nature of the cross-cultural adaptation phenomenon. It seeks to achieve a balance between the two distinct common goals of social science: *understanding* and *prediction* (Dubin, 1978, pp. 9-10). Understanding is sought through a comprehensive *description* of the nature of cross-cultural adaptation that maximally corresponds to the actual experience of the stranger. At the same time, prediction is sought through a system of *explanation* to be identified based on consistent patterns of the specific aspects of the phenomenon through logically deriving functional linkages between and among theoretical units (factors) that collectively influence the process of cross-cultural adaptation. Understanding as a scientific goal is achieved via a thorough and accurate system of description of how a certain phenomenon being investigated operates in reality, what key elements constitute the phenomenon, and how these elements interact and evolve over time. The degree to which such understanding is provided by a given theory is assessed in terms of its (descriptive) *power*.

On the other hand, prediction means that we can foretell the value of the elements that make up a phenomenon, or that we can anticipate the condition or state of a phenomenon as a whole. In both instances the focus of a predictive theory is on the outcome, and the degree to which a prediction is provided by a given theory is judged in terms of its (predictive) *precision*.

Many of the social psychological models of cross-cultural adaptation have not met both of these theoretical goals. Motivated primarily by practical needs to predict "overseas success," as noted in Chapter 2, researchers have tended to focus on one or more "dependent" variables, such as "satisfaction" and "attitude toward the host society." The primary theoretical benefit of their studies has been a simple inventory of supposed "causes" of the dependent variable(s) under consideration. The "variable-oriented" approaches have given rise to "precision paradox" (Dubin, 1978, pp. 23-26), or the situation in which we can achieve precision in predicting certain outcomes without understanding how the outcomes are produced.

Other conceptualizations of cross-cultural adaptation have contributed mainly to promoting our *understanding* of the phenomenon. Sociological theories such as Gordon's (1981) taxonomic "models of pluralism" and anthropological theories such as Hsu's (1981) ethnographic description of cultural change in Chinese Americans are designed mainly to help us understand the adaptation process. Such theories are not intended for use in making specific predictions as to which factors contribute to what adaptive changes in individual strangers. This kind of theoretical shortcoming represents "power paradox" (Dubin, 1978, pp. 26-30); that is, a given theory can achieve powerful understanding of a social phenomenon without being able to predict how the phenomenon is played out in specific situations.

Given these two theoretical goals, the present theory offers a system of both description (for the goal of understanding) and explanation (for the goal of prediction). First, cross-cultural adaptation is conceived as an evolutionary *process* of change, and the theory describes this process in which individuals transform themselves over time. Second, the theory identifies a multidimensional and interactive *structure* of constituent factors that help explain different levels (or rates) of change that individuals achieve over time. By theorizing the process and its structure, the theory seeks to achieve the goals of understanding and prediction simultaneously.

The procedures for the present theory building are consistent with those commonly practiced in the social sciences (see Blalock,

1969, 1989; Dubin, 1978). First, grounded in the three open-systems assumptions identified earlier, a number of principles pertaining to the cross-cultural adaptation process will be determined in the form of *axioms*. These axioms are generalizable statements that identify patterns of interaction between constructs. Axioms are employed in the present theory as propositions that are assumed to be true and that are untested or untestable. Specifically, an axiom states the relationship between two or more units of a model for the entire range of values over which the units are related by the law. For example, an axiom is stated, "A is positively related to B." Strictly speaking, such an axiom would be untestable because of the impossibility of controlling for all relevant theoretical units.

This theorizing scheme differs somewhat from the one proposed by Blalock (1969, 1989), who argues for the use of axioms to delineate causal relationships between concepts. Blalock's system is principally based on the deductive process of establishing a series of causal axioms (e.g., "A causes B" and "B causes C"). In the present scheme, axioms serve as principles that describe the nature of cross-cultural adaptation and identify reciprocal functional relationships between and among concepts. Instead of linear causal reasoning of "independent" and "dependent" variables, reciprocal associations are emphasized throughout, consistent with the present systems view of cross-cultural adaptation as a dynamic, interactive, and multifaceted/multidimensional phenomenon. The notion that event A helps "cause" event B, but not vice versa, is put aside because it could be equally claimed that B precedes A depending on where one chooses to break the continuity of the process of cross-cultural adaptation.

Once axioms (or principles) are identified, they serve as the basis for explicating *theorems*. Theorems postulate the likelihood that certain change in a theoretical unit (or units) will occur given certain change in a certain other unit (or units): If one axiom relates constructs A and B, and a second C and D, then additional propositions can be deduced connecting these two axioms. Stated in terms of covariations ("The more . . . , the more . . ." or "The more . . . , the less . . ."), these theorems set forth the value of one unit that is positively or negatively associated with a corresponding value of another. Based on one or more of the theorems, specific research *hypotheses* can be explicated for empirical testing. Because hypotheses and theorems (from which hypotheses are derived) are linked to axioms and assumptions as shown in Figure 3.2, empirical validation of hypotheses (and thus theorems) is assumed to indirectly validate (or invalidate) the axioms and, ultimately, the basic assumptions themselves.

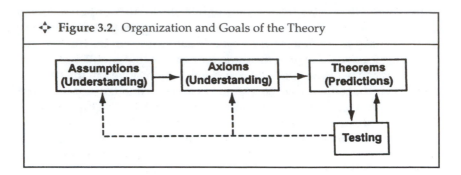

Figure 3.2. Organization and Goals of the Theory

Empirical Grounding

Consistent with the position of Blalock (1969, 1989) and Dubin (1978), the present theory is not restricted by empirical evidence. At the same time, it is thoroughly grounded in and strengthened by the extensive research evidence that has been made available across disciplines. Throughout this presentation, I will continually move back and forth between deductive reasoning and inductive-empirical proofs. The theory informs, as well as is informed by, the research evidence on individual strangers' cross-cultural adaptation that it purports to describe and explain. I will also utilize anecdotal stories and testimonials of immigrants and sojourners available from nontechnical sources such as reports, biographies, letters, diaries, dialogues, commentaries, and a host of other materials in magazines, newspapers, fiction and nonfiction books, radio programs, and television programs. Although these individual stories do not meet the prerequisites of scientific data, they serve as vital sources of insight into the "lived experiences" of cross-cultural adaptation. The practical and participatory experiences expressed in these stories offer credible, sensitive, and close-up witness to what is actually occurring in reality. Verbatim quotations from such stories are woven into the theoretical presentation to serve as realistic illustrations of its abstract concepts.[4]

This theoretical rendition of cross-cultural adaptation begins with a detailed description of cross-cultural adaptation as an evolving *process* of personal transformation that unfolds over time (Chapter 4). This depiction places the locus of cross-cultural adaptation squarely in individual strangers and the psychodynamics they experience as they interact with new milieus. The focus then switches to the *structure* of cross-cultural adaptation as the theory attempts to explain differential rates or degrees of adaptation among different individuals under different circumstances and environments (Chapter 5). Here, dimensions of key factors that interactively work to facilitate or impede the rate of adaptive change in strangers are identified and examined. Each dimension in the adaptation structure is fully elaborated in the subsequent chapters (Chapters 6 through 10), followed by discussion of a number of special considerations for future research that are guided by the present theory (Chapter 11). Included in this discussion are the specific aspects of the cross-cultural adaptation process that have received less than full research attention in the past, issues of maximizing theory-research correspondence in conceptual domains and in linking data, as well as research methods that are epistemologically consistent with the nature of cross-cultural adaptation articulated in the theory. The book ends with a detailed consideration of practical insights generated from and consistent with the present theory. These insights are offered for individual strangers who endeavor to maximize their success in adapting to new cultural environments (Chapter 12).

The Process of
Cross-Cultural Adaptation

No construction without destruction.

Kenneth Burke,
"Communication and the
Human Condition," 1974

By holding his breath, he loses it. By letting it go, he finds it.

Alan Watts,
The Wisdom of Insecurity, 1951

Adaptation is fundamental to human existence. As Ruben (1983) observes: "Living systems act instinctively to meet the challenge or threat and to restore balance and harmony. Once regained, equilibrium continues until the system is controlled by new environmental demands" (p. 137). Every new experience, particularly the drastic and disorienting ones that strangers encounter in a new environment, leads to new learning and growth. The unique character of the human mind, after all, is its plasticity—the capacity to face challenges and, in doing so, acquire new knowledge and insights. Situations of cross-cultural adaptation bring profound and all-encompassing challenges to strangers as they soon realize that many of their previously taken-for-granted assumptions and life tools, such as language and social norms, are no longer relevant or appropriate.

How do strangers undergo such changes in circumstances? What is the nature of their cross-cultural experiences? How do such experiences change them? To address these issues, this chapter will first examine the dynamic relationship between the individual and the culture, the process of becoming a cultural being through childhood socialization. The process of adapting to a new culture will then be described and explained in detail.

Cultural Adaptation

It can be said that all of us are born into this world knowing little of what we need to know to function acceptably in human society. Nor are we born prepared to engage in the various activities out of which our sense of reality and self is constructed. Instead, we *learn* to relate to our social environment and its culture, that is, the universe of information and operative linguistic and nonlinguistic communication rituals that gives coherence, continuity, and distinction to a communal way of life. The familiar culture is the "home world," which is associated closely with the family or "significant others." The unwritten task of every cultural environment is to organize, integrate, and maintain the psychological patterns of the individual primarily in the formative years of childhood. In Sapir's (1937) words, "Every cultural pattern and every single act of social behavior involves communication in either an explicit or implicit sense" (p. 78). Peterson, Jensen, and Rivers (1965) also note the intertwining of culture and communication: "Communication is the carrier of the social process. It is the means man has for organizing, stabilizing, and modifying his social life. . . . The social process depends upon the accumulation and transmission of knowledge. Knowledge in time depends upon communication" (p. 16).

Enculturation, Communication, and Cultural Adaptation

Through continuous interaction with the various aspects of the cultural environment, the individual's internal system undergoes a progression of quantitative and qualitative changes by integrating culturally acceptable concepts, attitudes, and actions; thus the individual becomes fit to live in the company of others. This internalized learning enables the individual to interact easily with others in the cultural community who share similar images of reality and self. The process by which persons adapt to surrounding cultural forces throughout the years of socialization is commonly called *enculturation*. Enculturation shapes a child's "mind" such that it becomes programmed into the group psyche, or what has been referred to as the "collective unconscious" (Jung, 1959; see also Barnlund, 1994). Such psychic programming gives the individual status as a recognizable member of that group and assigns to him or her a role in the life of the community.

The continuous new learning that takes place in the individual occurs in and through *communication*. Communication is the central pillar of all human learning. We learn to speak, listen, read, interpret, and understand verbal and nonverbal messages in such a fashion that we and the others with whom we interact can recognize, accept, and respond to those messages. Once acquired, communicative abilities serve us as an instrumental, interpretive, and expressive means of coming to terms with our environment. As Ruesch and Bateson (1951/1968) note:

> When persons convene, things happen. People have their feelings and their thoughts, and both while they are together and afterwards, they act and react to one another. They themselves perceive their own actions, and other people who are present can likewise observe what takes place. . . . as a result of such experiences people's views of themselves and of each other may be confirmed, altered, or modified. (pp. 5-6)

A crucial feature of the communication-enculturation process is the bonding between and among individuals, which includes the forming of groups (Dance & Larson, 1976). In this process, individuals acquire cultural membership through which they "find a place" in society. In each culture, people are connected to one another through a common system of encoding and decoding. Cultures vary in language and verbal behavior; in manners of movement; in ways of sitting, standing, and gesturing; in postures; in tones of voice and facial expressions; and in ways of handling time, space, and materials. It is culture that programs a society's members to interpret verbal and nonverbal messages by defining what is real, what is true, what is right, what is beautiful, and what is good. Culture conditions individuals to certain patterns of thinking, feeling, and behaving in varied social transactions. Frank (1975) describes the inseparable relationship between culture and communication as "arising from the patterned transactional relations" (p. 128) of all individuals, each of whom carries on continual interactions with other members of the group. All the varied cultural patterns, rituals, institutional practices, and symbols of group life appear as different modes of communication in and through which each person can approach, negotiate, and seek consummation of his or her own personal and social goals.

Implied in this communication-enculturation process is the *adaptation* of human systems. Each individual acquires a personality and a culture in childhood, long before he or she is capable of comprehending either of them (Barnlund, 1994). The enculturation of the human psyche is so pervasive that most behaviors rarely rise to the level of consciousness. Culture is imprinted on each individual as a pattern of perceptions, attitudes, and behaviors that is accepted and expected by others in a given society below the level of conscious thought. We are programmed by culture from the very day we are born and are largely unaware of the hidden cultural programming that shapes many of our mind-sets and behavioral patterns. We hardly realize that our invisible culture influences how we solve problems and how our economic and governmental systems are put together and function. In this process of human development, successive levels and forms of equilibrium are conceived of as levels of cultural adaptation. Conversely, maladaptation reflects a substantial level of mismatch between the individual's internal world and the external milieu (Ford & Lerner, 1992).

Three Facets of Cultural Adaptation

The enculturation process underlies individuals' development of the ability to organize their activities with the activities of others in the society. This ability, often called *communication competence* or *social competence,* comprises the cognitive, affective, and operational (or behavioral) capabilities by which individuals organize themselves in and with their sociocultural milieu (Kim, 1991). Through communication competence, individuals are able to integrate themselves with the reality and the reality with themselves. In Ruben's (1975) words, it is the ability of "sensing, making-sense-of, and acting toward the objects and people in one's milieu. It is the process by which the individual informationally fits himself into (adapts to and adapts) his environment" (pp. 168-169). Communication competence, as such, represents the individual's "mentation" (Dance & Larson, 1976) and operates largely on the unconscious level (Hample, 1987). The general criteria for communication competence can be viewed as two interrelated elements: appropriateness and effectiveness (Spitzberg & Cupach, 1984).

The development of an individual's communication competence within his or her cultural community occurs side by side with the degree of the individual's *functional fitness* and *psychological health*. When an individual's internalized communication symbols and meanings more or less match those of the rest of the given cultural community, that individual's social existence is functionally linked to that community (Dance & Larson, 1976). Through communication, cultural "programs" are incorporated into individuals' nervous systems. The "internalization" of communication is associated with the development of understanding and empathy. It also serves as the foundation for mediation between the person and others in the society, helping the person manage and control life activities with enough autonomy. Through the use of culturally sanctioned communication patterns, people perceive themselves, and are perceived by others, as socially "normal" or "healthy" individuals.

As individuals incorporate cultural patterns into their psyches, they also develop *cultural* (or *ethnic*) *identity*. Through the development of communication competence and functional fitness, the internalized cultural patterns become *the* world, with strong emotional and protective overtones. Individuals develop selfhood that is connected to their culture as they incorporate its worldviews, beliefs, values, norms, and concerted communication practices. Cultural identity, as such, refers to a self-definition and definition by others and serves as a frame of reference or a system of knowledge and meaning—an extended conceptual horizon against which the individual assesses his or her own thoughts and actions. Cultural identity, in turn, helps differentiate one group from other groups (De Vos, 1993; De Vos & Suárez-Orozco, 1990b) and breeds a sense of fellowship, or "we-feeling." Like gender identity, a fully formed cultural identity becomes a *given* or *ascribed* entity rather than an acquired one (Grotevant, 1992, pp. 75-78; Phinney & Rosenthal, 1992, p. 145). It connotes a kind of temporal continuity or common symbolic "tradition" linking group members to a "common future" (Nash, 1989).[1]

Cross-Cultural Adaptation

The development of cultural communication competence, functional fitness, psychological health, and cultural identity is instrumental to an individual's achievement of social efficacy. Each is an internalized cultural imprinting that remains largely unrecognized, unquestioned, and unchallenged—that is, until the person finds him- or herself in a new, unfamiliar, and different cultural milieu. In many ways, entering a new culture means starting an enculturation process all over again. Life in a new culture presents situations that deviate from the familiar and assumed, and the newcomer is faced with things that do not follow his or her unconscious cultural "script." Strangers become more aware of the previously taken-for-granted mental and behavioral habits to which they are accustomed. As Boulding (1956/1977) notes, the human nervous system is structured in such a way that "the patterns that govern behavior and perception come into consciousness only when there is a deviation from the familiar" (p. 13). Strangers do not experience the full impact of such deviation until they have "cut the apron strings" and established themselves as separate from the "culturally fixated existence" (Hall, 1976, p. 225).

In this separation, strangers experience a series of psychological "crises" because they lack a sufficient level of understanding of the symbols and activities of the new world. As Parrillo (1966) explains:

> For the natives . . . every social situation is a coming together not only of roles and identities, but also of shared realities—the intersubjective structure of consciousness. What is taken for granted by the native is problematic for the stranger. In a familiar world, people live through the day by responding to daily routine without questioning or reflection. To strangers, however, every situation is new and is therefore experienced as a crisis. (p. 3)

Indeed, encounters with a new culture bring many surprises, large and small. Some of the surprises may awaken or shake strangers' previously taken-for-granted self-concepts and collective ethnic identity and bring the anxiety of temporary rootlessness. Strangers in a new environment are confronted with situations in which their mental and behavioral habits are called into question, and they are forced to suspend or even abandon their identification with the cultural patterns that have symbolized who they are and what they are. Such inner conflicts, in turn, make individuals susceptible to external influence and compel them to learn the new cultural system. This activity of learning is the very essence of *acculturation* (Shibutani & Kwan, 1965, p. 470) or "resocialization" (Bar-Yosef, 1968), that is, the acquisition of the native cultural practices in wide-ranging areas, particularly in areas of direct relevance to the daily functioning of the strangers—

from attire and food habits to behavioral norms and cultural values. In many ethnically diverse societies, the cultural patterns widely regarded as standard are mainly those of the dominant culture. In the United States, for example, the standard cultural patterns are mainly those of Anglo-Americans. Although acquiring minority cultural patterns is a part of the overall adaptation process of newcomers, the most forceful pressure to conform generally comes from the dominant group.

Adaptation in the new environment is not a process in which new cultural elements are simply added to prior internal conditions. As new learning occurs, *deculturation* (or unlearning) of at least some of the old cultural elements has to occur, in the sense that new responses are adopted in situations that previously would have evoked old ones. The act of acquiring something new is inevitably also the act of "losing" something old, in much the same way as "being someone requires the forfeiture of being someone else" (Thayer, 1975, p. 240). As the interplay of acculturation and deculturation continues, the newcomer undergoes an internal transformation. Of course, a change in basic values is extremely difficult, slow, and rare. Common adaptive changes in strangers take place in more superficial areas, such as overt role behavior. A person can be pressed to conform to requirements in social interactions, but cannot be forced to accept and appreciate the underlying values, even in a "total institution" such as prison (Goffman, 1961). Despite such difficulty, a new culture undoubtedly exerts substantial influence on the psychological and social experiences of strangers. Through group support, institutional legitimation of the new identity, and the presence of new significant others to replace or substitute for the old, strangers adopt the cultural patterns of the host environment. The inevitable uncertainties that confront strangers are susceptible to explicit or subtle conformity pressure from the host environment. The routine operations of the society demand that the strangers conform to ways of thinking and acting that are consistent or compatible with the prevailing cultural practices of the environment. The mainstream language of the host environment is often imposed on the stranger as well.

To the extent that there are discrepancies between the demands of the host environment and the strangers' internal capacity to meet those demands, and as long as there are pressures to conform, the strangers are compelled to learn and make changes in their customary habits. Clearly, individuals need ongoing validation of their "place" in a given environment, and the inability to meet this basic human need can lead to symptoms of mental, emotional, and physical disturbance. Long-term settlers generally have a greater need to conform than do temporary sojourners, but no stranger is completely immune to having to understand, and manage, the various communication patterns operating in the host culture.

The direction of acculturative and deculturative change in strangers is ultimately toward *assimilation,* a state of the highest degree of acculturation into the host milieu and deculturation of the original cultural habits that is theoretically possible. Assimilation is thus an "ideal" state characterized by the maximum possible convergence of strangers' internal conditions to those of the natives (Kincaid, 1988; Kincaid, Yum, Woelfel, & Barnett, 1983). As such, assimilation can be located at the extreme end of the cross-cultural adaptation continuum that eludes the reality of many long-term settlers. Because change in internalized core values and beliefs is slow and difficult, complete assimilation is rare. Yet a considerable degree of assimilation can be observed over generations, most conspicuously in interethnic marriages. According to Lind (1995), the European ethnic groups that seemed so distinct at the beginning of the 20th century have almost completely faded away. Lind documents that four-fifths of Italian Americans, half of American Jews, one-third of Hispanics, and one-half of Asian Americans have married outside their officially designated categories since 1950. Lind further reports that the number of children born to Black-White marriages quintupled between 1968 and 1988, and a growing number of mixed-race Americans are now lobbying for their own "multiracial" category.

Page (1994) also observed this assimilative trend in a study of the 781 Japanese and their children who first made the long trip to Brazil in 1908 to serve as contract workers on coffee plantations. The great majority of these travelers hoped to earn and save enough money to return to Japan, and so resisted assimilation. They continued to speak Japanese, read Japanese-language newspapers, and founded Japanese schools for their children. Yet the present third-generation Japanese Brazilians are on the whole fully integrated into Brazilian society and enter into racially mixed marriages as freely as do other Brazilians. Nearly half of them have wed Brazilians who are not of Japanese descent and participate in Afro-Brazilian religions. Katsunori Wakisaka of the Center for Nippo-Brazilian Studies states, "Today we have a population of more than one million persons of Japanese descent who are integrated into Brazilian society and the Brazilian system of values, who work and suffer every day like any other Brazilian citizens and who have contributed, like all the other immigrant groups, to the modernization of Brazil" (quoted in Page, 1994, p. 41).

Studies focusing on historical change in immigrant communities also have demonstrated the acculturative, deculturative, and assimilative trend, both within and across generations. A study of Indian immigrants in the United States found that, along with changes in other areas, the immigrants' originally vegetarian food habits underwent significant changes over time, toward increasingly nonvegetarian habits (Gupta, 1975). A study conducted by the American Jewish Committee found a significant increase in members' merging into non-Jewish organizations and a substantial decrease in their Jewish identification (Zweigenhaft, 1979-1980). Masuda, Matsumoto, and Meredith (1970) found that ethnic identification of Japanese Americans in the United States gradually decreased from the first generation to the third. Likewise, Triandis, Kashima, Shimada, and Villareal (1986) and Suro (1998) have found both acculturative and deculturative trends among Hispanics in the United States: Long-term Hispanics showed diminished Hispanic "cultural scripts" in their judgments and increased social interactions with non-Hispanics. Namazi (1984) similarly observed an assimilative trend among Mexican, Cuban, and Middle Eastern immigrants. In Canada, McCauley (1991) has documented decreasing traditional forms of behavior in the French and English Canadian populations of Penetanguishene in southern Ontario. In addition, according to a study of language maintenance and shift by Morgan (1987), Haitian migrants in the Dominican Republic shifted, over time, from their native language, Creole, to the host language, Spanish, rather than maintaining Haitian Creole or establishing both languages in a state of balanced bilingualism.[2]

Figures 4.1 and 4.2 summarize the interplay of acculturation, deculturation, and assimilation. Assimilation is shown as the process by which strangers gradually acquire a new cultural system while losing some of their original cultural habits. For most people, even for

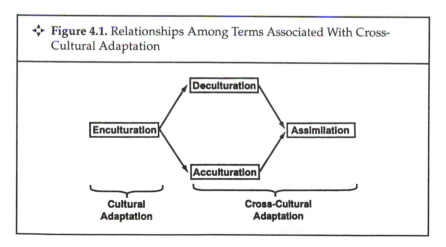

❖ **Figure 4.1.** Relationships Among Terms Associated With Cross-Cultural Adaptation

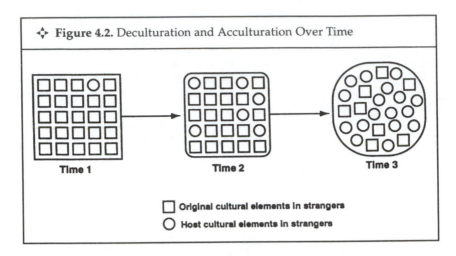

✦ Figure 4.2. Deculturation and Acculturation Over Time

Time 1   Time 2   Time 3

☐ Original cultural elements in strangers
○ Host cultural elements in strangers

natives, complete assimilation is a lifetime goal, and individuals vary in the level of overall adaptation achieved. The adaptation of strangers, therefore, is properly thought of as falling at some point on a continuum ranging from minimal acculturation and deculturation to maximum acculturation and deculturation.

The Stress-Adaptation-Growth Dynamic: A Process Model

The concurrence of acculturation and deculturation in the direction of assimilation brings about an internal *transformation* in individual strangers—a gradual opening of more or less culturally fixed existence to an open-ended intercultural synthesis (Dyal & Dyal, 1981). Unlike native-born members of the host culture, who often attempt and succeed in changing portions of the environment to better suit their needs, strangers bear the burden of making adjustments themselves almost exclusively. The power of individual strangers to change the dominant culture is minuscule, at least in the short run, when compared to the pervasive influence of the host culture on them. Clearly, a reason for the essentially one-sided change is the difference between the size of the population sharing a given stranger's original culture and that of the native population. To the extent that the dominant power of the host culture controls the daily survival and functioning of strangers, it presents a coercive conformity pressure on strangers to acculturate into the existing cultural order.

Adaptive change, then, inevitably causes stress in the stranger's psyche—a conflict between the desire to retain old customs and keep the original identity, on the one hand, and the desire to adopt new ways to seek harmony with the new milieu, on the other (Boekestijn, 1988; Zaharna, 1989). This conflict is essentially between the need for acculturation and the resistance to deculturation, the push of the new culture and the pull of the old, and between the existing conditions inside the stranger and the demands of the external environment. It is, then, a conflict that is not unlike the experience of members of older generations, who find themselves resisting the newly prevailing norms of the changing times and feeling left out unless they go along with such new forces. The internal turmoil created by the forces of acculturation and deculturation inevitably produces forms of temporary personality disintegration, or even "breakdown" in extreme cases. As parts of his or her internal organization undergo changes, the stranger is, temporarily at least, in a state of flux or disequilibrium, which is reflected in many emotional "lows" of uncertainty, confusion, and anxiety.

Stress, as such, is a manifestation of the generic process that occurs whenever the capabilities of the individual are not adequate to the demands of the environment. Stress is a direct function of the lack of fitness between the stranger's subjective experiences and the prevailing modes of experience among the natives. Naturally, stress is severest during the initial phases of cross-cultural adaptation, as demonstrated in culture-shock studies (see Chapter 2). Conservative estimates suggest that within the first year in a new culture, an individual may experience nearly one-third of what Holmes and Rahe (1967) identify as the 43 most significant life changes. Episodes of such temporary internal disturbances have been amply documented in research findings (e.g., Chan & Lam, 1987b; Ying & Liese, 1991), as well as in many fictional and nonfictional first-person accounts and ethnographic essays depicting a bewildering array of often painful experiences undergone by strangers in foreign lands (e.g., Dublin, 1993; Enguidanos-Clark, 1986; Foner, 1987).[3]

Because humans are characteristically homeostatic, individuals strive to hold constant a variety of variables in their internal structure to achieve an integrated whole. The natural tendency of open systems to resist the evolution that accompanies the destruction of the old structure, and to look "backward" to the original culture and its habits, is an essential aspect in the dynamics of evolution. To this end, defensive responses are activated in strangers under stress. They try to hold on to the existing internal structure (old cultural habits) through some form of protective psychological maneuvering (Brody, 1969; Lazarus, 1966; Lazarus, Cohen, Folkman, Kanner, & Schnefer, 1980; White, 1976). They attempt to avoid or minimize the anticipated or actual "pain" of disequilibrium through selective attention, self-deception, denial, avoidance, and withdrawal, as well as through compulsively altruistic behavior, hostility, and cynicism. The specific nature of a stranger's defensive responses to acculturative pressure is partly shaped by his or her predisposition. Ill equipped to deal with such inconsistencies, most strangers experience states of mental, emotional, and physical disturbance and confusion that vary in their degree of severity.

Yet no open system can stabilize itself forever. If it could, nothing would come of evolution. The state of misfit and a heightened awareness in the state of stress are the very forces that propel individuals to strive to overcome their predicament and partake in active development of new cultural understanding and habits. This is possible as strangers engage in forward-looking moves, striving to meet the challenge by acting on and responding to the environment (Piaget, 1963). Through these activities, some aspects of the environment may be incorporated into a stranger's internal structure, gradually increasing its overall fitness to the external realities. What follows the dynamic stress-adaptation disequilibrium is a subtle *growth*. Periods of stress pass as the stranger works out new ways of handling problems, owing to the creative forces of "self-reflexivity" of human mentation (Jantsch, 1980, pp. 162-172; Kirschner, 1994, p. 165). A crisis, once managed, presents the stranger with an opportunity for new learning and for strengthening his or her coping abilities. As Moos and Tsu (1976) note, "Every crisis presents both an opportunity for psychological growth and a danger of psychological deterioration" (p. 13).

Stress, adaptation, and growth thus highlight the core of strangers' cross-cultural experiences in a new environment. Together, they constitute a three-pronged *stress-adaptation-growth dynamic* of psychic movement in the forward and upward direction of increased chances of success in meeting the demands of the host environment. None of the three occurs without the others, and each occurs because of the others. Stress, in this regard, is intrinsic to complex open systems such as humans and essential in their transformation process—one that allows for self-organization and self-renewal (Masterpasqua & Perna, 1997; Ruben, 1983).

The stress-adaptation-growth dynamic plays out not in a smooth, linear progression, but in a cyclic and continual "draw-back-to-leap"

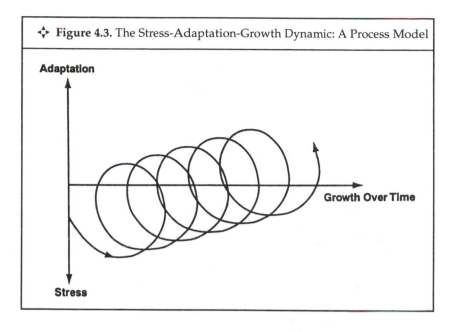

✦ **Figure 4.3.** The Stress-Adaptation-Growth Dynamic: A Process Model

representation of the present articulation of the interrelationships among stress, adaptation, and growth. Strangers respond to each stressful experience by "drawing back," which in turn activates adaptive energy to help them reorganize themselves and "leap forward." As growth of some units always occurs at the expense of others (Crowe, 1991; Weinberg, 1959/1987), the adaptive journey follows a pattern that juxtaposes novelty and confirmation, attachment and detachment, progression and regression, integration and disintegration, construction and destruction. The process is continuous as long as there are new environmental challenges. Indeed, no living structure can be permanently stabilized (Jantsch, 1980). The forces of attachment, progression, integration, and construction define the overall directionality of the forward and upward psychic movement of intercultural transformation toward greater adaptation and growth.

The above depiction of the intercultural transformation process, represented by the stress-adaptation-growth dynamic, echoes Dubos's (1965) view that "the problems of human adaptation could be presented as a dialectic between permanence and change" (p. 2). It converges with Hall's (1976) idea of "identity-separation-growth dynamics" and Phinney's (1993) conception of the "differentiation-conflict-integration" process.

Similarly, Jourard (1974) describes the same dynamism in terms of "integration-disintegration-reintegration":

> Growth is the dis-integration of one way of experiencing the world, followed by a reorganization of this experience, a reorganization that includes the new disclosure of the world. The disorganization, or even shattering, of one way to experience the world, is brought on by new disclosures from the changing being of the world, disclosures that were always being transmitted, but were usually ignored. (p. 456)

The stress-adaptation-growth model further resonates with Mezirow's (1984, 1991) notion of "transformation learning" of adults. Mezirow emphasizes the capacity of adults to develop a higher level of self-understanding and, in so doing, "emancipate" themselves from the constraints of various limited, conventional perspectives. The model reflects a dialectic relationship between the "opposite" forces of push and pull, change and stability, engagement and disengagement. Most strangers can, and do, maintain a balance between these two forces, out of which comes a qualitative transformation (see Graafsma, Bosma, Grotevant, & de Levita, 1994; Kroger, 1993; Weick, 1969; Wrightsman, 1994).[4] In the words of Dabrowski (1964):

> Disintegration is a generally positive developmental process. . . . The disintegration process, through loosening and even fragmenting the internal psychic environment, through conflict within the internal environment and with the external environment, is the ground for birth and development of a higher psychic structure. Disintegration is the basis for developmental thrusts upward, the creation of new evolutionary dynamics, and the movement of the personality to a higher level. (p. 5)

Once strangers enter a new culture, the cross-cultural adaptation process is set in full motion. The strangers' habitual patterns of cognitive, affective, and behavioral responses undergo adaptive transformations. Through the processes of deculturation and acculturation, some of the old cultural habits are replaced by new ones. The strangers acquire increasing proficiency in self-expression and the fulfillment of their various social needs. Although most strangers desire and even make deliberate plans for achieving successful adaptation in their host environment, such desire and plans are not necessary for adaptation to take place. Even those who interact with natives with the intention of confining themselves only to superficial relationships are likely to become, given sufficient time, at least minimally adapted to the host culture "in spite of themselves" (Taft, 1977, p. 150).

In this transformative process, large and sudden adaptive changes are most likely to occur during the initial phase of exposure to a new culture. Such drastic changes are themselves indicative of the severity of adaptive difficulties and disruptions, as has been demonstrated in culture-shock studies. At the same time, as Jantsch (1980) points out, "the higher the resistance against structural change, the more powerful the fluctuations which ultimately break through—the richer and more varied also the unfolding of self-organization dynamic at the platform of a resilient structure." (p. 255). Over a prolonged period, however, as strangers go through a progression of internal change, the fluctuations of stress and adaptation are likely to become less intense or severe, leading to an overall "calming" of strangers' internal condition. Accordingly, the generic, prototypical depiction of the stress-adaptation-growth dynamic presented earlier can be modified to reflect a diminishing severity in its fluctuation over time (see Figure 4.4).

Of course, not all individuals are equally successful in making transitions. The maintenance and restoration of equilibrium are possible

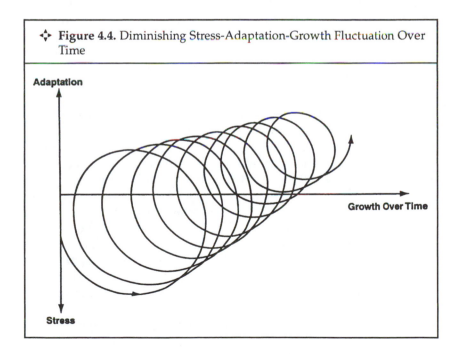

❖ **Figure 4.4.** Diminishing Stress-Adaptation-Growth Fluctuation Over Time

only to the extent that individuals' existing inner resources allow. When confronted with the definitive failure of their existing adaptive resources, some individuals may experience states of extreme panic, causing serious and prolonged damage to their psyches (Hettema, 1979). Some people may strongly resist change, thereby intensifying the stress level so much that they are unable to avoid a "negative adaptation cycle" (Giles, Coupland, Coupland, Williams, & Nussbaum, 1992)—a reverse (or regressive) process of change in the direction of increased stress, maladaptation, and psychic degeneration.

Yet most strangers in alien cultures have demonstrated an impressive capacity to manage cross-cultural encounters successfully. Research data offer some direct and indirect evidence that stressful experiences may lay the groundwork for subsequent adaptive growth. A study of Canadian technical advisers in Kenya revealed that those who would ultimately be the most effective in adapting to the new culture underwent the most intense culture shock during the transition period (Ruben, 1980; Ruben & Kealey, 1979). Eaton and Lasry (1978) found that more upwardly mobile immigrants had experienced greater stress than had those who were less upwardly mobile. Among Japanese Americans (Marmot & Syme, 1976) and Mexican American women (Miranda & Castro, 1977), better-adapted immigrants have been found to have a somewhat greater frequency of stress-related symptoms (such as anxiety and need for psychotherapy) than their less-adapted counterparts. In a study of international college students, Redmond and Bunyi (1993) found that those students who identified with others exhibiting a strong social "decentering" tendency reported the highest levels of stress from their intercultural experience. In a study of a Cuban community in the Washington, D.C., area, Rivera-Sinclair (1997) found a positive relationship between psychological orientation to be integrated into the American culture ("biculturalism") and level of stress ("anxiety"). Gebart-Eaglemont (1994) found that immigrants in Australia experienced less stress as they achieved greater acculturation. This finding led the researcher to conclude that adaptation exerts a "buffering effect" on stress. Likewise, Ward and Kennedy (1994) found notable psychological stress in those international students in Singapore who attempted to integrate in Singaporean society, and Gil, Vega, and Dimas (1994) found that foreign-born Hispanic teenagers who were undergoing the cross-cultural adaptation process had higher levels of stress than did their American-born bicultural counterparts.

Additional empirical data supporting the stress-adaptation-growth dynamic have been reported in studies of immigrants and foreign students, who have been found to demonstrate increased levels of adaptation once they have successfully managed the initial phase. For example, based on cross-sectional analyses of data comparing various adaptation indicators, long-term immigrants and sojourners alike appear to develop an increased understanding of similarities between the host culture and the home culture as well as an expanded behavioral capacity to manage themselves, function effectively, and experience less feeling of alienation in relation to the host society (e.g., Kim, 1976, 1977, 1979a, 1980, 1989, 1990). De Verthelyi (1995) provides additional evidence that initial stress leads to acculturation. In studies of the spouses of international students, De Verthelyi observed manifestations of widespread stress during the initial weeks and months of the sojourn, such as feelings of sadness, loneliness, self-doubt, confusion, and frustration. Language difficulties accentuated this initial stress. Within the first 6 months after arrival, however, the subjects reported that their stress experiences had subsided and had been replaced by a positive change of mood. In addition, Steen (1998) found that American exchange students studying abroad experienced a series of stress-adaptation-growth cycles throughout their time abroad, "eventually achieving a sense of integration and unity with the host community" (p. 1).

Taken together, these and related research findings clearly suggest the viability of the present theoretical articulation of the interrelatedness of stress, adaptation, and growth, and the general upward and forward movement of psychic evolution that accompanies the stress-adaptation-growth dynamic.

Three Facets of Intercultural Transformation

Emerging in the process of intercultural transformation described above are three interrelated facets of internal change in strangers: increased functional fitness in carrying out daily transactions, improved psychological health in dealing with the environment, and a movement from the original cultural identity to a broader, "intercultural" identity. These three facets are to be considered as developmental continua on which individual strangers can be placed at different locations reflecting the different levels of intercultural transformation they have achieved at given points in time.

Functional Fitness

Strangers conduct continuous "experiments" in the host environment. They instinctively strive to "know their way around," so that they may effectively control their own behavior in relation to the behavior of others. Through repeated activities resulting in new learning and internal reorganizing, strangers achieve increasing functional fitness between their internal responses and the external demands of the host environment. Well-adapted strangers have accomplished a desired level of appropriate and effective ways of communicating with and relating to the host environment—particularly with those individuals with whom the strangers carry out their daily activities. As they achieve increased communication competence, they are also better able to meet their personal needs, and experience greater contentment, confidence, and self-esteem. Maladaptation during initial phases, in turn, reflects the strangers' lack of an internal capacity to deal with new challenges. As Seeman (1983) states:

> [The] most frequently mentioned aspect of personal effectiveness centered on a conceptual framework which emphasized synthesis and integration. There was wide agreement that special qualities of organization and function of the individual as a whole characterized the phenomenon of personal effectiveness. The individual's capacity to regulate the total personal system, the harmonious interplay of part processes, and the existence of adequate communication channels were all required as conditions of effective functioning and optimal utilization of personal resources. (p. 231)

The development of functional fitness, therefore, is directly linked to the development of the ability to communicate in accordance with the local cultural norms. An increased capacity to communicate allows strangers to increase their participation in the local society, through which they gradually move away from the "intergroup posturing" (Kim, 1991) that often predominates in social encounters across cultures. Instead, they are increasingly better able to interact with local people with less psychological distance and stereotyping. This change in strangers can be further explained in terms of Tajfel and Turner's (1979) idea that various relationships can be characterized as varying in "intergroupness" or "interpersonalness":

> At one extreme . . . is the interaction between two or more individuals which is fully determined by their interpersonal relationships and

individual characteristics and not at all affected by various social groups or categories in which they respectively belong. The other extreme consists of interactions between two or more individuals (or groups of individuals) which are fully determined by their respective memberships of various social groups or categories, and not at all affected by the individual personal relationship between the people involved. (p. 34)

The development of functional fitness has been documented extensively in studies of sojourners as well as studies of immigrants. In a longitudinal study, for instance, Ward, Okura, Kennedy, and Kojima (1998) found that psychological and sociocultural adaptation problems of Japanese students in New Zealand decreased over time. The overall trend of increasing sense of control and satisfaction has also been observed among Korean immigrants (Kim, 1976, 1977, 1978b) and Indo-Chinese refugees (Kim, 1979a, 1980, 1989, 1990). Likewise, Szalay and Inn (1988) examined the "subjective meaning systems" of Puerto Ricans and Anglo-Americans in New York and compared these to the meaning systems of Puerto Ricans in San Juan. Findings from this study demonstrated a progressive convergence of the meaning systems of Puerto Ricans in New York toward those of Anglo-Americans.

Psychological Health

Everyone requires the ongoing validation of his or her social experience. Being unable to meet this basic human need can lead to symptoms of mental, emotional, and physical disturbance. The shifting of the self-world relationship brings about heightened levels of inner conflict due to the gap between internal and external reality. As suggested by Zajonc (1952) and by Dollard, Miller, Doob, Mower, and Sears (1963; cited in Blalock, 1982, p. 14) in their theoretical articulations of the linkage between frustration and aggression, the psychological health of strangers is directly associated with their ability to communicate and their functional fitness in the host environment. In the absence of adequate communication competence and functional fitness, strangers are subject to frustration, leading to symptoms of poor psychological health. Indeed, the very meaning of the term *culture shock* employed in studies of temporary sojourners suggests lack of psychological health, stemming from the poor fit between a stranger's intrapsychic system and that of the natives (see Chapter 2). Issues of psychological health have also been investigated in psychology and psychiatry in terms of mental illnesses among long-term settlers. The severity of disturbance, in particular, has been noted in initial phases of resettlement in the form of negative self-image, low self-esteem, low morale, social isolation, depression, dissatisfaction with life in general, and a feeling of being a helpless victim of circumstance, among others (e.g., Furnham & Bochner, 1986; Torbiorn, 1982, 1988; Vega, Kolody, & Valle, 1987; Williams & Westermeyer, 1986; Ying & Liese, 1991).

Extremely traumatic stress reactions of strangers may take the form of escapism or mental illness symptoms. Psychiatrists in recent years have concerned themselves with the clinical description of emergent mental illnesses among immigrants. There has been growing recognition that the development of mental and behavioral disorders in immigrants is due not so much to innate characteristics as to severe lack of fit between individuals and the receiving community. Stress is particularly acute among those whose native cultures differ radically from that of the host community, especially when there is a strong pressure for rapid assimilation and the strangers are unable, or unwilling, to join familiar groups that might offer tension reduction and flexibility in coping with cultural change (David, 1969).

Clearly, there is an inherent and enduring "danger" of psychic disintegration, particularly during the initial phase, for those individuals who are unable to endure the stresses of the new environmental challenges. When confronted with the definitive failure of their existing adaptive resources, some may experience states of extreme panic, causing serious and prolonged damage to their internal systems. Certain individuals, although in the minority, may strongly resist change, thereby increasing the stress level and making the stress-adaptation-growth cycle intensely difficult. According to Ruesch (1957/1972), the condition of psychosis can be interpreted to be the result of a person's misinterpretation of messages received from the environment. Also, the condition commonly labeled neurosis can be viewed to be a result of unfortunate attempts to convey messages in social situations without success. Similarly, schizophrenic individuals can be viewed as those incapable of discerning the multiplicity of messages.

Most strangers, however, are able to achieve, over time, a higher level of psychological health and a subsiding level of disturbances in dealing with the host environment. In this process, they experience reduced defense reactions, such as withdrawal, denial, and hostility, as they follow the trajectory of the stress-adaptation-growth dynamic described earlier (see Figures 4.3 and 4.4). In this process of continual psychological "ups and downs," they achieve an increased internal integration—a sense of inner cohesiveness and

confidence. Researchers have gathered abundant evidence that supports this increasing trend in strangers' psychological well-being (e.g.,
Church, 1982; Nishida, 1985).[5]

Intercultural Identity

Along with functional fitness and psychological health,
intercultural transformation is reflected in the gradual development of
an intercultural identity. The term *intercultural* is employed here to
reflect the boundary-crossing nature of such development in identity.
In facing the challenges of cross-cultural adaptation, strangers experience what Zaharna (1989) calls "self-shock," a "shake-up" of their
sense of connection to their original cultural group and an incorporation of psychological ties with a broader humanity. Although rooted in
the original cultural identity, the emerging identity presents a more
complex process of interpretive activity inside a stranger. Just as cultural
identity serves as a linkage between a person and a specific cultural
group, the emerging identity links a person to more than one cultural
group. According to Adler (1982), this newly forming identity is based
"not on 'belongingness,' which implies either owning or being owned
by a single culture, but on a style of self-consciousness that situates
oneself neither totally *a part of* nor totally *apart from* a given culture"
(p. 391).

The psychological movement of strangers into new dimensions of
perception and experience produces "boundary-ambiguity syn-
dromes" (Hall, 1976, p. 227), in which the original cultural identity
begins to lose its distinctiveness and rigidity and the emergent identity shows an increasing *interculturalness.* This is a form of "self-
transcendence," the reaching out of an open system "beyond the
boundaries of one's own existence" (Jantsch, 1980, p. 183). Unlike the
original cultural identity that had been largely programmed into the
stranger through childhood socialization experiences, the emerging
identity is one that develops out of the many challenging and often
painful experiences of self-reorganization under the demands of a new
milieu. Through prolonged experiences of trial and error, the stranger
begins to "earn" a new, expanded identity that is more than either the
original cultural identity or the identity of the host culture.

Intercultural identity, as such, is not a fixed psychological state but
a developmental continuum on which strangers travel (Kim, 1988,
1995b, 1997b; Kim & Ruben, 1988). As they undergo adaptive changes
in host communication competence (most notably, language

competence), their internal conditions change from a monocultural to an increasingly multifaceted character. At the same time, the host cultural elements are increasingly incorporated into their self-concept. In this process, the strangers' identities become more flexible. No longer rigidly bound by membership to the original culture, or to the host culture, their identities begin to take on a greater *interculturalness* (Kim & Ruben, 1988; Sarbaugh, 1988), including the vital component of emotional self-identification that reaches beyond a particular group.

The development of an intercultural identity does not come about without certain "costs" that may be deemed too high by some. The process is filled with ambivalence and internal conflict between loyalty to the original identity and the necessity to embrace a new one. Ursula Bender, a German who came to the United States when she was 23 years old, lived in the United States for 25 years and then returned to West Germany in 1987. Five months after her return to Germany, she was interviewed for a radio program by author and radio talk-show host Studs Terkel (1987). In this interview, Bender expressed just such an internal dilemma:

> Marginal, I don't feel, but border I think that's true . . . a border person looking for a playground. . . . I feel there is a certain amount of loneliness that I experience that has to do with my feeling German . . . the understanding of all of a sudden saying maybe I am not so German— maybe I'm not as German as I thought—I hung on to this German passport for 25 years—thinking you don't change passports like . . . you don't shed nationality that easily.

The formation of intercultural identity as depicted here challenges the conventional, categorical conceptions that largely ignore the dynamic nature of cultural identity by focusing only on the negative consequences of cross-cultural contact and adaptation, such as "marginalization," "alienation," and negative images of the original group (e.g., De Vos, 1990b; De Vos & Suárez-Orozco, 1990b). In contrast, the present approach to identity resonates closely with a growing recognition of flexible, evolving, and differentiated identities (see Berry, 1980; Brewer & Gardner, 1996; Deaux, Reid, Mizrahi, & Ethier, 1995; Phinney & Rosenthal, 1992; Ting-Toomey, 1993).[6] Phinney and Rosenthal (1992), for example, have examined and theorized about the process in which ethnic minorities form "dual identity" or "bicultural identity." Along the same line, Berry (1980) has argued that it is possible for those who cross cultures to maintain or enhance their ties with both groups. Studies of Asian Indians in Britain (Hutnik, 1986), Armenian Americans

(Der-Karabetian, 1980), Chinese Americans (Ting-Toomey, 1981), and Greek and Italian Australians (Rosenthal & Hrynevich, 1985) all have shown coexisting identities without evidence of conflict between them.

Consistent with these differentiated conceptions of identity, I view intercultural identity development as being rooted in, embracing, and not discarding the original cultural identity—just as acquiring knowledge and skill in the host language does not necessarily result in corresponding loss in the original language (Arnberg, 1987; Beardsmore, 1986; Boekestijn, 1988; Phinney & Rotheram, 1987). Adaptation means the resolution of internal stress that promotes the qualitative transformation toward growth—a greater maturity and psychic integration as well as an increased capacity to cope with varied environmental challenges. In this sense, strangers "owe" their adaptive transformation to the host environment because, in Dobzhansky's (1962) words, "evolutionary change *comes from* the environment" (p. 17). Despite the pivotal importance of the original cultural identity in the psychosocial functioning of an individual stranger, the acculturative forces of the host environment stimulate the adaptive alteration of that identity in the direction of a higher level of psychic integration. Whatever the specific method of resolving an identity conflict, cumulative experiences of cross-cultural adaptation bring about an emerging identity that is broader than the original.

We witness such development in successfully adapted individuals who have achieved creative resolution of their inner identity conflicts, who recognize that the boundaries of a cultural identity are not impermeable, and who understand that cross-borrowing of identities is often an act of appreciation that leaves neither the lender nor the borrower deprived, symbolically or otherwise. Among such individuals is Mary Catherine Bateson, author of *Composing a Life* (1989), whose insight touches on the complexity and richness of her own identity:

> I had spent my senior year of high school in Israel and had come back to the United States to start college with a deep sense of dividedness, of having first found a new sense of myself in Israel and then having left that clarity behind. The new task was to combine and translate, to put an American gentile identity with my Israeli experience and to use my college education to shape them into some new whole. . . . Each of us has repeatedly had to pose the question of who we are. (pp. 212-213)

In the present conception of identity development, there is no contradiction between maintenance of a positive cultural identity and the development of a flexible intercultural identity. The notion that a person has to choose one or the other is false. Although identity development is often a difficult process filled with confusion and self-doubt, ultimately, the constitution of an individual stranger's identity becomes increasingly intercultural. This transformation is not always a matter of conscious decision; rather, it is simply an aspect of the natural psychic evolution beyond the boundaries of childhood enculturation.

Axioms

We have so far examined the process of personal transformation in a new cultural environment—from being a cultural outsider to becoming increasingly fit in performance, psychologically healthier, and more intercultural in identity. As strangers overcome multitudes of challenges and frustrations and undergo the alteration of their internal conditions along the way, they develop a personhood broadened beyond their original psychocultural parameters. Grounded in the dynamic, interactive, and integrative perspective of an open-systems theory of the nature of human behavior, the present theory explains how such an intercultural transformation occurs. At the core of this explanation is the stress-adaptation-growth dynamic, which acts as the prime mover of strangers toward greater control and freedom in the new environment. Cross-cultural adaptation, as such, is a continual back-and-forth and downward-and-upward movement in the direction of increasing adaptation and growth. Through various temporary setbacks and experiences of asymmetry between themselves and the external conditions, strangers are able to come out victorious, with increased capacity to see situations, others, and themselves with new eyes.

The theoretical description presented thus far in this chapter is summarized in the following five axioms. These axioms are proposed as a set of broad, generalizable principles of cross-cultural adaptation:

- ◆ *Axiom 1:* Cross-cultural adaptation involves both acculturation and deculturation, an eventual possible outcome of which is assimilation.

- ◆ *Axiom 2:* Underlying the cross-cultural adaptation process is the stress-adaptation-growth dynamic.

- ◆ *Axiom 3:* The stress-adaptation-growth dynamic brings about an intercultural transformation in the stranger.

◆ *Axiom 4:* As the stranger undergoes intercultural transformation, the severity of fluctuation in his or her stress-adaptation-growth dynamic subsides.

◆ *Axiom 5:* Intercultural transformation is manifested in increased functional fitness, psychological health, and intercultural identity.

The spiral representation of the adaptation process is not intended as a replacement for existing descriptions such as the U-curve or W-curve, discussed in Chapter 2. Rather, it extends them into a model that is more inclusive and general in profiling the intrapsychic dynamic that potentially applies to short-term as well as long-term strangers who find themselves having to function in an alien environment. The model further allows a reconciliation of the two divergent views of cross-cultural adaptation: (a) one held by many investigators of the culture-shock phenomenon, which emphasizes the problematic nature of cross-cultural adaptation, and (b) the contrary approach, which emphasizes the learning and growth aspects of the same experiences. These two views are reconciled in this model as it recognizes that the adaptation process is *both* stressful and growth promoting, and that adaptive change occurs in the dynamic tension between these two competing psychological forces. In this approach, various culture-shock experiences are viewed as the generic stress responses that occur whenever the capabilities of a person are not sufficiently adequate to the demands of an unfamiliar environment. Stress, moreover, is a necessary condition for adaptive transformation, activating the inner drive to make changes and thereby realize growth in the stranger's psychic resources.

Moreover, the model bridges the existing division between the assimilationist and pluralist views concerning the degree and directionality of change in strangers. It does so by taking the open-systems view that cross-cultural adaptation (and, indeed, all other aspects of human adaptation) is something natural and inevitable as long as strangers are engaged communicatively with a given host milieu. Through communication, strangers acquire at least some degree of new cultural learning (acculturation) and, at the same time, lose some of their original cultural patterns (deculturation). The model thus ameliorates the ideological divide that has dominated the contemporary academic and political discourse concerning the "fate" of strangers, including ethnic minorities. It reaffirms the basic premise underlying this theory that we humans are never "finished products": We refine, we rearrange, we revise, and we evolve. In this fundamental context, cross-cultural adaptation as portrayed is simply a special case of the ever-present human learning and development process. Strangers weather many disorienting dilemmas and, in time, "stretch" themselves out of the boundaries of their original cultures. In this creative process of self-reinvention, strangers discover new forms and symbols of life with which to forge new identities.

The Structure of
Cross-Cultural Adaptation

Evolution essentially is a vast operation of interlocking changes.

Gregory Bateson,
Steps to an Ecology of Mind, 1951

Building on the essential nature of the process of cross-cultural adaptation depicted in Chapter 4, we now turn to differential adaptation rates at which different strangers move along in attaining higher-level functional fitness, psychological health, and intercultural identity. Clearly, some strangers make smooth and speedy transitions, whereas others suffer from prolonged inability to find ways to overcome their cross-cultural predicaments. Some may strongly resist the idea of having to change their original cultural habits, thereby raising psychological barriers that work against their own transformation. The state of extreme stress eases over time for most strangers, whereas this may become a chronic condition for some, leading to enduring alienation.

Given that adaptive changes in individual strangers fall along a continuum, the question to be addressed is, Why do some strangers adapt faster than others? Or, given the same length of time, why do some strangers attain higher levels of adaptation than do others? In this chapter, a number of key dimensions and factors will be identified and linked together into a system of logical relationships that, when taken

71

together, form a kind of structure in the dynamic process of cross-cultural adaptation. We return to the premise that communication lies at the heart of cross-cultural adaptation—just as it is the very process through which all individuals acquire their original cultural patterns during childhood. Both the quantity and the quality of strangers' communication activities in a new environment are crucial to the success of their adaptation. As Lewis (1948) has observed, an individual's "effective membership in his society directly depends upon his ability to communicate with his fellows; in turn his power of communication is a primary factor in his development as an individual" (p. 12).

Personal Communication: Host Communication Competence

Strangers' communication activities can be conceptualized as having two basic, inseparable dimensions: personal communication and social communication. Ruben (1975) defines *personal communication* as "private symbolization" and all the internal mental activities that occur in individuals that dispose and prepare them to act and react in certain ways in actual social situations. Personal communication is linked to *social communication* when two or more individuals interact with one another, knowingly or not. Ruben thus conceives of social communication as the process underlying "intersubjectivization," a phenomenon occurring as a consequence of "public symbolization." The personal and social communication processes can be compared to what Geyer (1980) refers to as the "off-line functions" and the "on-line functions" of computer systems (p. 32).

Strangers realize successful adaptation only when their internal communication systems sufficiently overlap with those of the natives. The capacity of the personal communication system serves as the innermost dimension in the structure of cross-cultural adaptation, enabling strangers to organize themselves mentally, motivationally, and emotionally in and with their sociocultural milieu, developing ways of seeing, hearing, understanding, and responding to the environment appropriately and effectively. As they become more competent in the host communication system, they are better able to discern the similarities and differences between their original home culture and the host culture and are able to act accordingly. For the natives, such capabilities were acquired early in life and are programmed into their internal communication systems such that communication practices occur in an automatic manner. For immigrants and sojourn-ers, the linguistic and nonlinguistic symbols, codes, and meanings of the host communication system must be learned and internalized.

Through trial and error, strangers develop their abilities to relate to the host milieu. These abilities are collectively identified here as *host communication competence*—the overall capacity of the stranger to receive and process information appropriately and effectively (decod-ing) and to design plans to initiate messages or respond to others (encoding) in accordance with the host communication system. Once acquired, host communication competence facilitates cross-cultural adaptation in direct and significant ways. It serves as an instrumental, interpretive, and expressive means of coming to terms with the envi-ronment. It enables strangers to develop their view of the way things are carried out in the host environment and the way they themselves need to think, feel, and interact with that environment. As Ruesch (1957/1972) notes, "One of the criteria for successful communication is the mutual fit of over-all patterns and constituent parts, integration, synchrony, and smoothness so that no particular person is overbur-dened with or completely relieved of work, and thus the exchange of messages becomes efficient, clear, economical, and well timed" (p. 34). Until strangers have acquired communication competence that matches that of the natives, they are handicapped in their ability to meet their physical, material, psychological, and social needs and goals. To quote Ruesch and Bateson (1951/1968): "The ability to communicate success-fully becomes synonymous with being mentally healthy" (p. 87). The lack of such ability manifests itself in various forms of miscom-munication (Banks, Gao, & Baker, 1991; Gass & Varonis, 1991; Tyler & Davies, 1990).

What, then, are the key elements that constitute the concept of host communication competence? What specific capabilities do strangers need to communicate successfully in the host environment? Many ele-ments have been identified previously—from the most obvious lan-guage competence and knowledge about the norms of the host culture to the ability to act in ways that are effective and appropriate in the host environment. Such elements have been commonly grouped into cogni-tive, affective, and operational (or behavioral) categories (e.g., Spitzberg, 1989; Spitzberg & Cupach, 1984; Wiseman & Koester, 1993).[1] Even though the three categories are simultaneously present and inseparable in actual communication situations, they are treated here as distinct categories for the purpose of organizing various aspects of communication abilities in a coherent framework. Each facet of host communication competence is viewed on a continuum, on which dif-ferent strangers can be plotted and compared. At the lowest end of each continuum is a hypothetical state of zero competence, a complete inability to communicate in a new cultural environment. At the highest end are those individuals whose capacity to communicate with native members of the host society is at the highest possible attainment.

Social Communication

Host communication competence is directly and reciprocally connected to participation in the interpersonal and mass communication activities of the host environment. Interacting with natives face-to-face requires a degree of host communication competence on the part of strangers. At the same time, host interpersonal communication activities provide strangers with points of reference for checking and validating their own behaviors and the behaviors of the natives. As such, both the quantity and the quality of strangers' new social experiences are largely a function of their host communication competence. In turn, each social experience offers strangers an opportunity to cultivate their host communication competence.

Social communication activities occur on many levels. On the macro level, social communication takes place via newspapers, television, movies, and other forms of mass communication. Social communication also takes place at the micro level, in such places as homes, neighborhoods, workplaces, classrooms, and airports. Micro-level social communication also occurs when strangers make simple, passing observations of people on the street, or when they engage in serious dialogue with close friends. These and many other social communication activities can be grouped into two categories: *interpersonal communication* activities, that is, various direct, face-to-face interactions with people in an immediate social environment; and *mass communication* activities, or experiences with the larger social environment through mediated channels of communication, such as radio and television programs, magazine and newspaper articles, movies, museum exhibits, theater performances, audiotapes, videotapes, and posters. For strangers, interpersonal communication activities offer opportunities for more personalized and thus "meaningful" involvement with members of the host culture, whereas mass communication activities help them participate in "para-social interactions" (Horton & Wohl, 1979, p. 32) beyond the ordinary reaches of their daily life.

Host Social Communication

Communication activities involving native-born members of the host environment, in particular, play a vital role in the cross-cultural adaptation process. Communication in interpersonal relationships, especially significant ones, is central to strangers' securing information and insight into the mind-sets and behaviors of local people. Through formal and informal contacts, strangers find social support in handling difficulties as well as opportunities for language and culture learning and for finding additional contacts (Adelman, 1988; Jou & Fukada, 1995; Takai, 1991; Wellman, 1992). Interpersonal networks exert social control by determining the language strangers must use and by conveying implicit or explicit messages of cultural values and social approval or disapproval (Heckathorn, 1990; Ho & Sung, 1990; Milroy, 1982, 1987).

Most strangers, when they move to a new culture, must begin to form a new set of relationships. They find themselves without an adequate support system when they are confronted with highly uncertain and stressful situations. Uprooted from their supportive ties in the home country, strangers themselves are also keenly aware of the vital role that interpersonal relationships play by offering a "personal community" (Hirsch, 1981) through which they can receive informational, technical, material, and emotional support for their functioning in the new environment (Eckenrode & Gore, 1981; Gottlieb, 1981). In a survey of Indo-Chinese refugees in the United States, almost all respondents expressed a strong need for communication training and cultural orientation (Kim, 1980). In the same study, a similar view was expressed by the social and educational service agencies and organizations serving refugee resettlement. Agency personnel considered communication barriers to be one of the most serious problems impairing their service delivery to refugee clients.

The crucial importance of participating in *host interpersonal communication* activities has been amply emphasized. In anthropological studies, interpersonal communication has been regarded as a "given" (or necessary) condition for "acculturation" (e.g., Herskovits, 1958, 1947/1966). In sociological and social psychological studies, host interpersonal communication has been examined mainly in terms of the number of relationships strangers develop and maintain with natives. The main purpose has been to create indices of "social integration" or "social assimilation" of ethnic individuals or communities (e.g., Marden & Meyer, 1968).

Along with host interpersonal communication, *host mass communication* facilitates the adaptation of strangers. As Gordon (1964) has observed, mass media (along with public schools) exert "overwhelming acculturation powers" over immigrants' children (pp. 244-245). Shibutani and Kwan (1965) support this view, indicating that "the extent to which members of a minority group become acculturated to the way of life of the dominant group depends on the extent of their participation in the communication channels of their rulers" (p. 573). Access to, exposure to, and use of the mass media of the dominant group influences strangers' cultural learning and social participation (Subervi-Velez, 1986). Similar observations can be made about the situations of temporary sojourners, although little attention has been paid to the role of such sojourners' mainstream mass communication activities.

Generally, host mass communication activities require little or no involvement in personalized relationships with specific individuals. They are governed by little mutual obligation, effort, or responsibility on the part of the spectator. This difference exists because mass communication experiences offer little opportunity for instant feedback, whereas face-to-face situations always do (Chaffee & Mutz, 1988; Rogers, 1979; Schramm, 1979). Accordingly, the strangers' mass communication activities are vital to their cultural/language learning, particularly during early phases of the adaptation process when they have less direct access to the natives.

Ethnic Social Communication

In addition to host social (interpersonal, mass) communication activities, strangers' social communication activities often involve their coethnics (or conationals) and the experiences of their home cultures. In many countries, strangers today have at least some access to *ethnic interpersonal and mass communication* processes involving their home cultures. Whether they take the form of British compounds in India, American military posts in West Germany, Puerto Rican barrios in New York City, Chinatown in Tokyo, or Japanese student associations in Canadian universities, ethnic communities provide strangers with access to their original cultural experiences. Particularly in large cities in countries that have experienced sizable influxes of immigrants, many aliens have organized some form of "mutual aid" or "self-help" community groups. Such ethnic organizations render assistance to newcomers who need material, informational, emotional, and other forms of social support (DeCocq, 1976; Tran, 1987). In larger ethnic communities, ethnic media (including newspapers, radio stations, and television programs) perform various informational, educational, entertainment, and social services for their members (Miller, 1987). Because many strangers initially lack host communication competence and do not have access to the resources they need to be self-reliant, they tend to seek out and rely heavily on ethnic community assistance. The relatively stress-free ethnic communication experiences this allows strangers to delay or avoid confronting more stressful communication activities involving members of the receiving community, as Tanaka, Takai, Kohyama, Fujihara, and Minami (1994) found in a study of international students in Japan.

Despite the short-term support function, ethnic social communication activities tend to discourage the long-term development of host communication competence and participation in host social processes, thereby deterring strangers' long-term adaptation to the host cultural system itself (Padilla, 1980b; Subervi-Velez, 1986; Walker, 1993; Yang, 1988). In the case of certain temporary sojourners, such as American military personnel in Okinawa, daily duties confine social communication activities almost exclusively to interaction with coethnics. Such specially arranged ethnic "islands" in the midst of the host environment structurally limit the necessity for strangers to engage in activities involving local people or in local mass communication activities.

Whether by choice or by circumstance, strangers' heavy and prolonged reliance on coethnics sustains their original cultural identity while limiting opportunities to participate in the social communication activities of the host environment (Burgess, 1978). This means that, to the extent that strangers communicate with coethnics, they are more likely to maintain perspectives different from the normative patterns of the host culture and to experience difficulty in understanding and relating to the host environment. Indeed, the longer strangers avoid or participate only minimally in the communication processes of the host environment, the longer it will take for them to acquire host communication competence. Strangers cannot remain ethnic while also becoming highly adapted to a new culture. Instead, they are likely to remain inadequate in the host environment, to continue experiencing psychological instability in dealing with local people, and to hold on to their original ethnic identity.

It is, of course, possible for the two interrelated constructs, ethnic interpersonal communication and ethnic mass communication, to facilitate cross-cultural adaptation in the initial phases as long as the coethnics involved are themselves well adapted. In such cases, strangers' adaptation can be facilitated by the information and assistance offered by coethnics to help guide the development of host communication competence and host social communication activities. Such adaptive functions of ethnic communication serve many newcomers well by softening the stress of crossing cultures. In time, however, the adaptive function of ethnic social communication diminishes, and, instead, it begins to interfere with the stranger's adaptation to the larger environment. This pattern can be seen in the social communication activities of many elderly immigrants whose daily interactions are restricted for the most part to a narrow circle that includes family members, coethnic friends, and, when available, ethnic media. Their constrained intercultural communication activities are contrary to the activities of such sojourners as missionaries and Peace Corps volunteers, who, soon after arrival in the host culture, immerse themselves in their daily duties of working with local people and thus achieve a considerable level of adaptation in a relatively short period.

Environment

As long as strangers remain in contact with and participate in the host environment, the environment serves as the cultural and sociopolitical *context* for their communication activities. As such, the host environment helps shape the nature of the strangers' adaptation process. On the macro level, it exerts influence on the process largely through mass communication activities. Also, strangers' significant interactions with the host environment take place in the immediate social milieus in which they carry out their daily activities, such as their workplaces, neighborhoods, and communities. For many, the environment also includes coethnics, especially in communities that are large and highly organized, such as the Vietnamese community in Chicago. For others, such as the American community in Tokyo, the ethnic community is small and loosely organized, offering only limited access to the home culture.

Given the mixed nature of the new environments in which many strangers find themselves today, we need to examine both the host sociocultural environment and the subenvironment consisting of coethnics. Specifically, the present theory focuses on three environmental conditions: host receptivity, host conformity pressure, and ethnic group strength.

Host Receptivity

Host receptivity is reflected in the degree to which a given environment is open to, welcomes, and accepts strangers into its social communication networks and offers them various forms of social support. This concept incorporates other similar concepts, such as "interaction potential" (Kim, 1976, 1988, 1995a) and "acquaintance potential" (Cook, 1962), that have been employed in studies concerning strangers' access to host social communication networks. Societies and communities offer different degrees of receptivity for different groups of strangers. Ethnically homogeneous and geographically isolated societies (such as Japan) offer relatively fewer opportunities for strangers to develop close interpersonal relationships with local people. Within a society, members of certain groups are more warmly received than others. For instance, Canadian visitors arriving in a small town in the United States are likely to find a largely receptive environment, whereas the same small town may show less receptivity toward visitors from a lesser-known and more visibly different culture.

Differences in host receptivity can be further traced to various plausible reasons, including cultural and racial similarity/difference, compatibility/incompatibility, relative status, and the nature of the historical or current relationship (friendly or hostile) between the stranger's home country and the host society in the case of immigrants, or between the stranger's ethnic group and the dominant ethnic group in the host community in the case of domestic migrants. These and related factors may induce different levels of receptivity on the part of the receiving community toward particular strangers.

Host Conformity Pressure

Along with receptivity, the host environment influences the communication activities of strangers by exerting "conformity pressure" (Zajonc, 1952). Conformity pressure is the extent to which the environment challenges strangers to adopt the normative patterns of the host culture and communication system. Rooted in the expectations or assumptions that the natives routinely have about how strangers should think and act, host conformity pressure shapes the extent to which the host environment challenges strangers to adopt its normative communication practices. As the findings of a study of Hispanic and Black communities in Canada suggest, experiences of discrimination tend to serve as a motivating force for ethnic minorities to change their original cultural habits and conform to those of the mainstream culture (Ruggiero, Taylor, & Lambert, 1996).

Host conformity pressure is often reflected in the level of intolerance, prejudice, and discrimination aimed at strangers. Of course, given historically rooted sociopolitical reasons, different host environments show different levels of tolerance to strangers and their ethnic or cultural characteristics. For example, heterogeneous and "open" environments such as the United States tend to hold pluralist ideologies and related norms and policies concerning ethnic differences. Such ideological climates exert less pressure on ethnic minorities to change their habitual ways. Within the United States, ethnically heterogeneous metropolitan areas such as Los Angeles and Miami tend to place fewer demands on strangers to conform to the mainstream cultural practices than do small, ethnically homogeneous rural towns. Even within a given city, certain neighborhoods may be more homogeneous and thus may expect more conformity from strangers.

Ethnic Group Strength

The degree to which a given host environment exerts receptivity and conformity pressure on a stranger works interactively with the strength of the stranger's ethnic group. One way to examine the strength of an ethnic group is to assess its *ethnolinguistic vitality*. In research on the influence of the social milieu and the collective consequences of fluency in a second language, ethnolinguistic vitality has been defined by three structural variables: (a) the status of a language in a community, (b) the absolute and relative numbers of the language's users, and (c) institutional support (e.g., government services, schools, mass media) for the ethnic language (Giles, Bourhis, & Taylor, 1977; Giles & Byrne, 1982; Giles & Johnson, 1987). As such, ethnolinguistic vitality has been examined as an objective environmental condition linked to what Giles et al. (1977) propose as the "subjective ethnolinguistic vitality," or perceived legitimacy of the position of the ethnic group. For example, speakers who perceive the subordinate position of their group as legitimate are likely to adjust their communication behaviors to converge with those of the out-group.

Further insights into ethnic group strength are provided by sociologists Clarke and Obler (1976), who identify three general stages of ethnic group development. The first stage is *economic adjustment*, which occurs upon arrival of the group until its members become an integral part of the permanent economy. The second stage is *community building*, or the development of the community leadership and institutional resources used to assert the ethnic group's identity and interests. This stage of ethnic community development corresponds to the concept of "institutional completeness" offered by other sociologists (Breton, 1964, 1991; Breton, Isajiw, Kalbach, & Reitz, 1990; Goldenberg & Haines, 1992). The third stage is the period of *aggressive self-assertion*, which develops into the group's conventional use of the existing political system and other activities aimed at strengthening ethnicity and a collective ethnic identity among group members. It is in this third stage of development that some ethnic groups actively pursue identity politics (Aronowitz, 1991). Certain ethnic groups in a given society may play up their ethnic identity as a rallying point to assert themselves as separate from the identity of the larger society. Such group-level identity posturing tends to pressure group members to avoid developing relationships with out-group members through subtle or explicit forms of conformity pressure and the threat of the social exclusion of those who are successful in out-group relationships by labeling them, for example, "deserters" or "betrayers" (De Vos & Suárez-Orozco, 1990a, p. 256).

In light of these considerations, a strong ethnic group is likely to offer its members a strong ethnicity-based subculture within the larger host environment. An inverse relationship is expected between an ethnic group's strength and its individual members' cross-cultural adaptation in the host society. The adaptation-impeding influence of ethnic group strength is intensified when the group pursues political aspirations of building an identity separate from, or even in conflict with, the identity of the larger environment. Despite the likelihood that a strong ethnic group can help facilitate the cross-cultural adaptation of strangers during the initial phase, such a group tends to discourage its members' adaptation to the host milieu as it encourages ethnolinguistic maintenance. A strong ethnic community may even exert subtle or explicit political pressure on its members to conform to ethnic norms and thereby discourage members' active involvement outside the community. Conversely, strangers who have already successfully adapted to the larger society are likely to find their ethnic communities less relevant to their everyday existence.

Together, the three environmental conditions described above— host receptivity, host conformity pressure, and ethnic group strength— help define the relative degree of "push and pull" that a receiving society offers to strangers. An environment offering an optimal influence on strangers' adaptation is one in which the native population welcomes and supports the strangers while expecting them to conform to local norms. An optimal environment may also include an ethnic community that provides strangers with support during the initial transition period without exerting its own conformity pressure on group members.

Predisposition

Along with the above-described environmental conditions, the internal conditions of the strangers themselves affect the process of cross-cultural adaptation. Each stranger begins the adaptation process with a unique temperament and sensibilities. Some may be filled with determination to succeed in the adaptive journey, whereas others may find themselves bitterly resenting it. Some may be very malleable and open to new experiences, whereas others may feel they are too old to make changes in their lifetime habits. Some may find themselves "blending" well, whereas others may stand out oddly against the mainstream ethnicity of the native population. These predispositional conditions serve as a kind of blueprint for what follows in the new environment. The internal conditions with which a stranger begins life in the new environment help set the parameters for subsequent adaptive changes. The present theory organizes these various preexisting conditions into three categories: preparedness for change, factors of ethnicity, and personality characteristics. Together, these concepts help define the degree of a stranger's "adaptive potential" (Kim, 1976, 1988, 1995a) or "permeability" (De Vos, 1990a) into the host environment.

Preparedness for Change

Strangers come to a new environment with differing levels of preparedness (or readiness) for learning and adapting to life in that environment. Preparedness contributes to the overall internal capacity to take on the challenges of the host milieu. Affecting strangers' preparedness is the range of *cultural learning* they may have had prior to relocation. Well-informed individuals tend to have more realistic expectations about the cross-cultural experience (Black & Gregersen, 1990; Searle & Ward, 1990) owing to formal schooling or training as well as media exposure to and experiences in dealing with people in different cultural and subcultural communities through travel and other personal contacts.

Strangers' preparedness is often influenced by the circumstances under which their cross-cultural moves take place. A particularly important circumstantial factor is whether the move is *voluntary* and carefully *planned* or involuntary and unplanned. Voluntary, long-term immigrants are likely to make a greater effort to prepare themselves for relocation before they enter the host environment than are those who are reluctant immigrants or those who are forced by circumstances to leave their home countries.

Ethnic Proximity

The fact that strangers arrive in a new environment with differing ethnic backgrounds has bearing on their subsequent adaptation in the host environment. *Ethnicity* is an inclusive term that refers to combinations of cultural, racial, linguistic, national, and religious backgrounds, all pertaining to the distinctiveness of a people. As Phinney and Rosenthal (1992, p. 145) note, the particulars of the stranger's ethnicity influence his or her adaptation process in two interrelated manners: through difference and through compatibility. The term *ethnic proximity* is employed here to refer to the degree of the stranger's overall ethnic similarity and compatibility relative to the mainstream ethnicity of the natives.

First, each ethnicity presents a level of *similarity* (or difference), that is, the group characteristics that stand out against the backdrop of the predominant or mainstream ethnicity of the natives. Often, salient ethnic characteristics work against the stranger's adaptation as they introduce a psychological barrier between the stranger and the natives. The quality of "standing out," of being different, makes it particularly difficult for the stranger to ease into the host social milieu. Outstanding physical attributes such as height, skin color, facial features, and physique often add to the overall "foreignness" of strangers and to the psychological distance between the stranger and the local people. An Irish immigrant in the United States, for instance, presents less of a psychological strain to native-born Caucasian Americans than does someone from India or Pakistan. Such visible ethnic differences adversely affect the degree to which local people are inclined to welcome and interact with the stranger. Supporting this observation is a recent study conducted by Vazquez, Garcia-Vazquez, Bauman, and Sierra (1997), who found that skin color played a significant role in acculturation in their sample of Mexican American students.

Second, each ethnicity creates a level of *compatibility* with the host environment. A stranger whose cultural values and norms are highly compatible with those of the natives is likely to find the host environment less stressful. Such compatibility also enables the stranger to acquire host communication competence more smoothly and to participate in host social communication processes with greater ease. For example, Japanese business executives in the United States generally face a greater amount of challenge in overcoming their cultural and language barriers than do their British counterparts. Japanese compatriots working with American colleagues in a Japanese subsidiary in the United States have been found to have many workplace cultural values and practices that are extremely incompatible with those of their American counterparts (Kim & Paulk, 1994a, 1994b).

Adaptive Personality

Along with ethnicity, strangers enter a host environment with a set of personality traits that tend to endure and remain unchanged throughout life. At a given time, personality serves as the basis upon which the individual pursues and responds to new experiences with varying degrees of success. Of particular interest here are those personality resources that would help facilitate the strangers' adaptation by enabling them to endure challenges and to maximize new learning—both of which are essential to their intercultural transformation.

Openness is such a trait. In the systems perspective, openness is defined as an internal posture that is receptive to new information (see Gendlin, 1962, 1978; McCrae & Costa, 1985). Openness, like a child's innocence, enables strangers to minimize their resistance and to maximize their willingness to attend to new and changed circumstances. Openness further enables them to perceive and interpret various events and situations in the new environment without making ethnocentric judgments. As a theoretical concept, openness is a dimension of personality that enables strangers to seek to acquire new knowledge, to participate in the communication processes of the new environment, and to expand the range of their aesthetic sensibilities and their repertoires of habitual behaviors. It incorporates other similar but more specific concepts, such as *flexibility, open-mindedness,* and *tolerance for ambiguity.*

Strength is another personality trait that facilitates cross-cultural adaptation. It is a broad concept that represents a range of interrelated personality attributes, such as *resilience, risk taking, hardiness, persistence, elasticity,* and *resourcefulness.* As such, personality strength is the internal capacity to absorb "shocks" from the environment and to bounce back without being seriously damaged by them. It entails those responses to life that "set the stage for both persistence (or continued integration) and change of personality" (Stewart & Healy, 1985, p. 118). Low levels of strength are expressed in shyness, fearfulness, and distress in uncertain situations. In contrast, individuals with high levels of strength tend to be stimulated by new challenges.

Personality strength is a function of *positivity*—an affirmative and optimistic outlook of mind, or the internal capacity to defy negative prediction (Dean & Popp, 1990). Strangers with positive personalities can better endure many stressful encounters because of their tendency to believe that things will turn out as they should. Positivity is a kind of idealism—a belief in possibilities and a faith in the goodness of life and people in general. It is the opposite of defeatist cynicism. Positivity thus encourages acceptance of others despite differences and is manifested in self-esteem, self-trust, and "general self-efficacy" (Harrison, Chadwick, & Scales, 1996).

Together, openness, strength, and positivity help define the inner resources with which strangers can facilitate their own adaptation process with persistence and flexibility, as has been characteristic of many Jewish immigrants in the United States (see Zenner, 1991). Strangers who are open, strong, and positive are less likely to give up easily and more likely to take risks willingly under challenging situations in the host environment. They are better equipped to work toward developing host communication competence, as they continually seek new ways to handle their life activities. In doing so, they are better able to make necessary adjustments in themselves and facilitate their own intercultural transformation. A serious lack of these personality attributes, on the other hand, handicaps strangers' adaptive capacity and acts as a self-imposed barrier against adaptation.

Linking Dimensions and Factors:
A Structural Model

This chapter has identified a structure of cross-cultural adaptation by locating the key dimensions and factors that facilitate or impede the process. We began with the dimension of personal communication, which is most central to strangers' adaptation. The cognitive, affective, and operational facets of strangers' *host communication competence*

(Dimension 1) serve as the very engine that moves them along on the adaptive journey. Inseparably linked with host communication competence is the dimension of *host social communication* (Dimension 2), through which strangers participate in host interpersonal and mass communication activities. *Ethnic social communication* (Dimension 3) is added to emphasize the role of distinct, subcultural experiences of the strangers with coethnics. Interacting with the personal and social communication dimensions are the conditions of the new *environment* (Dimension 4), including the receptivity and conformity pressure of the host environment as well as the strength of the ethnic group. The strangers' own *predisposition* (Dimension 5) in terms of preparedness for change, ethnic proximity, and adaptive personality sets the initial parameters for the subsequent unfolding of the personal and social communication activities. Collectively and interactively, these five dimensions influence, and are influenced *by*, the adaptive changes in the direction of *intercultural transformation* (Dimension 6). As explained in Chapter 4, strangers undergo internal changes toward greater functional fitness and psychological health in relation to the host environment and toward the development of an intercultural identity.

The structure of cross-cultural adaptation and its constituent components identified above is presented in Figure 5.1. This is an interactive model in which all of the linkages indicate mutual (and not unidirectional) causations, reflecting the open-systems principle that emphasizes reciprocal functional relationships between and among a system, its parts, and its environment. The least interactivity is likely between predispositional conditions (of preparedness, ethnicity, and personality) that a given stranger brings to the cross-cultural adaptation process. Personality traits tend to remain relatively unchanged during an individual's lifetime. Nevertheless, at least some of the enduring predispositional attributes undergo the processes of change as strangers experience disequilibrium and integration and a gradual adaptive transformation through periods of significant changes or intense life crises (Horowitz, 1991; Stewart & Healy, 1985). Experiences of facing the challenges of a new and unfamiliar cultural environment involve such events. Extensive research has documented, for example, that exposure to strong environmental influences changes even genetically "fixed" temperaments such as shyness (Wrightsman, 1994). Similar changes are expected in some ethnic traits, such as cultural values and aesthetic sensibilities (including sensibilities and tastes in food, clothing, music, and humor).

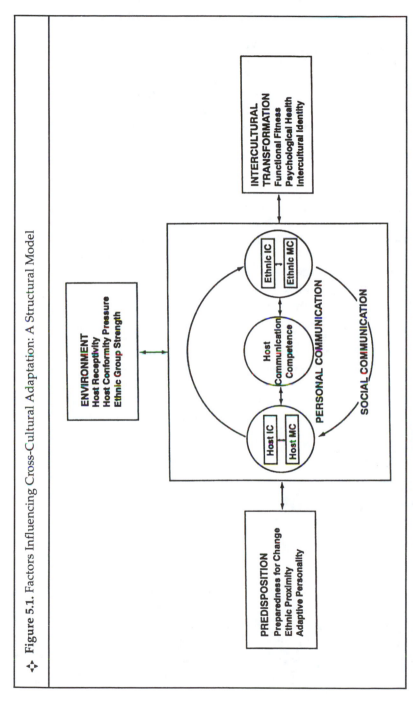

❖ **Figure 5.1.** Factors Influencing Cross-Cultural Adaptation: A Structural Model

Note: IC = interpersonal communication; MC = mass communication.

The present structural model offers an overall description of reasons for differential rates or levels of intercultural transformation within a given time period. The dimensions and factors incorporated in this model help predict the successes as well as the failures in cross-cultural adaptation. Some of the theoretical dimensions and factors may be more pertinent than others for explaining and predicting particular situations in which specific strangers may find themselves. In some cases, for example, the strangers' adaptive successes may be almost entirely due to their personal strength and openness, which enable them to overcome even the most severely hostile environment. In other cases, strangers may accomplish little cross-cultural adaptation because their fellow coethnics insulate them almost completely from having to face the host cultural challenges. Yet others may adapt poorly mainly due to their lack of host communication competence, particularly their inability to comprehend and respond to members of the host culture and their unwillingness to undergo a strenuous new cultural and language-learning experience.

In reality, all of these forces work together interactively to facilitate or impede each stranger's adaptation process. As in a locomotive engine, the workings of each unit operating in this process affect and are affected by the workings of all other units. Out of this dynamic interface among the dimensions and factors arise the fluctuating psychological experiences of stress, adaptation, and growth depicted in Chapter 4. These experiences, in time, help strangers advance toward increasingly intercultural personhood—a condition in which they are at ease with the host environment and its cultural patterns, their cultural origins, and, indeed, their ongoing transformation as well.

Assumptions, Axioms, and Theorems

All in all, the present theory is founded on the three open-systems assumptions and three boundary conditions discussed in Chapter 3 (see Tables 5.1 and 5.2). Humans are assumed to have an innate drive and capacity to adapt and grow. Adaptation of an individual to a cultural environment occurs in and through communication. Adaptation is a complex and dynamic process that brings about a qualitative transformation of the individual. Based on these basic premises, the 5 axioms identified in Chapter 4 help define the principal nature of the process of

TABLE 5.1 Boundary Conditions

1. The strangers have had a primary socialization in one culture (or subculture) and have moved into a different and unfamiliar culture (or subculture).

2. The strangers are at least minimally dependent on the host environment for meeting their personal and social needs.

3. The strangers are at least minimally engaged in firsthand communication experiences with that environment.

TABLE 5.2 Assumptions

1. Humans have an innate self-organizing drive and a capacity to adapt to environmental challenges.

2. Adaptation of an individual to a given cultural environment occurs in and through communication.

3. Adaptation is a complex and dynamic process that brings about a qualitative transformation of the individual.

cross-cultural adaptation. The theoretical delineation of the structure of cross-cultural adaptation in this chapter adds 5 more axioms. Altogether, these 10 axioms serve as the general principles operating in the cross-cultural adaptation process (see Table 5.3).

Based on the 10 axioms, 21 theorems are extrapolated to explain the differential degree or rate at which cross-cultural adaptation takes place across different individuals and environments (see Table 5.4). Although many more theorems can be logically deduced from the axioms, only those that are of direct relevance to the present purpose of describing and explaining the cross-cultural adaptation process and its structure are presented here. These theorems are stated in empirically testable predictive statements specifying the positive or negative nature of associations among the constructs identified in the six dimensions of the structure of cross-cultural adaptation.

Together, the 21 theorems help to integrate many of the existing concepts and issues that have been separately investigated in the past. The theory makes it possible to integrate the field because of the systems concepts it employs. These concepts are sufficiently generic and abstract to accommodate other, more narrowly defined concepts. The

TABLE 5.3 Axioms

1. Cross-cultural adaptation involves both acculturation and deculturation, an eventual possible outcome of which is assimilation.

2. Underlying the cross-cultural adaptation process is the stress-adaptation-growth dynamic.

3. The stress-adaptation-growth dynamic brings about an intercultural transformation in the stranger.

4. As the stranger undergoes intercultural transformation, the severity of fluctuation in his or her stress-adaptation-growth dynamic subsides.

5. Intercultural transformation is manifested in increased functional fitness, psychological health, and intercultural identity.

6. Intercultural transformation facilitates, and is facilitated by, host communication competence.

7. Intercultural transformation facilitates, and is facilitated by, participation in host social (interpersonal and mass) communication activities.

8. Extensive and prolonged participation in ethnic social (interpersonal and mass) communication activities deters, and is deterred by, intercultural transformation.

9. Environmental conditions (host receptivity, host conformity pressure, and ethnic group strength) influence, and are influenced by, the stranger's intercultural transformation.

10. The stranger's predispositional conditions (preparedness for change, ethnic proximity, and adaptive personality) influence, and are influenced by, his or her intercultural transformation.

---

term *stranger* incorporates existing terms such as *immigrants, refugees,* and *sojourners.* The term *adaptation* broadly incorporates more specific terms such as *assimilation, acculturation, integration,* and *adjustment.* In addition, the theory consolidates two previously separate areas—studies of *long-term* and *short-term* adaptation. Conceptualizing adaptation as a continuous, evolutionary process of the internal transformation of a person, the present theory considers the distinction between long- and short-term adaptation irrelevant.

The multidimensional and multifaceted structure model reflects the open-systems perspective on human communication, which emphasizes the principal features of the inseparable and interactive

TABLE 5.4 Theorems

1. The greater the host communication competence, the greater the host interpersonal and mass communication.

2. The greater the host communication competence, the lesser the ethnic interpersonal and mass communication.

3. The greater the host communication competence, the greater the intercultural transformation (functional fitness, psychological health, and intercultural identity).

4. The greater the host interpersonal and mass communication, the lesser the ethnic interpersonal and mass communication.

5. The greater the host interpersonal and mass communication, the greater the intercultural transformation (functional fitness, psychological health, and intercultural identity).

6. The greater the ethnic interpersonal and mass communication, the lesser the intercultural transformation (functional fitness, psychological health, and intercultural identity).

7. The greater the host receptivity and host conformity pressure, the greater the host communication competence.

8. The greater the host receptivity and host conformity pressure, the greater the host interpersonal and mass communication.

9. The greater the host receptivity and host conformity pressure, the lesser the ethnic interpersonal and mass communication.

10. The greater the ethnic group strength, the lesser the host communication competence.

11. The greater the ethnic group strength, the lesser the host interpersonal and mass communication.

12. The greater the ethnic group strength, the greater the ethnic interpersonal and mass communication.

13. The greater the preparedness for change, the greater the host communication competence.

14. The greater the preparedness for change, the greater the host interpersonal and mass communication.

15. The greater the preparedness for change, the lesser the ethnic interpersonal and mass communication.

(continued)

TABLE 5.4 Continued

---

16. The greater the ethnic proximity, the greater the host communication competence.

17. The greater the ethnic proximity, the greater the host interpersonal and mass communication.

18. The greater the ethnic proximity, the lesser the ethnic interpersonal and mass communication.

19. The greater the adaptive personality, the greater the host communication competence.

20. The greater the adaptive personality, the greater the host interpersonal and mass communication.

21. The greater the adaptive personality, the lesser the ethnic interpersonal and mass communication.

---

relationship between an individual and the environment. This holistic perspective on adaptation serves to integrate sociological and anthropological factors and psychological factors in explaining the cross-cultural adaptation of individual strangers. It brings together the *macro-level* analyses that have long been applied to issues of ethnic community, interethnic relations, social integration, and ethnicity and the *micro-level* analyses that have typically been conducted in social psychology and communication for exclusively intrapersonal issues such as culture-shock reactions, psychological adjustment, attitude toward the host society, and culture learning.

In merging micro- and macro-level factors, the theory allows a reconciliation of two divergent views: the view held by many investigators of the culture-shock phenomenon, which emphasizes the *problematic nature* of cross-cultural adaptation experiences; and the contrary view, which emphasizes the aspect of cross-cultural *learning and growth*. These two approaches are joined in the present theory as it recognizes both the stressful and growth-promoting functions of the cross-cultural adaptation process and the transforming effect of the dynamic tension between these two competing psychological forces. Relatedly, the structural model bridges the division between *assimilationist* and *pluralist* views concerning the degree and directionality of adaptive change. It does so by taking the systems-theoretic view that cross-cultural adaptation (and, indeed, all other aspects of human adaptation) is something that occurs naturally and inevitably through communication, as strangers achieve new learning (acculturation) while losing some of their original cultural practices (deculturation).

The assumption that adaptation is a natural and inevitable phenomenon is by no means a denial of the fact that the ideological climate of the host environment is consequential to individual strangers' adaptation processes. On the contrary, the present structural model incorporates such ideological influence in two ways. On the individual level, a given stranger's personal ideological position has to be a part of the affective aspect of his or her host communication competence. A stranger with an assimilative orientation is more likely to be determined to partake in the host social communication processes than is someone with a pluralist orientation. At the macro level of the environment, the assimilative or pluralist ideological climate is clearly a defining element of its receptivity and conformity pressure toward strangers. The same should hold true when we examine the strength of an ethnic minority group with which a given stranger interacts and/or identifies him- or herself. By incorporating both positions, the present theory maintains its ideological neutrality and balance. It has no particular predetermined cultural or political end in mind. Instead, it explains how a particular ideology can influence the individual stranger's adaptation process.

The two models depicting the process and the structure of cross-cultural adaptation emphasize the *dynamic, integrative,* and *general* nature of the reality of cross-cultural adaptation. The process model offers a systematic account of the evolutionary process of intercultural transformation over time. The structural model provides a comprehensive structure of cross-cultural adaptation through which to understand and predict the psychological, sociological, and anthropological forces operating in the adaptation process. Both models are general in that they present a wide range of applicability, including the adaptation experiences of both short-term and long-term strangers from any cultural origin, to any new destination, for any voluntary or involuntary reason.

These theoretical characteristics are grounded in the systems-based communication approach—an approach that uniquely offers a special avenue for unifying diverse perspectives in the social sciences. This approach allows a theoretical account that focuses not on the person or the group (environment), but on the "circuit" of communication that connects the two entities. In the words of Ruesch and Bateson (1951/1968):

Communication is the only scientific model which enables us to explain physical, intrapersonal, interpersonal, and cultural aspects of events within one system. By the use of one single system we eliminate the multiplicity of single universes, the multifarious vocabularies, and the controversies which arise because we, the scientists and clinicians, cannot understand each other. (p. 5)

Part III

Elaboration of the Theory

Personal Communication

We live, so to speak, in co-evolution with our own mental products.

Erich Jantsch,
The Self-Organizing Universe, 1980

*If what we can express in any present moment cannot be compre-
hended, or if what we can comprehend at that moment is not being
expressed, our existence as humans is threatened.*

Lee Thayer,
"Knowledge, Order, and
Communication," 1975

The evolutionary process of cross-cultural adaptation is punctuated
by tribulations and triumphs. Large or small, each struggle and
each triumph brings about a degree of internal transformation—no
matter how minuscule or insignificant. The very engine that drives this
transformative process is strangers' host communication competence,
or their overall capacity to engage themselves in host social communication processes in accordance with the host communication system.
Host communication competence, as such, serves as a "self-propelling"
and "self-perpetuating" agent that empowers strangers to participate
and maximize successes in social processes of the host environment
(Barker, Barker, & Hauser, 1988). Thus the present theory places the
personal communication dimension at the very center of the structure
of cross-cultural adaptation as a factor that affects (and is affected by)

all other dimensions of factors operating in the cross-cultural adaptation process (see Figure 5.1).

Host Communication Competence

Considerable divergence is seen in the existing academic conceptions of *communication competence* (a concept also variously called *interpersonal communication competence, interpersonal competence, social competence,* and *human competence*) and *intercultural communication competence* (or *intercultural competence* and such related terms as *intercultural skills* and *intercultural effectiveness*), in particular. Some have used the term *competence* interchangeably with notions of successful performance or performance outcomes demonstrated by favorable judgments of the encoder's communication quality based on *perceived* effectiveness and/or appropriateness (e.g., Gudykunst, 1983; Spitzberg, 1988, 1989; Spitzberg & Cupach, 1984). Others have viewed competence as an internal capacity or a set of identifiable capabilities associated with (but not identical to) performance outcomes such as perceived effectiveness (e.g., Dinges, 1983; Dinges & Lieberman, 1989; Kealey & Ruben, 1983; Kim, 1991; Ruben, 1989).

The latter approach is taken in the present conceptualization of host communication competence, following the original notions of competence employed by Chomsky (1968, 1986) and Hymes (1979). Communication competence is conceived to be always interactional and thus a necessary but not sufficient condition for a successful performance or its outcomes. This view is based on the fact that the actual performance and its outcomes in any communication encounter are affected not only by the individual's own internal capacity to communicate but by many other contributing factors—such as the other interactant's communication competence and biases arising from the nature of the relationship and compatibility of self-interests between the interactants. A similar case can be made regarding a professional race car driver who may not be able to avoid accidents due to various circumstances, such as hazardous road conditions, mistakes made by other drivers, or the driver's own momentary inattention.

This conception of host communication competence combines the "culture-specific" and "culture-general" dimensions (Hammer, 1989; Kim, 1991). The culture-specific dimension entails a set of abilities to encode and decode linguistic and nonlinguistic codes and practices specific to a given cultural or subcultural community. Strangers must acquire knowledge of such codes and practices in order to understand, respond to, and coordinate their social interactions with fidelity. To be successful in running a company in France, for instance, an American businessman must equip himself with an in-depth knowledge of the local communication system. At the same time, strangers also need to be equipped with culture-general communication competence. Culture-general or "intercultural" communication competence involves the ability to communicate in all types of encounters, regardless of the specific cultural context. Included in intercultural communication competence are the ability to manage various differences between communicators, cultural or otherwise, and the ability to deal with the accompanying uncertainty and stress. Such generic ability helps strangers to tolerate and appreciate their differences instead of responding to others with "intergroup posturing" (Kim, 1991).

Specifically, host communication competence can be conceptualized in terms of three interrelated kinds of components: cognitive, affective, and operational. Although these components do not necessarily develop simultaneously and at the same pace, development in one aspect facilitates development in the others, so that an overall balance and integration may be achieved over time. The cognitive, affective, and operational components are interdependent and simultaneously present in actual communication situations (Barker et al., 1988; Booth-Butterfield, 1991). They are treated here as separate categories solely for the purpose of organizing various adaptive communication abilities in a coherent framework. This three-pronged conception of host communication competence corresponds to Kuhn's (1975) model of a communication system. Kuhn describes the state of an individual communication system by its "detector," "selector," and "effector" processes. The detector process is the concept-perception function that processes information, the selector process is related to the goal or value function of the individual, and the effector process involves the physical ability to carry out the selected behavior. This scheme is also consistent with other existing conceptions of communication competence, such as Spitzberg and Cupach's (1984) notions of "motivation," "knowledge," and "skill"; Taft's (1977) "cognitive," "dynamic," and "behavioral" dimensions; Brislin, Landis, and Brandt's (1983) concepts of "thinking," "affective reactions," and "behavior"; and Grove and Torbiorn's (1985) "clarity of the mental frame of reference," "emotional adequacy," and "applicability of behavior."

Cognitive Components

The cognitive components of host communication competence are the mental capabilities of comprehension and "sense-making" ability to ascertain the meanings of various verbal and nonverbal codes. On the whole, cognitive competence reflects the capacity to identify and understand messages in different situations of interaction with the environment. Through cognitive competence, strangers can achieve "coorientation," a convergence of their subjective meaning systems with those of the natives (Kincaid, 1988; Kincaid, Yum, Woelfel, & Barnett, 1983). Strangers cannot have any meaningful communication with the natives unless they recognize and understand at least some of the natives' verbal and nonverbal communication codes and practices.

Knowledge of Host Communication System

Cognitive competence includes knowledge of the communication system operating in the host environment. One of the most salient factors of cognition in cross-cultural adaptation, of course, is knowledge of the host *language*. Knowledge of the host language means not just linguistic knowledge, such as knowledge of phonetics, syntax, and vocabulary. It also entails pragmatic knowledge about the everyday use of the language, including the many subtleties in the way the language is spoken and interpreted in various formal and informal social engagements.

The language of a given society represents the real as well as perceived social, political, and ideological pressures on cultural strangers and linguistic minorities (Clachar, 1997; Reid & Ng, 1999). Language is a communication medium for turning a power base into influence. In turn, the creation and maintenance of power occurs in and through language. Any language is a veil over the reality of a culture based on an agreement among the users about what there is to be seen and how it should be seen. As Whorf (1952) notes, a linguistic system is "not merely a reproducing instrument for voicing ideas but rather is itself the shaper of ideas, the program and guide for the individual's mental activity, for his analysis of impressions, for his synthesis of his mental stock in trade" (p. 5; quoted in Hoijer, 1985, p. 211). Language is the primary conduit for the adaptation of strangers. The extent of strangers' knowledge of the host language corresponds to the extent of their new cultural learning and engagement in the new social processes

(Clément, Noels, & Karine, 1994; Cohn & Wood, 1982; McAllister, 1986; Noels, Pon, & Clément, 1996). Knowledge of the host language is not limited to the ability to express and comprehend new information. It enables strangers to access the accumulated records of the host culture and to learn to *think* in the way the native speakers think (Brown, 1991). In Lewis's (1948) words:

> The constant intention of every society is to socialize its members.... language is the primary means of the socialization of the individual. As he becomes increasingly a member of a linguistic community, language plays a larger and larger part not only in his social life but in his personal behaviour, feeling, and thought. His effective membership in his society directly depends upon his ability to communicate with his fellows; in turn his power of communication is a primary factor in his development as an individual. (p. 12)

The development of host language competence, in turn, brings status and power for strangers, both psychologically and socially. A person speaks not only to be understood but also to be empowered—believed, obeyed, respected, and distinguished. Hence the full definition of host language competence is the right to speech, that is, to legitimate the language of authority. Host language competence thus serves as a primary agent of social currency with which strangers can access the mainstream culture and pursue personal and social goals. Strangers with little or inadequate linguistic competence are often subject to subtle discrimination. Testifying to this fact is a personal account by novelist Jan Novak, a native of Czechoslovakia who emigrated to Chicago in 1969 following 10 months in Austrian refugee camps. This account shows how Novak's development in English-language competence brought about a broader cultural change in her unconscious mind and a range of personal freedom to express herself as a writer:

> I was sixteen when I left Czechoslovakia and seventeen when I arrived in the United States. I didn't speak any English at all, and I started writing poetry—in Czech about Czechs for Czechs. After a time I went to school and began translating my work into English. That is to say, I was still writing in Czech about Czechs, but I was now writing for Americans. Ten years into my stay in the States I noticed that in my dreams even Czechs were speaking English. I think that at that point my unconscious mind was sort of switching gears. I was also getting tired of the tedious and redundant business of translation. So I started to write in English, and I found I was ready for it; work just came pouring out. And my verbal life became more exciting

because of this change. At that point, I was writing in English, still about Czechs, for Americans. I made the final plunge in my last book, which has no Czech characters, so now I am writing about Americans in English for Americans. (in Brodsky, 1990, pp. 115-116)

Considerable research attention has been devoted to the significance of language orientation in promoting cross-cultural adaptation. Early on, DeFleur and Cho (1957) included "language behavior" as one of the crucial areas in their "index of acculturation." Almost all subsequent studies of cross-cultural adaptation have included language competence and have presented empirical evidence for the paramount importance of host language competence in various adaptation situations. For example, Nishida (1985) found that the English competence of Japanese students in the United States was closely related to their interactional effectiveness. H. K. Kim's (1991) laboratory study of intercultural dyads showed that nonnative individuals who were perceived as competent in the host language were more liked by native individuals than those who were perceived to be less competent. Relatedly, surveys of South Asian refugees in the United States have shown that those who were fluent in English had labor force participation rates similar to or higher than those of the American population as a whole; the unemployment rate of those who spoke limited English was twice the national average; and those who spoke no English had an even higher rate of unemployment (Jaeger & Sandhu, 1985; Office of Refugee Resettlement, 1984). Language proficiency has also been found to be positively related to indicators of psychological adjustment. LaRose and Gebart-Eaglemont (1994), Epstein, Botvin, Dusenberry, Diaz, and Kerner (1996), and Noels et al. (1996) are among the many researchers who have reported a significant positive association between indicators of language competence and indicators of psychological adaptation.[1]

Accompanying the host language are the *nonverbal codes*, the rich repertoire of vocal and physical ancillary codes that are ritualized in the communication practices of the natives. The adequacy and effectiveness of communication is governed not only by words but also by the use of more or less standardized behaviors, ceremonies, rituals, and norms. Implicit, nonverbal messages such as facial expressions and body movements, vocal patterns, and spatiotemporal behaviors establish the emotional and attitudinal undercurrents of interactions, regulate the flow and rhythm of social interactions, and help define the nature of the relationships among interactants (Argyle, 1975). Like language, many nonverbal codes are shaped by cultural conditioning from early childhood. Once acquired, nonverbal codes act to encourage, inhibit, or otherwise alter the direct expression of emotional experiences. Ekman and Friesen (1971) call these factors *display rules*—that is, cultural expectations about emotional expressions. Nonverbal codes thus regulate the "rhythms" of interactions and "action chains" such as gesturing or other body movements signifying turn taking and turn yielding or initiating and terminating interactions (Hall, 1976, 1979, 1983).

The verbal and nonverbal codes and rules of the host culture define the local *communication rules* about "correct" or "right" behavior. These rules enable the natives to make sense of events, activities, and actions in their society. Communication rules function as directives that govern the flow of messages from one person to another and limit the possibilities of actions of the participants. Such rules also identify recipes that specify how a given social goal may be achieved and render the behavior of each person more or less predictable and understandable to others. Communication rules apply to all levels of behavior, both verbal and nonverbal as well as formal and informal. Some are explicitly coded within the written or spoken language, as in the case of grammatically correct writing or organizational rules and regulations. Most other rules, however, are implicit; they deal largely with the nature of interpersonal relationships, such as involvement and intimacy, dominance and status, and cooperation and accommodation. In each situation, from asking a friend for help to seeking to resolve a conflict in a relationship, nonverbal behaviors reflect the normative cultural rules and elicit specifiable responses with often measurable social consequences.

Clearly, strangers must learn and understand these implicit communication codes and the processes of the host culture, just as they need to learn the host language, if they are to become successful in communicating with the host environment. Many embarrassing and awkward moments do, indeed, occur when strangers lack the nonverbal knowledge of the host culture and remain "out of sync" with the natives. Even with outstanding knowledge of English, for example, many foreign students on American campuses experience discomfort in communicating with Americans due to lack of fluency in paralinguistic patterns such as accent, intonation, tempo of utterance, and placement of pauses. Such deviations from the normative speech patterns are coupled with other nonverbal inadequacies, such as inappropriate or awkward kinesic patterns, including facial expressions, eye behavior, hand gestures, body posture, body movement, and interpersonal spatial behavior. Nonverbal inadequacies may be further experienced in temporal behaviors that are critical to the perception, structuring, and management of time and that are manifested in the way the natives plan, pace, and punctuate formal and informal social transactions.

Cultural Understanding

The task of acquiring host communication competence by learning the communication codes and rules of the mainstream culture is a monumental and lifelong task. It entails much more than "mastering" the language alone, as strangers face the special challenge of learning the covert, subtle, implicit, complex, and context-bound uses of the language as well as of the host nonverbal codes. Gradually, making almost imperceptible gains, strangers can develop more complete host communication competence only through direct participation in host interpersonal and mass communication processes. The crucial place of the development of cognitive competence in strangers' adaptation has been widely recognized since the Social Science Research Council (1954) defined cross-cultural adaptation as primarily a matter of "perceptual reality" (p. 993).

Achieving full knowledge of the communication codes and rules of the host environment requires a general and deep understanding of the cultural and subcultural milieu that provides the context for specific situations. As Gumperz and Cook-Gumperz (1982) point out, grammar and accent are less often the cause of poor communication in interethnic encounters than is the lack of ability to make a logical argument in accordance with the host cultural logic. Strangers need to go beyond simply knowing verbal and nonverbal patterns; they need to understand the cultural mind-sets (Fisher, 1988) operating in the host environment. A deeper-level understanding of the local culture involves knowledge of its historical, political, economic, religious, and educational institutions as well as its values, ideologies, arts, sciences, technologies, attitudes, beliefs, values, and reciprocal role requirements. If, for example, strangers are to adapt to a predominantly Muslim culture, they need to have an understanding of the Muslim heritage underlying the various public and private social dynamics of that culture. Cultural understanding helps strangers to share the natives' shared memory, to interpret the hidden, unspoken assumptions operating in the natives, and to see how and why the natives communicate in the ways they do (Sechrest, Fay, & Zaidi, 1982).

Initially, strangers' knowledge of the host culture tends to be simplistic, informed by gross stereotypes rather than accurate and detailed distinctions. Many of strangers' "think-as-usual" patterns become unworkable in their dealings with the host environment. The inadequacy of their verbal and nonverbal patterns can create discomfort, if not outright communication "breakdown." In this uncertain situation, securing adequate information about the environment is an obvious necessity for the adaptive process. A conflict that took place in Monterey Bay, California, between Vietnamese refugee fishermen and the local fishing community illustrates this point. As Orbach and Beckwith (1982) relate, the Vietnamese entered the community and undertook independent fishing operations without understanding an informal local rule concerning loose geographic areas where particular fishermen or groups had preferential rights to set fishing traps. Because this rule was beyond the reach of the Vietnamese entrants into the industry—especially those who were not knowledgeable in English—the conflict led to incidents of "citizens' arrests" of Vietnamese, the vandalizing of Vietnamese fishermen's equipment, and the sinking of their boats.

Through repeated social interaction with the host environment, however, strangers become increasingly proficient in understanding the host culture. Such development is reflected in the advanced form of language use, which requires understanding not only of the language's phonemic, syntactic, and semantic rules, but of its pragmatic rules that reflect the cultural and subcultural connotations of linguistic expressions in situ. In particular, slang, idiom, jokes, humor, satire, metaphors, and other forms of language usage are highly nuanced and contextual, requiring substantially intimate knowledge of the relevant cultural experiences of the native speakers (Lee, 1994; Ruidl, 1982). Understanding such language usage is difficult for strangers even when they have extensive formal "textbook knowledge" of the host language. It is only through extensive and continuous exposure to and participation in host social processes that they are able to develop a deeper understanding of the pragmatics of the host language. Thus fluency in idiomatic communication is an indicator of relatively high-level acculturation. In a study of Asian new arrivals in Hawaii, Ruidl (1982) found a positive correlation between idiomatic fluency and close friendships with Americans.

The cultural knowledge of any structurally complex group can never be complete, even for a lifelong member of the group. Thus strangers' understanding of the host cultural system can be assessed only in relative terms. Yet strangers must understand the cultural rules operating in the host environment to the extent necessary and possible in order to deal with the challenges of the host culture. In the case of the Vietnamese fishermen mentioned above, the strangers learned the rules the hard way. In time, and after repeated contacts, strangers' cultural understanding will increase so that they may not only understand the natives' communication rules, but even participate in the implementation of the rules. As the strangers improve their ability to "fill in" the unspoken assumptions behind host communication behaviors, they become better able to manage their daily activities.

Cognitive Complexity

Knowledge of the host communication system and understanding of the host culture accompany the development of cognitive complexity, that is, the refinement of an individual's "cognitive schemas" or "structures of meaning" (Kelly, 1955). Whereas knowledge and understanding aspects of cognitive competence involve primarily the informational base of cognition, the concept of cognitive complexity addresses the structure (or pattern) of information processing. Cognitive complexity has been recognized in psychology in terms of "differentiation" and "integration." According to Schroder, Driver, and Streufert (1967, 1975), individuals with complex cognitive structures tend to differentiate or particularize (Billig, 1987) their perceptions and are adept at consolidating different information "pieces" into a coherent and meaningful whole. The development of an integrative cognitive system occurs when an individual's "self-schemas" form a cohesive structure out of seemingly diverse and even opposite traits and characteristics (Horowitz, 1991). Strangers' cognitive integration increases their capacity to know "how" they know what they know with regard to the host milieu. We may consider the content aspect of strangers' cognitive competence as the substance of their ideas that constitute the requisite information necessary to perform various social transactions.

Accordingly, cognitive simplicity (or low-level cognitive complexity) is reflected in simplistic, stereotypical, and incohesive perception and interpretation. A low level of cognitive complexity is closely linked to ignorance (Allport, 1954) as well as depersonalized (or impersonal), stereotypical, and simplistic opinions about out-group members based on in-group membership (Francis, 1976; Tajfel & Turner, 1979, 1986). Cognitive simplicity has also been found to be associated with lack of prejudice, contact, attribution errors, in-group favoritism, and out-group discrimination (Brewer, 1979, 1986; Clark, 1985; Jaspars & Hewstone,

1982; Pettigrew, 1979, 1982; Weigel & Howes, 1985). By implication, strangers with high-level cognitive complexity are more knowledgeable about the host culture and language and have developed a psychological orientation that is more personalized, less based in stereotypes, and less prejudicial toward the natives. As strangers gradually attain cognitive complexity, they can better differentiate along more dimensions and categories between their original culture and the host culture. Strangers with higher cognitive complexity thus are able to perceive events and issues unfolding in the new environment in a more realistic manner and to detect subtle variations and nuances in social situations.

The development of strangers' cognitive complexity in understanding the host culture and communication system is a cumulative process. As Schroder et al. (1967, 1975) explain, cognitive complexity in a given content area is not static over time but can develop with new learning experiences. Initially, strangers' perceptions and interpretations of the environment tend to be simplistic and unrealistic as they sort events and people into certain categorical molds. Gross stereotypes serve as salient screening devices, helping them maintain the easiest and most economical cognitive structure. This is a case of the principle of "least effect" at work: Simplified images give strangers something to hang on to in the absence of more detailed knowledge of the host environment and help them cope with uncertainty. Strangers' cognitive development is closely linked with their increased competence in the host language and culture (see Hogg, 1996), allowing for a greater "perceptual readiness" (Bruner, 1957)—a closer match between their mental images and the reality of the host milieu and their experiences with the natives.

Extensive research evidence links cognitive complexity and other indicators of cross-cultural adaptation. Seelye and Wasilewski (1981), in a study of immigrant children (ages 6-13), observed positive associations of increased cognitive complexity with increased flexibility in interpersonal interaction, a flexible coping style, a repertoire of linguistic and psychomotor behavior patterns peculiar to the host culture, and an understanding of the efficacy of different behavioral options within each situation. Research on adult immigrants and sojourners has also shown that, in general, strangers' perception of the new culture becomes more complex and refined over time along with increased host language competence, and that such perceptual development is closely linked to increased social participation in the new environment. Coelho (1958), for example, found that Asian Indian students, over a 3-year period in the United States, showed increasingly differentiated perspectives on the American culture, with corresponding detail, variety, and scope. Such cognitive development, in turn, was significantly related to the numbers of American friends the students reported having during the same period. A study of Chinese immigrants by Lindgren and Yu (1975) also showed an enhanced understanding of American culture with increased exposure to the host culture. My own research with Korean immigrants also shows a trend of increasing cognitive complexity measured in terms of the immigrants' ability to identify similarities and differences between Korean and American friendship patterns (Kim, 1976, 1977).

Together, the three interrelated cognitive components of host communication competence—knowledge of verbal and nonverbal codes, cultural understanding, and cognitive complexity—help define the overall congruence between the strangers' subjective meaning system and that of the natives. Such semantic congruence increases over time as strangers become better adapted to their new environment (Szalay & Inn, 1988), serving as a key to the development of functional fitness, psychological health, and intercultural identity.

Affective Components

Strangers' cognitive development is closely linked with their affective development—that is, the emotional and motivational "drives" or "reflexes" toward successful adaptation in the host environment. Taft (1977) identifies affective competence as the ability of strangers to relate to the "dynamic" aspect of culture that allows individuals to meet their "self-expressive needs." Along with cognitive competence, affective competence facilitates cross-cultural adaptation by providing an emotional and motivational capacity to deal with the various challenges of living in the host environment. Included in affective competence is flexibility in cultural identity, which is reflected in the willingness to learn the host language and culture and to make some changes in original cultural habits. Also included in affective competence is strangers' ability to appreciate and empathize with the emotional and aesthetic sensibilities of the natives.

At the heart of affective competence are strangers' attitudes toward the host environment and toward themselves. Strangers who feel positive and respectful toward local people tend to maintain less psychological distance from them than do those who may resent or have little genuine interest in understanding them. In addition, strangers often lack affective competence when they feel insecure, ambivalent, or confused about their own cultural identity or feel marginal because of the sense that they are rejected by the native members of the host environment. As such, affective competence serves strangers as their motivational and attitudinal readiness to accommodate the host environment, with all its challenges and promises. It further helps strangers to develop a capacity to participate in the values and emotional/aesthetic experiences of the local people. Through affective competence, strangers can understand the often subtle and hidden meanings embedded in various messages from the host environment; this ability enriches their experiences with the natives.

The concept of affective competence thus embraces various existing concepts that have been employed in communication and social psychological studies, including "ambiguity tolerance" (Ruben & Kealey, 1979; Tamam, 1993), "empathy" (Ruben & Kealey, 1979; Tamam, 1993), "empathic motivation" (Burleson, 1983), "psychological distance" (Amir, 1969), "intergroup anxiety" (Gudykunst, 1995; Stephan & Stephan, 1985, 1989, 1992), "ethnocentrism" (Brewer & Campbell, 1976), and "prejudice" (Allport, 1954; Weigel & Howes, 1985). These and related concepts are integrated in the present theory into three main components: adaptation motivation, identity orientation, and aesthetic/emotional orientation.

Adaptation Motivation

Adaptation motivation—the will or willingness to participate and become functionally fit in the host environment—involves an internal quarrel between the individual's self-command to act and his or her resistance to acting. Adaptation motivation influences, and is influenced by, how strangers envision their relationship with the host environment. This psychological posture underlies strangers' self-guiding propensity to imagine what does not yet exist, including what they would like to achieve in the host environment. In some cases, no external pressures may be as strong as self-motivation in influencing strangers' behavior. The more intense the strangers' motivation to adapt, the more they are likely to make an effort to learn about and participate in the host environment with enthusiasm and perseverance.

The anticipation-based nature of adaptation motivation, indeed, is likely to be a key factor that differentiates the extent of cross-cultural adaptation of temporary sojourners from that of permanent settlers (immigrants and refugees). Sojourners, thinking of their visits abroad as transitory (e.g., limited to the period of an assignment), may not consider any serious commitment to adaptation. With little motivation, they may not find it important or worthwhile to learn the host communication systems and participate in the host communication processes (Aitken, 1973). Coelho's (1958) findings in his study of Asian Indian students in the United States substantiate this observation: Coelho observed significant differences in adaptation motivation between students planning to stay in the United States and those planning to return to India. Other studies have documented a positive relationship between adaptation motivation and other aspects of cross-cultural adaptation. Selltiz, Christ, Havel, and Cook (1963) found that foreign students in the United States varied considerably in their interest in getting to know Americans and that such variations were associated with the students' actual social relations with Americans. Taylor and Simard (1975) found the lack of interaction between ethnic groups in Canada to be more a function of motivation than of language capacity per se. Similarly, Martin, Bradford, and Rohrlich (1995) provide evidence that successful exchange student experiences are related more to expectation than to acculturation. Many other social psychological researchers have documented the critical importance of motivation in second-language learning (e.g., Gardner, 1985, 1991; Gardner & Clément, 1990). Relatedly, van den Broucke, de Soete, and Böhrer (1989) found a significant association between lack of motivation and unsuccessful social functioning of exchange students as indicated by serious complaints about the students' maladjustment by host family members, school officials, or the students themselves.

Similar observations have been made about certain immigrant groups in the United States. Massey (1987) reports that, in the case of Mexican immigrants in the United States, ties to Mexico (especially through owning property there) are a factor associated with the likelihood of return migration. In comparing the adaptation of Cuban and Puerto Rican immigrants in the United States, Friedrich (1985) found that Cuban refugees, realizing that they could not go home before long, accepted the United States as a permanent home. Friedrich interprets this realization as the main reason for Cubans' relatively higher economic adaptation rate compared with Puerto Ricans (many of whom are free to come and go between the mainland United States and Puerto Rico). Likewise, Suro (1998) has attributed the relatively slower pace of socioeconomic mainstreaming of Hispanic immigrants (compared with Asian and European immigrants) in the United States to differences in adaptation motivation stemming from the ease with which they can visit and maintain ties with their home countries.[2]

Identity Flexibility

Closely related to adaptation motivation is flexibility in identity—a basic psychological-social orientation of individual strangers with respect to themselves, their original cultural group, and the host culture at large. A flexible self/other orientation helps to engender greater openness and lessen unwarranted prejudicial cynicism toward new cultural experiences. Included in a flexible identity orientation is the stranger's willingness to accept the identity of the host culture. In contrast, a rigid identity orientation engenders closed-mindedness and a defensive and critical posture. As social identity theorists have explained, individuals' identity orientation tends to rigidify when they feel that their in-group identities are threatened by an out-group. Their desire to distinguish their own identities from other group identities leads to "in-group favoritism" (or tendency to favor in-group members over out-group members) and "in-group bias" (or unreasonable and unjustifiable forms of in-group favoritism). Such psychological tendencies are likely to polarize in-group/out-group differences and to generate intense "intergroup posturing" (Kim, 1991), increasing discriminatory behaviors toward out-groups (Perreault & Bourhis, 1998) and thus hindering openness to new cultural learning. In a study of Portuguese immigrants and first-generation Canadians of Portuguese descent, for example, Lanca, Alksnis, Roese, and Gardner (1994) found that the degree of an individual's ethnic identity was significantly correlated with his or her preference for the Portuguese language over English or French.

The psychoanalytic notion of a "frustration-aggression" mechanism (Berkowitz, 1962; Zajonc, 1952) offers further understanding of rigidity in identity orientation in the face of conformity pressure from the host environment. The theory contains the assumption that frustration—the blockage of a goal—is followed by some form of aggression. This aggression may not always be directed toward the actual source of frustration. Instead, the aggression may be "displaced" onto a different target; it may also be subtle, indirect, and delayed. In the case of strangers experiencing difficulties in the host environment, at least some of their frustrations stem from their inability to meet personal and social goals. They are likely to experience bitter and angry hostility toward the conditions of the host environment and to be less engaged in host social communication processes. Such an outlook would increase an individual's psychological insecurity (or other similar experiences, such as fear and uncertainty), self-alienation, "minority status stresses" (Saldaña, 1994), and withdrawal from the host environment. Strangers who are insecure are likely to prefer their own language (Edwards, 1985, 1994), seek support from less "threatening" coethnics rather than from natives (Lazarus, 1966), and engage in aggressive and hostile responses to out-group members even under mildly threatening conditions (Eastman, 1985; Francis, 1976; Hutnik, 1986; Hutnik & Bhola, 1994). Furthermore, identity rigidity and related defensive behaviors have been found to provoke defensive postures in out-group members as well. Bourhis, Giles, Leyens, and Tajfel (1979), for instance, found a close linkage between identity insecurity and interethnic conflict, suggesting different types of "divergent speech behavior" (that distances the speaker from an out-group interaction partner) resulting from the feelings of insecurity generated by perceived threats from out-groups.

Flexible identity orientation, in contrast, is closely related to a positive intergroup orientation. Punetha, Giles, and Young (1988) found that Sikh, Hindu, and Muslim immigrants in Britain with a smaller psychological distance from the natives showed a stronger desire to adapt to British society and a weaker desire to maintain separate identities of their own. Similarly, Zimmermann (1995), in a study of international students on an American college campus, found a significant positive correlation between the subjects' identification with the new environment and indicators of psychological adjustment, host interpersonal communication, and host language competence. Ward and Searle (1991) likewise found that American business managers in the United States and in Thailand assessed their overseas experiences more positively than did their Japanese counterparts in both countries; the researchers attribute this finding to the greater identity flexibility on the part of Americans. More recently, Eschbach and Gomez (1998) have reported a positive correlation between identity flexibility ("identity switching") by Hispanic high school students and the students' families' economic status.

Aesthetic Coorientation

Along with the strength of adaptation motivation and flexible identity orientation, strangers' affective coorientation is reflected in the extent to which they are able to fulfill their aesthetic needs in the host environment, or their capacity to participate in such experiences of the natives. The system of aesthetics is an important aspect of shared life experiences in a given cultural group and thus a vital component of its cultural identity (Fischer, 1961; Jung, 1964; Leuthold, 1991;

Maquet, 1979). Mansell (1981) describes the importance of the aesthetic/emotional fulfillment of individuals in an alien culture:

> The concept of aesthetic awareness is linked with ineffable, intuitive feelings of appreciation and celebration. This form of awareness creates a consciousness which transforms individuals' perceptions of the world and imports a sense of unity between self and surrounding.... It is in this transformative mode of experiencing that many people create access to the momentary peaks of fulfillment which makes life meaningful. (p. 99)

Strangers often find it difficult to gratify their aesthetic needs. Because natives' experiences are spontaneous, unstructured, and mostly unspoken, inexperienced strangers cannot adequately meet their aesthetic needs when they find their own sensibilities incompatible with those of the natives. Strangers whose aesthetic sensibility, for instance, is rigidly tied to a certain narrowly defined kind of music may find the types of music popular in the new environment uninteresting or even unbearable. Such strangers can fulfill their aesthetic need only when they are able to participate emotionally in the strange texture and rhythm of the local music without resistance and prejudice. The inability to participate in this way often forces strangers to turn to their original ethnic cultures to compensate for their unfulfilled needs.

Through repeated exposure to varied social situations and communication encounters, strangers gradually familiarize themselves with, accept, and appreciate local aesthetics. To a large degree, the development of aesthetic coorientation with the host culture parallels the process in which members of older generations reluctantly accept the sensibilities of members of younger generations. As strangers develop their aesthetic/emotional coorientation with local people, they are increasingly better able to empathize with the surrounding cultural productions, including art, music, and sports, as well as to appreciate the culture's everyday experiences of fun, joy, humor, and happiness, and of anger, despair, frustration, and disappointment. In this development, the strangers' communication experience becomes richer and more meaningful to them. Their sense of connection to the host environment becomes more complete and fuller, and they are better able to be a part of the "collective unconscious" of the natives—their myths, rituals, and habits. In this visceral connection, strangers no longer stand outside the domain of the host culture; they are now on their way to meaningful

engagements with the natives as friends and neighbors with a sufficient level of comfort and satisfaction.

Operational Components

Strangers' host communication competence is ineffectual until its cognitive and affective components are coupled with its "operational"
components (Taft, 1977) of communication competence, "enactment
tendencies" (Buck, 1984), or "skills" (Taft, 1977). Collectively, *operational competence* refers to the capacity to express one's cognitive and
affective experiences outwardly through specific behaviors. This
capacity allows strangers to carry out successful social transactions in
accordance with the prevailing cultural and subcultural norms operating in specific situations (Ruben, 1976; Ruben & Kealey, 1979). No matter how competent strangers may be cognitively and affectively, they
cannot be successful in their interactions with the host environment
without a corresponding operational competence. Operational competence is conceptually differentiated from actual communicative performance: Whereas operational competence involves strangers' "internal
capacity" to carry out behaviors externally in accordance with the host
cultural patterns, actual behaviors are necessarily a function not only of
the strangers' operational competence but also of many other external,
circumstantial factors, including the behavior of the other person and
the nature of the relationship involved.

Technical Skills

Among the primary components of operational competence are
technical skills. As a basic aspect of operational competence, technical
skills are essential to an individual's carrying out daily activities in general and performing social roles in particular (Taft, 1977). Technical
skills range from basic language skills, job skills, and academic skills to
skills in locating appropriate information sources and solving the various day-to-day problems. Studies of sojourners and immigrants in the
United States and Canada have shown that the lack of technical ability
to solve various routine tasks (such as driving a car, finding directions,
filing taxes, and seeking information and assistance from appropriate
sources) correlates significantly with psychological problems (see, e.g.,

Diggs & Murphy, 1991; Mendenhall & Oddou, 1985; Wong-Rieger, 1984, 1987).

Technical competence, of course, expands as strangers go through trial and error. As they learn the pragmatics of the host environment, they are able to internalize integrated sequences of appropriate acts and activities in a relatively smooth and spontaneous manner. As they achieve an increasing level of technical competence, they no longer go through mental "rehearsal" before performing. At this level, strangers find that their daily activities become less stressful and more gratifying.

Synchrony

Beyond technical skills, operational competence entails the capacity for synchrony, or the ability to carry out communication interactions with local people in ways that are compatible, congruent, and harmonious. Two close friends, for example, often confide in each other, speaking "in one voice," each "echoing" the other's patterns of communication. Hall (1976, 1979, 1983) provides extensive documentation of paralinguistic and other types of nonverbal convergence patterns across cultures. Included in Hall's observations are temporal, spatial (proxemic), paralinguistic, and kinesic convergence patterns, all of which constitute the concepts of "interaction rhythm" and "action chains." In each culture, communicators "move" together, in part or in whole, in a synchronized manner so as to mirror or complement each other's nonverbal patterns in a kind of dance, such as the highly stylized "verbal listening" among Japanese and the more silent listening behavior among Americans (Miller, 1991). A more widely recognized example is the practice of bowing in Japan, in which two people's lowering of the head and the upper body follows a symmetrical or complementary form and rhythm of movement, accompanied by correspondingly synchronized vocal and facial expressions.

Synchrony in communicative interaction is reflected in two broad categories of behavioral adjustments: symmetrical (mirroring) and asymmetrical (complementary) (Kim, 1993). These synchronic behavioral types generally correspond to what Burgoon, Dillman, and Stern (1993) have identified as serving the function of fulfilling the corresponding interactional norms, "reciprocity" and "compensation." Further insights into the phenomenon of synchrony are offered in the notion of "convergence" in speech accommodation theory (Giles, Bourhis, & Taylor, 1977; Giles, Mulac, Bradac, & Johnson, 1987; Giles & Smith, 1979) and its newer, expanded version, communication accommodation theory (Gallois, Franklyn-Stokes, Giles, & Coupland, 1988; Gallois, Giles, Jones, Cargile, & Ota, 1995). According to Giles and his associates, individuals interested in the effectiveness of an intergroup encounter tend to make adjustments in their behavioral patterns (e.g., modification of dialect, vocabulary, vocal intensity, and length of pauses and loudness) in a direction toward those of another interlocutor. Another explanation of the convergence phenomenon has been offered in Kincaid's (1988) convergence theory, in which a gradual convergence of two initially differing cultural systems is predicted to occur as a function of continual contact and communication between the systems' members. In addition, Bernstein (1975) found that speakers tend to make convergent linguistic choices as well, specifically in terms of the lexical and syntactic characteristics called "elaborated" and "restricted codes."

Achieving synchrony in operational communication competence can be more challenging than acquiring technical skills. Strangers who are competent in technical skills may find it difficult to detect the subtleties in local communication patterns. In fact, the natives are often unable to identify and explain specific patterns in their own communication practices. It is only through prolonged exposure and participation in the social processes of the host environment that strangers are able to develop ease and proficiency in all aspects of the interaction process, including topic management and managing conversational give-and-take (Young, 1995). When this occurs, they are able to speak the host language with a fluency and style that flows smoothly with the way the natives speak. Strangers are able to achieve such social ease and proficiency when they are able to coordinate their actions and behaviors with those of the natives and attain highly personalized psychological relationships (Chen, 1990) with the natives.

Resourcefulness

Relatedly, operational competence includes resourcefulness, or the ability to reconcile cultural differences and come up with creative action plans in carrying out daily activities—from managing face-to-face encounters, initiating and maintaining relationships, and seeking appropriate information sources to solving various problems and finding ways to accomplish personal and social goals. This creative resourcefulness, in turn, enhances the quality of strangers' communication encounters with local people. Given strangers' understanding of the local customs and the differences between their own and the local practices, strangers must be resourceful in dealing with such differences. Resourcefulness further reflects a sense of security the strangers feel about their identity, cultural or otherwise, enabling them to negotiate differing identity orientations between themselves and those with whom they interact (Ting-Toomey, 1993). Because each social transaction presents a unique set of contextual conditions, there are few concrete rules that strangers can learn that can help them know how, say, an American businessman visiting a Japanese company should deal with apparent cultural differences between the United States and Japan in the way business is conducted. Resourceful persons figure out how to deal with such differences in ways that maximize their effectiveness in performing their role as negotiators. In a recent study of international students on an American college campus, Zimmermann (1995) found that the students' ability to be resourceful and flexible in interacting with American students was closely linked to their sense of being well adjusted to American life.

On the whole, resourcefulness, along with technical skills and synchrony, reflect a given stranger's behavioral competence—his or her capacity to select and enact behaviors that are likely to be effective and appropriate in various social situations. These three concepts also help consolidate more specific concepts that have been employed in defining communication competence, such as "behavioral complexity" (Applegate & Sypher, 1988), "behavioral flexibility" (Samter, Burleson, & Basden-Murphy, 1989), "message complexity" (Applegate & Sypher, 1988), "person-centered communication" (Applegate & Delia, 1980; Applegate & Sypher, 1988), "interpersonal management" (Applegate & Leichty, 1984), "interaction involvement" (Cegala, 1981, 1984), and "interaction management" (Koester & Olebe, 1988; Olebe & Koester, 1989; Ruben & Kealey, 1979).

Linking Cognitive, Affective, and Operational Components

The three facets of host communication competence elaborated in this chapter—cognitive, affective, and operational—are inseparable in reality (see Figure 6.1). Simultaneously and interactively, they shape a stranger's overall capacity to participate in the host environment and facilitate the stranger's participation in host social communication activities (Theorem 1) and long-term intercultural transformation

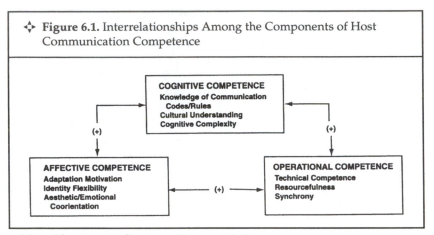

❖ **Figure 6.1.** Interrelationships Among the Components of Host Communication Competence

Note: Plus signs indicate positive associations.

(Theorem 3) while discouraging extensive and prolonged involvements in ethnic communication activities (Theorem 2). Strangers with an advanced level of cognitive competence (with greater knowledge of the verbal/nonverbal communication codes and cultural patterns of the host environment and a higher level of cognitive complexity in processing the information from the environment) are likely to be more motivated to interact with the natives, are more positive and flexible in their orientation toward themselves and the host environment, and are better able to understand and participate in the emotional and aesthetic experiences of the natives. The same strangers also tend to be skilled and resourceful in responding to new situations through effective and appropriate behaviors and are more in sync with the rhythms of the host communication processes. The interrelatedness of cognitive, affective, and operational components of host communication competence has been documented in empirical studies of immigrants (e.g., Kim, 1976, 1977, 1980) and sojourners (e.g., Maruyama, 1998; Maruyama & Kim, 1997; Zimmermann, 1995).

In time, strangers gradually increase their host communication competence. Through trial and error, and through cumulative learning and experience, they become better able to identify, understand, affirm, appreciate, and feel comfortable with the peculiar patterns and paradoxes in the host society. Through varied interfaces with the natives, and through exposure to host mass communication messages, strangers also become more keenly conscious of many of the peculiarities of their original cultural that they had previously taken for granted. They become better able to find different ways of responding to personal and social needs—from the simple acts of applying for a bank account and expressing gratitude to a friend to more complex transactions, such as managing a business and cultivating new friendships. As strangers' host communication competence increases, so do their "intersubjectivity" (Crossley, 1996; Schuetz, 1964, 1970) and "coorientation" (H. S. Kim, 1991; Pearce & Stamm, 1973), which enable them to relate to native members of the host culture more fully. Host communication competence thus serves as the central force behind strangers' gaining access to and control over the host environment. It facilitates strangers' development of an intercultural identity by enabling them to experience the deeper, emotional-aesthetic dimension of the local life and to be transformed in the process.

For most strangers, achievement of advanced host communication competence requires a continuous, lifelong endeavor. It is a process of personal development that leads to the attainment of the characteristics of "cosmopolitan communicators" (Pearce, 1989). As strangers achieve a significant level of interculturalness, they are better able to make deliberate choices of actions, with flexibility and objectivity, through the use of a sophisticated "metasystem." They attain a greater autonomy and harmony in relation to the host environment, as suggested in the story of Stephan Kovalski, told by Dominique Lapierre in *The City of Joy* (1985). Kovalski, one of the main characters in Lapierre's novel, is a Polish Catholic priest who arrives at a poverty-stricken sector of Calcutta, India, in August 1965, when he is 32 years old. He comes to share and ease the plight of the people of Calcutta who are suffering from poverty and disease. *The City of Joy* is based on Lapierre's own experiences as well as on 2 years of research he conducted in Calcutta and other places in Bengal. He was given access to personal diaries and correspondence, and the bulk of his research consisted of more than 200 lengthy interviews. These interviews, which Lapierre transcribed into English and French, are the basis for much of the dialogue and the testimonies in the book.

In this story, we see Stephan Kovalski's enormous achievement in developing cognitive, affective, and operational communication competence over the years, through daily observation and interaction with the local people. As the book progresses, Kovalski not only comes to understand intellectually but also becomes fully in sync with the emotional and aesthetic undercurrents of the local people's everyday lives. The following passage presents an incident in which his profound transformation can be witnessed:

His sad appearance was an indication that Kovalski's Indianization was almost under way. One day his neighbors recognized that the process was almost complete. It was at the conclusion of a marriage ceremony. Some Hindu friends had just married their last daughter to the son of one of his neighbors. Kovalski knelt down in front of the father and mother to do what possibly no other foreigner had done before him. He wiped the dust from their sandals and raised his hands to his forehead. This gesture was a way of saying to them, "Since my little sister has married my little brother, you are my parents. I have become a member of your family." (Lapierre, 1985, p. 222)

Social Communication

Struggle as we may, "fixing" will never make sense out of change.
The only way to make sense out of change is to plunge into it, move
with it, and join the dance.

Alan Watts, *The Wisdom of Insecurity*, 1951

Strangers cannot fully develop host communication competence, the main engine that drives the cross-cultural adaptation process, without participating in the social processes of the host milieu. Conversely, strangers' social participation is possible only to the extent that the strangers are able to communicate in accordance with the norms and practices of the local people. Every interpersonal or mass communication event offers strangers an opportunity to develop host communication competence. The message input from each social event offers a reference point against which strangers can compare their own communication patterns and, when necessary, correct those patterns. Adding complexity to the crucial linkage between strangers' host social communication and host communication competence are the ethnic ties that strangers develop and maintain with their coethnics. More often than not, strangers not only maintain contacts with the people close to them back home, but have access to networks of coethnics in the new environment.

Given the dual context of hosts and coethnics, this chapter examines a number of interrelated issues: How do strangers' involvements in interpersonal and mass communication with host nationals evolve?

How does strangers' participation in host interpersonal and mass communication processes facilitate their adaptation? How do strangers' involvements in ethnic interpersonal and mass communication activities change? How does strangers' prolonged reliance on ethnic communication systems deter their adaptation in the host environment?

Host Social Communication

Strangers' participation in the social processes of the host environment takes place mainly through interpersonal relationships with local people and exposure to the natives' mass communication processes. Broadly defined, *host mass communication* includes various ways and sites in and through which the host culture is disseminated and perpetuated, such as restaurants, schools, churches, supermarkets, highways, political campaigns, the fashion industry, theaters, museums, art galleries, and libraries, in addition to the commonly recognized mass media of radio, television, newspapers, and magazines.

Host Interpersonal Communication

Interpersonal communication in the context of relationships is central to social existence. Mostly on a voluntary basis, people mature through their relationships with others (Fogel, 1993; Palisi & Ransford, 1987). Having been removed from most of their long-standing friends, family members, and coworkers back home, strangers begin the process of constructing new sets of relationships with members of the native population. It is in and through such relationships that strangers participate in interpersonal activities with natives and are given opportunities to learn the host cultural practices and to engage in "corrective exchanges" (Moos & Mitchell, 1982; Norrick, 1991) with respect to the use of the host communication system (including its verbal and nonverbal codes), as communication in any given relationship almost always exerts some degree of social influence and control (Heckathorn, 1990; Ho & Sung, 1990; Milroy, 1982, 1987). Through personal contacts in their relationship networks, strangers observe and learn from nativeborn acquaintances and friends the standards of verbal and nonverbal communication practices, the underlying tacit assumptions, and the subtleties of the aesthetic and emotional sensibilities of the local people. Consciously or not, strangers rely on other network members for interpretation of various attributes and actions of others and of themselves. By conferring with the natives (or with ethnic friends who are successfully adapted), strangers can confirm or reject presumed meanings and motives in natives' communication behaviors. They learn not only what to do, but also how they are doing. Interpersonal networks further exert social control by determining the language strangers must use and by conveying messages of cultural values and social approval or disapproval.

Interpersonal communication experiences with natives also provide emotional support to strangers by helping to ease the loneliness, stress, and difficulty that strangers encounter (Fogel, 1993; Jou & Fukada, 1995; Marcia, 1993; Tanaka, Takai, Kohyama, Fujihara, & Minami, 1994). Strangers seek support in their efforts to find necessary information and to handle the difficulties they face; they also need help in finding additional contacts (Jou & Fukada, 1995).[1] The sense of security that strangers gain from supportive relationships with natives generally outweighs the difficulty and anguish that strangers may go through in establishing such relationships. Ordinarily, strangers' formation of relationships with natives is constrained by specific circumstances, such as the workplace, neighborhood, and other physical and social placements in which the strangers find themselves. For business managers from Japan assigned to a company subsidiary in the United States, for example, relationships with Americans are likely to be primarily with coworkers and other business contacts within the workplace. On the other hand, elderly parents of Russian immigrants who came to the United States to join their family may have little access to Americans with whom to develop relationships.

Relationship formation is also largely voluntary; it is a function of the mutual interest and willingness of all persons involved. Thus strangers' interpersonal communication activities are best revealed through certain identifiable patterns of *personal networks*—also called *interpersonal networks, social networks, communication networks, ego networks, egocentric networks,* and *personal communities.* The personal network has been investigated extensively in the fields of anthropology, sociology, and communication.[2] As Rogers and Kincaid (1981) observe: "The uniqueness of an individual's personal network is responsible for the uniqueness of his meaning. The codes and concepts available to interpret information are based on each individual's past experiences which may be similar . . . to another individual's" (p. 45). The convergence of cultural and communicative patterns in individuals' relational networks is further reinforced by the "contact hypothesis," which links increased interaction between members of different racial/ethnic groups to a narrowing of previously divergent attitudes (Amir, 1969; Amir & Chana, 1977; Worchel, 1979, 1986).[3]

Some of the concepts attached to personal networks are useful for the examination of the nature and configuration of strangers' involvement in interpersonal communication activities with local people and the relationship of that involvement to other aspects of cross-cultural adaptation. A personal network consists of "nodes"—that is, other persons with whom the "Ego" (the focal person at the center of a network) has relations—and the relations among these nodes. As such, a personal network can be examined in several ways. First, a network can be seen as being made up of all nodes, including the "core" or "first-order" nodes (others whom the Ego knows directly) and the "second-order" or "peripheral" nodes (those whom the Ego knows indirectly, through one or more of the first-order nodes) (Leenders, 1996; Morgan, Neal, & Carder, 1997). Second, a network can be defined somewhat narrowly to include only the "first-order" nodes—those people with whom the Ego is directly involved. Third, an even more restrictive approach can be taken in which the network is seen as comprising only the smaller, more influential "primary" nodes with "significant others," that is, those persons who substantially influence the formation, maintenance, or modification of the Ego's cultural and communication patterns (McDermott, 1980; Smith, 1976).

For the present purpose of understanding strangers' interpersonal communication activities in the context of cross-cultural adaptation, the second, moderately inclusive, view of the personal network is useful. Because of the potentially wide variance in the extent of strangers' involvement with local people, restricting analysis of their networks according to the third view would exclude the situations of many strangers whose host relational ties are limited to only superficial ones. On the other hand, the most inclusive approach of counting all first- and second-order ties would dilute the relevance of strangers' personal network patterns to an understanding of their adaptation.

Size/Proportion of Host Ties

For strangers with only a limited level of host communication competence, developing relationships with natives is a challenging or even threatening task. As Simard (1981) notes, relationship formation across ethnolinguistic boundaries is perceived to be more difficult than relationship formation within such boundaries. This perceived difficulty, according to Simard, is due not only to differences in language but also, and more important, to psychological barriers such as ethnic identity. Gudykunst (1983) found a similar result in his study of intra- and intercultural communication; that is, his respondents perceived initial conversations as developing more easily in in-group encounters than in out-group encounters.

Notwithstanding cross-cultural psychological barriers, strangers develop at least a limited number of interpersonal ties with host nationals over time. As their host communication competence improves, so does their self-confidence regarding participation in host interpersonal communication activities. The increased number of host ties, in turn, brings about an increased ratio of host ties to all ties included in the personal network (Kim, 1986, 1987). Although newly arrived immigrants and sojourners tend to be drawn to coethnics for social activities, over time they incorporate more ties with local people into their personal networks, replacing some of the ethnic ties.

Among an extensive pool of empirical data supporting the importance of ties with natives is Zimmermann's (1995) finding that talking with American students was "the single most important factor" in psychological adjustment to American life for a sample of international students. Likewise, Selltiz and associates found that sojourners in the United States who were more actively involved with Americans were more satisfied with their sojourn experiences and perceived the American society and people more favorably (Selltiz & Cook, 1962; Selltiz, Christ, Havel, & Cook, 1963). Other researchers who have studied sojourners in the United States and elsewhere have reported similar results, linking the number of host nationals in personal networks to various indicators of acculturation. Wen (1976) found that the degree of mental illness experienced by Chinese immigrants tended to vary with the degree of their non-Chinese relationships. Shah (1991) found a positive relationship between Asian Indians' social interactions with Americans and their psychological adaptation in the United States. The same relationship has been reported by Takai (1991) based on a study of international students in Japan, and by Noels, Pon, and Clément (1996), who conducted a survey of Chinese college students in Canada. In the case of American Indians, those with greater relational involvement with non-Indians have been found to be significantly "happier," higher in income level, and more intercultural (compared to cultural) in identity orientation than those with only limited involvement with non-Indians (Kim, Lujan, & Dixon, 1998a, 1998b).[4]

Relatedly, schooling in the host community has often been pointed out as a key means of status mobility among immigrants (De Vos & Suárez-Orozco, 1990a, p. 260). This finding may be explained by the fact that in schools and on college campuses, strangers are surrounded by, and form relationships with, local people. In contrast, strangers whose personal networks comprise primarily coethnics manifest a monocultural ethnic frame of reference, or what Suárez-Orozco (1990) calls a "dual frame of reference" (p. 280). Suárez-Orozco found in his research among Central Americans in an American inner city that, to a high degree, these immigrants remain psychologically in their homeland rather than in the host society. Likewise, many urban Italian immigrants in Belgium are reported to measure their condition not in terms of Belgian views of the "good life" but in terms of Sicilian standards (Suárez-Orozco, 1990, p. 280). Christie (1976) and Dosman (1972) also found that "elite" or "affluent" sectors of Native American Indian reserve communities in Canada were plugged into off-reserve networks (consisting of both Indians and non-Indians or representatives of the Bureau of Indian Affairs) and that such interethnic bonds helped make the transition to urban life a simpler and more stable process. In a study of Black graduate students, Adkins-Hutchison (1996) found similar evidence for the adaptation-facilitating function of host relational ties. The students' perceptions of their academic success and positive attitudes were positively associated with more mixed social contacts (with non-Black as well as Black faculty members and fellow graduate students). In a study of Ghanaian immigrants in Toronto, Owusu (1996) found that most of the immigrants lived in neighborhoods that offered close proximity to fellow Ghanaians, and that their lack of common interests was a principal reason for the weakness of their relationships with non-Ghanaians.[5]

Figure 7.1 shows the gradual change that takes place in the composition of strangers' personal networks from maximum homogeneity of ethnic ties to a greater heterogeneity of ethnic and host ties. This adaptive change in network composition generally corresponds with a common change in strangers' physical living arrangements, such as neighborhoods. Many newly arrived immigrants and sojourners live in close proximity to their coethnics in urban ethnic enclaves, such as Chinatown in San Francisco, Little Havana in Miami, and the Polish neighborhoods in Chicago (Lum, 1991). Studies of Korean and Southeast Asian immigrants, for example, have documented the gradual mainstreaming of neighborhood ethnics and the corresponding change in personal networks, with coethnic relationships diminishing as relationships with natives increase over time (Kim, 1976, 1980; Yum, 1982, 1983).[6]

Researchers have typically analyzed the personal networks of immigrants and sojourners simply by counting the numbers of ethnic and nonethnic ties, or by computing the ratios between the two

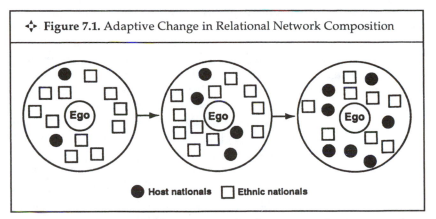

✧ **Figure 7.1.** Adaptive Change in Relational Network Composition

● Host nationals □ Ethnic nationals

Note: Network size is held constant in this figure to emphasize network composition.

relational categories. Few systematic attempts have been made to determine whether nonethnic ties must be limited to members of the dominant group in the host environment (e.g., Caucasian Americans in the United States). Nor is it clear whether an analysis of personal networks should include others from many different backgrounds, or whether they may all be from one group so long as it is different from the stranger's ethnic group. Empirical data show no apparent relationship between the increasing incorporation of other nonmainstream members of the host community in the Ego's personal network and the development of host communication competence and psychological and social dimensions of cross-cultural adaptation (e.g., Alba, 1976, 1978, 1990; Kim, 1976, 1980; Kim et al., 1998a, 1998b; Noels et al., 1996).

Strength of Host Ties

Once the overall composition of the stranger's personal network is identified, it is possible to examine the "strength" of the ties maintained with host nationals (as well as ethnic individuals) in the network. "Tie strength" (Granovetter, 1973)—that is, whether ties are "strong" or "weak"—incorporates at least the two interrelated relational characteristics of intimacy and centrality.

The *intimacy* of a given relationship is manifested in some form of mutual affective engagement, as in friendship or other close relationships such as romantic relationships (Hays, 1989; Koenig, 1990). According to Altman and Taylor (1973) in their "social penetration theory," relational intimacy is cultivated through the increasing breadth and depth of mutual self-disclosure of information and stabilization of the affective exchange. As such, relational development is seen as a progression in which partners make themselves increasingly accessible to each other's more private life experiences. Altman and Taylor compare this social penetration process to the peeling of the outer layers of an onion. The greater the surface area that becomes exposed to a relational partner, the greater the breadth of the relationship. Each of those areas, in turn, has underlying layers, with the inner core representing a person's basic needs, feelings, and values. The more a relational partner is able to penetrate into these inner aspects of personality, the greater the depth of the relationship. The intimacy of ties with natives in a stranger's personal network is variously expressed in the degree of solidarity, intensity, reciprocity, or bondedness. Intimacy is also manifested in the mutuality and commitment vested in the relationship between the involved parties—that is, the relative level of difficulty in breaking the relationship. Some of a stranger's relationships with natives may be public, impersonal, superficial, and casual, whereas others may be private, personal, and emotionally involved (see Kim, 1986, 1987; Marsden & Campbell, 1983; Wellman, 1982, 1983, 1992; Yum, 1984, 1988).

The relational intimacy discussed above is associated with, but does not necessarily coincide with, the *centrality* of host ties. Whereas intimacy emphasizes emotional mutuality and bonding in relationships, centrality points to the importance (or value) and potential social influence of a given person to the Ego, relative to others in the network (Brewer, 1992; Faust & Wasserman, 1992; Kameda, Ohtsubo, & Takezawa, 1997; Shook & Finet, 1987).[7] To an American businessman marketing American computer products in Japan, for instance, relationships with those Japanese in charge of local computer retail stores would be important to the Ego, but not necessarily intimate. Likewise, graduate students from Taiwan working toward doctorates at American universities would find their relationships with American professors to be some of their most important ties. Relatedly, those individuals central to the Ego are better able to "get in touch" with the Ego, find out what is going on, pass on information, and offer advice (Berkowitz, 1982, p. 18). Even though few studies of cross-cultural adaptation have employed centrality measures, centrality is potentially a useful indicator of the extent to which natives are integrated into the stranger's everyday life.

Over time, strangers develop stronger relational ties with host nationals, as depicted in Figure 7.2. Taken together, the intimacy and centrality of host ties in a given stranger's personal network at a given time are indicative of the advances he or she has made in the cross-cultural adaptation process. They represent the overall strength of relationships with natives and, hence, the enhanced quality of communication that the stranger enjoys with natives. The combination of intimacy and centrality of host relationships profiles the "social capital" of the stranger's functioning in the host environment. Strangers with many strong (intimate and central) ties to natives are likely to have incorporated a great many of the psychological and social attributes of the host culture. Indeed, they are often no longer viewed as "strangers" by the natives. Research findings support this observation. Selltiz et al. (1963) found that, as time went on, foreign students in the United States met more different kinds of people and visited American families more, and that, by the end of their first year, they had made at least one close American friend. The trend of increasing host tie strength has also been observed among other sojourner groups (e.g., Okazaki-Luff, 1991) and immigrants (e.g., Kim, 1976, 1989, 1990) and in the context of intermarriage, through which strangers develop intimate ties with host nationals through their spouses' relational networks (e.g., Alba, 1976, 1978, 1990; Friedrich, 1985; Tinker, 1973).

Although strong ties, particularly marital relationships, play a vital role in facilitating strangers' cross-cultural adaptation, weak ties (Granovetter, 1973; Weimann, 1983, 1989) should not be considered insignificant to the adaptation process. All relationships with host nationals serve as sources of information based on which strangers

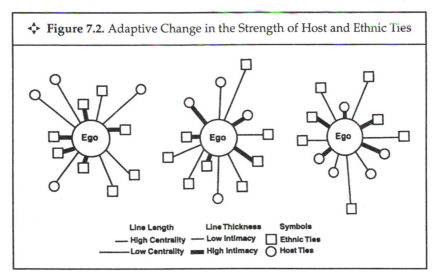

❖ **Figure 7.2.** Adaptive Change in the Strength of Host and Ethnic Ties

learn the host culture and communication patterns. In Weimann's (1983) analysis of relational patterns between members of different social groups (such as age and occupational groups) in a kibbutz community in Israel, weak ties were observed to serve as the most frequent "bridges" or "middlemen" between members of different groups (Wellman, Yuk-lin, Tindall, & Nazer, 1997). From a macro-level perspective, weak stranger-host ties serve the vital function of providing linkages between various ethnic groups. Along with mass communication processes, even weak relational linkages between strangers and hosts help spread information, innovations, and regulations of the host sociocultural system.

The two network characteristics examined so far—the extent to which host nationals are incorporated into the network and the tie strength of the stranger-host relationships reflected in the intimacy and centrality of such ties—serve as two main considerations when we examine strangers' interpersonal communication activities in the context of their cross-cultural adaptation. If their network compositions are primarily ethnic, that would indicate that the strangers' coethnics remain all-important to them, their group identity remains largely monocultural, and their functional fitness in the larger host environment is less than satisfactory. The identifiable patterns of strangers' personal networks at a given time, in turn, facilitate or constrain their subsequent adaptive learning and acquisition of host communication competence. Homogeneous ethnic personal networks diminish strangers' adaptation, whereas the inclusion and strength of host ties in strangers' personal networks facilitates subsequent adaptation by serving as the basis for further development of host communication competence.

Host Mass Communication

Adaptive functions of host mass communication have long been suggested in studies of immigrant adaptation. Some mass communication theorists have contributed theories and propositions that have direct relevance for the cross-cultural adaptation process. Gordon (1964), for example, has theorized that "the media's major socialization influence is on (1) the images and stereotypes we possess of our environment, our social systems; (2) the long-term value systems we possess; and (3) what we view as priority concern—by way of the media's agenda-setting function" (p. 13). Also, in his formulation of the mass communication process, Lasswell (1948/1964, p. 51) recognizes three major functions: surveillance of the environment, correlation of the components of society in making a response to the environment, and transmission of the social inheritance. Both Gordon's and Lasswell's views clearly point to the adaptation function of mass communication processes, which transmit not only topical events but also societal values, norms of behavior, and traditional perspectives for interpreting the environment—just as they contribute to the socialization of nonimmigrant younger generations. Shibutani and Kwan (1965) articulate this view when they state that "the extent to which members of a minority group become acculturated to the way of life of the dominant group depends upon the extent of their participation in the communication channels of their rulers" (p. 573).

Amount of Host Media Use

Because of the public nature of mass media, the scope of strangers' cultural learning can be extended beyond their immediate interpersonal environment through participation in the mainstream host mass communication processes. Through such participation, strangers learn about the broader range of host cultural elements—they are exposed to the culture's aspirations, traditions, history, myths, art, work, play, and humor, as well as current issues and events. Host mass communication experiences thus offer strangers an opportunity to complement their interpersonal communication experiences. Graves (1967) and Nagata (1969) both included the possession of a television set as one of the items in their indices of acculturation. DeFleur and Cho (1957) made a similar assumption for the adaptive function of radio; they used the amount of daily exposure to radio and television as key elements of "recreational behavior" (p. 249). As an extension of "visual orientation" for knowledge as well as entertainment, DeFleur and Cho employed moviegoing as one of the key indicators of "acculturation orientation" of Japanese immigrant women (p. 249). Relatedly, Spindler and Goldschmidt (1952) included moviegoing (together with radio use) as a component in their "index of social acculturation" among Menomini Indians.

Employing cross-sectional analyses in my own research, I have documented a significant increase over time in the use of American mass media by Asian immigrants in the United States (Kim, 1976, 1977, 1979b, 1980, 1989, 1990). Likewise, Chang (1972) found a recognizable difference in American mass-media use among three groups of Korean immigrants ("cultural assimilation group," "bicultural group," and "nativistic group"). Shah (1991) has drawn conclusions with respect to Asian Indians that are similar to those reached by Nagata (1969) with respect to first-, second-, and third-generation Japanese Americans. Other studies have revealed evidence for a theoretical linkage between increased host mass-media use and other aspects of adaptation, including adaptation motivation and development of host communication competence. Richmond (1967), who studied Canadian immigrants, observed that newspapers and magazines explicitly and implicitly "convey a knowledge of Canadian norms of behavior and social institutions, without which the immigrant will remain incompletely absorbed into the Canadian way of life" (pp. 138-139). Relatedly, Reece and Palmgreen (1996), Stilling (1997), and Chaffee, Nass, and Yang (1989) have all found the use of host mass media to play a positive role in strangers' acceptance of host cultural values, adaptation motivation, and socialization into the host political processes.[8]

Information-Oriented Use of Host Mass Media

Of the various types of host mass communication activities, exposure to information-oriented media content (e.g., news, news analyses, and editorials/opinions) is particularly significant in facilitating (and reflecting) cross-cultural adaptation. Compared with the use of entertainment-oriented media content, the use of information-oriented media content has been found to be far more strongly associated with formations of host relational ties (Kim, 1976, 1977, 1979b). This finding is reinforced by evidence found in other studies, including Reece and Palmgreen's (1996) work concerning Asian Indian graduate students at an American university. According to these investigators, the "need for acculturation" (or adaptation motivation) is significantly correlated with viewing of national news coverage.

While complementing the limited scope of cultural learning provided by interpersonal communication processes, the adaptive function of a specific mass communication experience is likely to be weaker than that of a specific interpersonal communication experience. Communication activities involving interpersonal relationships (particularly those involving face-to-face encounters) are high in intensity, providing strangers with unsolicited and simultaneous feedback messages that subtly, yet powerfully, let the strangers recognize inadequacies in their behaviors. Comparatively, the inherently unidirectional mass communication experience offers a more passive and private mode of communication, with little direct feedback or control over the interaction. Mass communication messages also depict largely undifferentiated (or stereotypical) images of the host culture at large.[9]

Within these and related constraints, however, mass communication experiences are positively associated with various aspects of cross-cultural adaptation. Clearly, strangers' participation in host mass communication processes fills the gap that strangers have in communicating with natives interpersonally. Mass communication experiences help strangers broaden their perspective on the host culture beyond their immediate interpersonal environment by providing information about the society at large. The intensity inherent in many face-to-face communication situations may be too stressful for strangers who are poorly equipped with host communication competence. They may shy away from participating in direct encounters with natives. In such situations, mass media provide alternative, less stressful channels of communication through which strangers with inadequate communication competence can absorb some elements of the host culture.

The supplemental adaptive function of mass communication experiences documented in a study of Korean immigrants in Chicago provides evidence for the relatively weaker adaptive function of mass communication (Kim, 1976, 1977). The statistical association between American mass-media consumption and cognitive complexity (in perceiving U.S. society), for instance, was found to be significantly weaker than that between interpersonal communication with Americans and cognitive complexity. The relatively weaker role of mass communication has been observed in the ethnicity-maintenance role of ethnic mass media compared with ethnic interpersonal involvements, according to Lam's (1980) study of Chinese immigrants in Toronto. This finding suggests that the adaptive function of host mass communication is likely to be significant, particularly during the initial phase of the adaptation process and among new arrivals whose need to learn the host language is high. During this phase, strangers have yet to develop sufficient host communication competence and often find their direct encounters with local people to be stressful. As they feel awkward and out of place in relating to the natives, their anticipated or actual negative feedback from the natives can be too overwhelming for them to face. They are, then, more likely to avoid or withdraw from direct interpersonal encounters when they can and, instead, resort to less-personal, less-direct mass communication as an alternative, virtually pressure-free, way of learning the host language, in particular, and about the host environment in general (Aames, Aames, Jung, & Karabenick, 1977).

Ethnic Social Communication

Strangers' participation in the social processes of the receiving community is complicated by their interactions with their coethnics. Many new arrivals' initial resettlement processes may be aided by ties with family and friends back home as well as with coethnics and ethnic organizations in the host community. Such ethnic social communication activities can be adaptation enhancing to the extent that they involve people who have already advanced in their adaptive experiences in the host environment. In most cases, however, communication within ethnic communities tends to impede, rather than facilitate, strangers' long-term cross-cultural adaptation to the host cultural milieu.

Short-Term Adaptation-Facilitating Function

New arrivals who experience a decline in emotional well-being often seek out ethnic communication. Faced with uncertainty and anxiety, strangers often seek refuge and opportunities to relieve their cross-cultural stress among ethnic friends and kin who share a common background and common experiences as strangers. Accordingly, many strangers initially gravitate toward places where they have at least some access to ethnic support systems through family, friends, or community organizations, such as churches and social clubs (Chan & Lam, 1987a; Hurh & K. C. Kim, 1990; Stopes-Roe & Cochrane, 1990; Ying & Liese, 1991). By locating themselves in or near an ethnic community, strangers can have some sense of "security" in an alien land. Through the emotional support strangers find in ethnic communication activities, they are able to avoid serious psychological "breakdown." As Albrecht and Adelman (1984) note, "Individuals will be most likely to perceive that those who share a stressful context will be more helpful as sources of support than those who do not share the context, provided that the stressful conditions are seen as reversible to some degree" (p. 20). Because the task of developing host communication competence is a monumental one, strangers often find host interpersonal communication experiences stressful and less than satisfying emotionally. Liu Zongren (1984), a Chinese journalist who had studied in the United States for 2 years, pointed out such frustration: "During my stay in the United States I had met many [American] people, some of whom had become very good friends. . . . they had helped me in every way they could to understand American life. But few of them really understood me or knew why I couldn't feel comfortable among Americans" (p. 200).

Among the most dramatic evidence for the role ethnic communication can play in strangers' mental health are the personal testimonials of some of the Jews who survived the Nazi concentration camps (e.g., Chodoff, 1976; Dimsdale, 1976; Kogon, 1958; Ostwald & Bittner, 1976; Steiner, 1967), American prisoners of war in Vietnam (e.g., Coffee, 1990), and Western hostages in the Middle East (e.g., Anderson, 1993; Keenan, 1992). Under the most harrowing conditions, these individuals were able to maintain their sanity and at least minimum control over their daily lives through some form of communication with other inmates—from sharing a room with a coethnic and sharing a secret underground communication network of tapping on the walls and coughing signals to receiving and sending letters to family and friends back home and hearing and reading news about the home country.

Many immigrants and sojourners begin seeking ethnic support systems even before they enter the host society. International students' choices of universities are often influenced by the availability of some ethnic ties at arrival. The Hmong refugees in the United States have been observed to rely on their own ethnic networks following the patterns of "group settlement" (Coombs, 1979) or "chain migration" (Price, 1968; Rex, Joly, & Wilpert, 1987; Zunz, 1977). Similarly, Krause (1978), in a study of Italian, Jewish, and Slavic immigrant women in Pittsburgh between 1900 and 1945, observed that ethnic friends, relatives, neighbors, and their own children played a vital role in the settlement of the immigrant women. Deusen (1982) and Valdéz (1979) have likewise reported Vietnamese and Puerto Ricans' high settlement in their respective ethnic networks of family, friends, and coworkers.[10]

The natural inclination for strangers to affiliate with coethnics is consistent with Albrecht and Adelman's (1984) views on support-seeking behavior. Based on uncertainty reduction theory (Berger, 1979; Berger & Bradac, 1982; Berger & Calabrese, 1975), Albrecht and Adelman hypothesized that people generally would seek support from those with whom they perceived less relational uncertainty. The same tendency would be seen among strangers, who would prefer seeking support from fellow coethnics whenever available to going through the uncertainty and anxiety of interacting with natives and taking the risk of performing inadequately in the unfamiliar modes of the host communication system. Although interacting with natives involves a great deal of psychological challenge, ethnic relations are less stressful, as they are formed on previously acquired and shared repertoires. Ethnic gatherings through churches or holiday festivities further provide strangers with opportunities to share familiar language, food, music, and private jokes without being constrained by cultural barriers. In participating in ethnic social activities, strangers are relieved from the strain of having to deal with the unfamiliar language and culture and are offered temporary solace and refuge.

Strangers' reliance on ethnic social communication and support systems is influenced by the degree of "institutional completeness" (Breton, 1964, 1991) of their ethnic community. As elaborated later in this chapter, institutional completeness is the degree to which the community has established its own religious, media, welfare, business, political, and other organizations. Inglis and Gudykunst (1982) have found the institutional completeness of an ethnic community to be significantly associated with the extent of ethnic relational ties. These researchers replicated an earlier study conducted with the large Korean community in the Chicago area (Kim, 1976) in Hartford, Connecticut, where the Korean community was much smaller and less institutionalized. Inglis and Gudykunst found that the Koreans in Hartford, indeed, were significantly less involved in coethnic ties than were those in the Chicago area.

The extensive reliance on other immigrants within the ethnic community has been observed frequently by researchers. Among the types of assistance made available for strangers in ethnic communities are the services provided by formal community organizations (e.g., Asian Human Services) and informal "self-help" patronage or "mutual assistance" systems among various immigrant and refugee groups largely invisible to the mainstream service organizations (Aames et al., 1977; Mortland & Ledgerwood, 1988). These formal and informal organizations are set up to offer technical and informational services in areas that range from housing and jobs to other necessities such as language training and immigration-related assistance. The Vietnamese Association of Illinois, for example, assists with many of its members' needs by providing translation services, housing information, transportation, and counseling (Kim, 1980). Ethnic religious organizations and social clubs help strangers develop contacts and friendships with other coethnics and provide advice concerning various questions that newly arrived individuals might have (DeCocq, 1976).

Similar supportive functions are also provided by ethnic mass communication systems. Ethnic media often provide at least some information about the host environment.[11] This informing function of ethnic media is often carried out through reports on immigration law changes, tax laws, etiquette, and other kinds of information that helps strangers adapt to the local community. Ethnic media have been a vital part of communication processes in many ethnic communities. Such has been the case in the United States since the first newspaper aimed at an ethnic population, the *Philadelphia Zeitung*, produced for the burgeoning German community in that city, began in 1732. According to Zubrzycki (1958), the ethnic (foreign-language) press in the United States peaked between 1884 and 1920, with 3,444 newspapers and journals catering mostly to Europeans. Many of the early ethnic newspapers have withered away, but the influx of Hispanics and Asians has given rise to dozens of new ones. Today, several hundred ethnic newspapers, in at least 40 languages, are reported to circulate in the United States (Sreenivasan, 1996). In some large cities, such as Chicago, Los Angeles, and New York, ethnic communities also have access to foreign-language radio and television programs for varying numbers of hours or days per week, in addition to their own newspapers, movies on videotape, music cassettes, and magazines available at neighborhood stores (Kelly, 1985; Miller, 1987; Subervi-Velez, 1986).

Along with community organizations, ethnic media serve as "gatekeepers" (Kurth, 1970; Lewin, 1951; Shoemaker, 1991) or "culture brokers" (Snyder, 1976). Through ethnic interpersonal ties and media uses, strangers are provided with indirect links to the host environment. In a study of the Spanish American community in Denver, Kurth (1970) found that newcomers looked to those ethnic friends and acquaintances with greater access to the mainstream Anglo community as "leaders" (p. 141). Similarly, Mortland and Ledgerwood (1988), in a study of a Southeast Asian refugee community in Boston, identified a patronage system mostly invisible to American service providers. The refugee patrons were an integral part of the refugee communication network, controlling the flow of information and resources between Americans (including service agencies) and the refugee population.

In addition, ethnic media serve an entertainment function in the community. By providing entertainment for community members, ethnic media help relieve the pressures that strangers feel in dealing with the host environment and help meet their needs for fun and relaxation (Ward & Kennedy, 1994). Ethnic media provide vital "emotional refueling" to newly arrived strangers, helping them to cope with uncertainties and the sense of uprootedness (Deusen, 1982; King, 1984; Krause, 1978).

Long-Term Ethnicity-Maintenance Function

Although ethnic support systems play a potentially vital role in cross-cultural adaptation, they become counterproductive beyond the initial phase of resettlement if strangers are to be better adapted to the host environment. The insulating effect of ethnic communication has been found to be stronger when strangers' ethnic ties consist primarily of coethnics who are themselves poorly adapted (Hsu, Grant, & Huang, 1993). In the case of Asian immigrant-owned small businesses, Bates (1994) has found that heavy use of ethnic support networks typifies less profitable, more failure-prone businesses. Ethnic social processes thus become a liability to cross-cultural adaptation when strangers depend on them heavily without direct and active involvement with the host environment at large (Anderson & Christie, 1978). Despite the informational, technical, material, and emotional support ethnic communities can provide, exclusive reliance on such assistance is likely to discourage direct participation in the host communication processes. Such would be the case when the ethnic communication sources upon which strangers rely are individuals who are poorly adapted to the host environment. Maladaptive communication of one stranger may breed maladaptive communication in another, through subtle or explicit forms of social pressure to conform to the ethnic culture. When the personal network reinforces ethnic communication patterns, the stranger's learning about the host culture and communication patterns is minimal.

Ethnic communication is likely to impede adaptation even further when strangers rely on it for a prolonged period beyond the phase of initial settlement. The relatively stress-free ethnic communication activities offer temporary relief, but no longer facilitate adaptation itself. There comes a point in the adaptation process when strangers' ethnic communication no longer serves the purpose of helping them adapt to the new environment or may even become a liability to their adaptive endeavor, competing with their host social communication activities. To acquire the host culture (acculturation) means to lose at least some of the original cultural patterns (deculturation). Each stranger has only so much time and energy to engage in communication activities, therefore his or her ethnic communication activities must be reduced in order to make room for host communication activities.

As Broom and Kitsuse (1955) argue, "A large part of the acculturation experiences of the members of an ethnic group may be circumscribed by the ethnic community" (p. 45). Likewise, Shibutani and

Kwan (1965) note: "To the extent that . . . a minority group participates in different sets of communication channels, they develop different perspectives and have difficulty in understanding each other" (p. 573). The subtle but intrinsic and lasting function of ethnic social communication lies in the maintenance of strangers' linkage to the homeland and mother tongue. Participation in ethnic communication reinforces the original cultural patterns in strangers as they continue to practice the verbal and nonverbal codes of the original culture and all its implicit rules and shared private meanings understood only by their coethnics. The notion that prolonged ethnic social communication activities deter cross-cultural adaptation is supported by the fact that most of these activities take place among individuals who are at an early stage of resettlement. In the process of becoming better adapted to the new life, these individuals are increasingly less active in ethnic community activities. Indeed, ethnic communities have been considered primarily as temporary holding stations where strangers tend to stay until they become more self-sufficient in the host environment at large. This view is consistent with the melting-pot symbolism of the integrationist and assimilationist views of cross-cultural adaptation.

Ethnic communication activities further impede adaptation by reducing the pressure on strangers to come to terms with the new situation in some way, and by providing a forum in which defensive reactions of fear, criticism, and hostility toward the host country are reinforced by similar reactions on the part of coethnics. Leslie (1992) studied immigrant groups in Canada and concluded that, although the networks of these individuals were dense and provided a great deal of support, they tended to have an insulating effect on the immigrants' interaction with the larger community. Likewise, Herberg (1989) identified ethnic language retention, ethnic residential concentration, and ethnic institutional completeness as key factors contributing to the maintenance and cohesiveness of ethnic groups in Canada.

An extensive body of empirical studies offers evidence supporting the long-term ethnicity-promoting and adaptation-impeding role of ethnic communication. Reliance on ethnic networks has been found to be associated with reliance on a nonstandard language (Gal, 1978) and a lack of sociocultural adaptation to the host milieu (Ward & Kennedy, 1994). Milroy (1980, 1982, 1987) has observed that a close-knit ethnic network structure is an important mechanism of language and culture maintenance, in that speakers are able to form a cohesive group capable of resisting pressure, linguistic and social, from outside the group. Milroy further suggests that a change in the ethnic group's nonstandard language maintenance would be associated with the breakup of such a structure. Likewise, Selltiz et al. (1963) found in their study of foreign students in the United States that ethnic contacts provided a setting in which strangers felt at home, where they did not need to worry about possible misunderstandings of their actions or fear possible rebuffs because of prejudice against people of their color or nationality. Krashen (1981) notes that first-language users tend to fall back on old knowledge when they have not yet acquired enough of the second language.[12]

Also, studies have shown that the level of interest in, and the perceived utility of, ethnic media among strangers is indicative of their lack of host communication competence and inability to participate in host interpersonal and mass communication processes. Ethnic communication activities have consistently been found to decrease as immigrants become more familiar with the host language and culture and are more extensively engaged in host social processes (e.g., J. Kim, 1980; J. Kim, Lee, & Jeong, 1982; Kim, 1976, 1978a, 1980, 1989, 1990; Kim et al., 1998a, 1998b; Ryu, 1978). Relatedly, the content of ethnic media themselves has been observed to evolve toward content that reflects more "mainstream" host cultural messages. As early as 1922, Park pointed out that if one examines the content of the ethnic press, "it is possible to estimate the extent to which the immigrant people have actually taken root in the United States and accommodated themselves to the forms, conditions and concrete purposes of American life" (p. 307). Echoing this point, Zubrzycki (1958) has noted that an increased acculturative role of the ethnic press parallels an increased maturity and success of particular ethnic groups in the host society.

Other studies have documented the interrelatedness among host communication competence, host social communication, and ethnic social communication. In reviewing studies on the adaptation of Japanese sojourners, Okazaki-Luff (1991) has concluded that, by and large, Japanese experience a great deal of difficulty in communicating with hosts and that they tend to maintain their coethnic interpersonal networks without developing meaningful host social networks. Shah (1991) likewise found in a study of Asian Indian "influentials" in the United States that the use of American communication channels contributed to adaptation, whereas the use of Asian Indian channels did not. Research data further indicate that sojourners who more strongly identify themselves with their home countries and are more involved in ethnic activities experience less satisfaction with their sojourns and are less successful in performing their daily tasks (e.g., Harrison, Chadwick, & Scales, 1996; Searle & Ward, 1990; Selltiz et al., 1963; Sewell & Davidsen, 1961).[13]

Ethnic mass media, in particular, have led their communities in their responses to international news events that involve their home countries. Even though ethnic media cover a limited amount of mainstream news and information, they tend to devote most of their content to news of the home country and of the ethnic community, thus propagating ethnic identity, pride, solidarity, culture, and language (Burgess, 1978; Marzolf, 1973, 1979). Content analyses of foreign-language newspapers with the largest circulations in Australia, Italy, Great Britain, and the United States have documented that, although the ethnic print media generally take the role of educating readers about the host society, they also serve as powerful agents to help their readers keep abreast of developments in the homeland, to shield against some of the external pressures of adaptation, and to advocate the national interests of the home country against the host country when conflict arises between the two (Shibutani & Kwan, 1965; Zubrzycki, 1958).

Even when ethnic media are based on the mainstream language of the host society, they still manage to facilitate the development of an in-group outlook that is distinctive from the rest of the society. Research findings generally support the ethnicity-maintaining and adaptation-deterring function of extensive and prolonged reliance on ethnic interpersonal and mass communication systems. Studies of Asian immigrants and Native Americans, for example, have shown insignificant or negative relationships among the degree of ethnic interpersonal and mass communication activities, development of host communication competence, and measures of functional fitness (e.g., upward socioeconomic mobility) and psychological well-being (e.g., perceived alienation) (see, e.g., Kim, 1976, 1977, 1980, 1990; Kim et al., 1998a, 1998b). In the case of Korean immigrants, the variance in the cognitive complexity measure explained by the degree of participation in interpersonal relationships with Americans has been found to be twice that explained by the degree of participation in interpersonal relationships with other Koreans. In the same study, no statistically significant association was observed between the degree of ethnic involvement and measures of host communication competence.[14]

The long-term ethnicity-maintenance function of ethnic communication has been further documented in terms of low education, low socioeconomic mobility, extensive ethnic interpersonal ties, limited host interpersonal ties, and limited host media use. Milroy (1980) presents specific cases of ethnic individuals in Belgium who actively sought upward mobility and deliberately avoided close ties within the ethnic community. These individuals saw extensive involvements with close ethnic ties as detrimental to their own or their children's opportunities for social advancement. Similarly, Jeffres and Hur (1981) found that ethnic individuals with lower socioeconomic status in Cleveland tended to be concentrated in ethnic neighborhoods and relied more on ethnic media as well as ethnic interpersonal communication; they resided more often in suburban areas, and turned more to the metro-area media and magazines.[15]

In addition, research evidence supports a positive association between the marital status of immigrants and their ethnic communication activities. Alba and Chamlin (1983), for example, found that those immigrants in their sample who were "in-married" (married to individuals of the same ethnicity) were more involved with coethnics for social support. Similarly, J. Kim (1980), in a study of Korean immigrants in Chicago, found that those married to Koreans demonstrated lower adaptation rates. Research has further shown that, over the years, among immigrants and sojourners alike, there is a trend toward increased participation in both interpersonal and mass communication activities of the host society and decreased participation in ethnic interpersonal and mass communication activities. In studies of Southeast Asian refugees in Los Angeles (Deusen, 1982) and in Illinois (Kim, 1979a, 1980, 1989, 1990), refugees' reliance on American social services has been found to decrease in accordance with the length of time spent in the United States.[16] In addition, Clément, Noels, and Karine (1994) conducted a longitudinal study of Francophone and Anglophone university students attending a bilingual university in a Canadian city where Anglophones are the majority group. In this study, the investigators found Francophone students' use of English media and identification with the Anglophone group to increase over time, along with a corresponding decrease in their use of French media and identification with the French Canadian group.

Linking Factors of Host and Ethnic Social Communication

The various types of social communication activities examined in this chapter and the nature of the interrelationships among them are summarized in Figure 7.3. Interpersonal and mass communication activities of strangers involving the natives and the host society at large are positively associated and mutually reinforcing. Likewise, strangers' involvements in ethnic interpersonal and mass communication

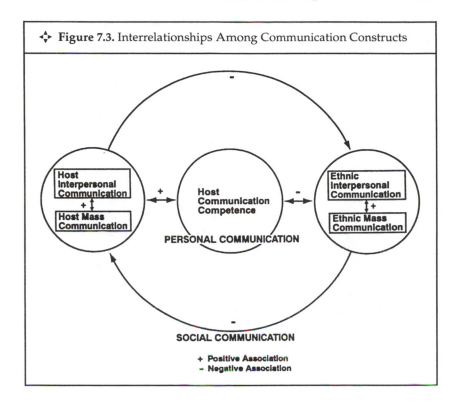

✧ Figure 7.3. Interrelationships Among Communication Constructs

processes are mutually reinforcing. Active participation in host inter-personal and mass communication processes is positively associated with the development of host communication competence (Theorem 1) and intercultural transformation (Theorem 3). On the other hand, heavy and prolonged involvement in ethnic social communication activities impedes the development of host communication competence (Theorem 2), discourages active involvement in host social communication (Theorem 4), and ultimately limits strangers' intercultural transformation (Theorem 6). Initially, the technical, informational, material, and emotional support of ethnic communication activities may be invaluable for strangers' adaptation as they struggle to cope with enormous uncertainty and uprootedness. Yet such supportive ethnic communication experiences by themselves cannot make strangers acquire the necessary host communication competence. In the long run, ethnic communication reinforces strangers' ethnicity, not adaptation, particularly if it is not supplemented or replaced by host social communication activities.

More recent research on ethnic communities, however, has tended to challenge the normative pattern of gradual social integration and assimilation of long-term residents. With the recent surge of cultural pluralism and assertion of ethnic identity in the United States, ethnic communities have come to be viewed by some as a more permanent solution to immigrants' social and cultural needs independent of the host society, where strangers and their children should be free to maintain their ethnicity and cultural identity. Social scientists, reflecting the ideological shift in U.S. society at large toward cultural pluralism, have expressed views that are opposite from the integrationist or assimilationist view, arguing for the vital importance of ethnic communities in serving the needs of ethnic individuals beyond the initial period. This pluralist view places less emphasis on the necessity of adaptation to the larger society and more on the preservation of the original culture.

Setting aside the ongoing ideological debates, there is an important place for strangers' ethnic involvements during their initial phase of cross-cultural adaptation. In the long run, however, strangers' continued heavy reliance on ethnic communication is counterproductive to their adaptation to the host society—if, indeed, such adaptation is their goal. Strangers cannot remain rigidly ethnic and also want to become highly adapted to the host culture. No new cultural learning (acculturation) can occur without unlearning some of the old habits (deculturation). An illustration of this fact can be seen in the lives of elderly immigrants whose everyday activities occur almost exclusively within the circle of their families and ethnic communities. They have little knowledge of the host language and culture. They mostly depend on interpreters if they must communicate with host nationals. Even after many years, these immigrants remain almost the same as they were when they first followed their children and moved to the host country. Contrast this lack of adaptation with the extraordinary level of adaptation achieved by many Peace Corps volunteers and missionaries whose relational networks in the host society consist mainly of local people.

Postulating the duality of the functions of ethnic communication—the short-term supportive function and the long-term function of deterring cross-cultural adaptation—is neither to endorse the assimilationist position nor to deny the validity of the pluralist position. It is simply to point out the cumulative influences of prolonged ethnic involvement in reinforcing ethnicity—following exactly the same theoretical principle that underlies the adaptation-facilitating function of host social communication activities. The maintenance of original cultural attributes may serve many useful purposes for individuals and groups who value and desire cultural preservation. For the purpose of cross-cultural adaptation, however, it delays the acquisition of host communication competence and meaningful engagement in host communication processes. As Boekestijn (1988) points out, many strangers experience a dilemma when faced with the duality of host and ethnic social communication and struggle with balancing their needs to retain their ethnicity and to adapt to the host society.

The choice remains one that each individual can and must make. Ultimately, such a decision requires an understanding that shared communication, intra- or interethnic, leads to shared knowledge and understanding, and vice versa (Carley, 1991). Given this principle, each stranger must take into consideration the nature of the relationship he or she desires to establish with the host environment; the psychological, social, and other "costs" he or she is willing to invest; and the "returns" that involvements in host and ethnic social communication respectively provide for the personal goals he or she aspires to achieve in the host society. Liu Zongren (1984), the Chinese journalist quoted earlier, has expressed his own experience of this dilemma when he sensed conformity pressure from his countrymen:

> I had been so absorbed in my studies of American life and language that I never took the time to go out with my Chinese roommates to a movie or to a park. . . . I had made more and more American friends and was involved with them in social events, visits, and short trips. When my Chinese friends made plans for a weekend, they stopped counting me in their group. Some, both the Chinese visiting scholars and a few Chinese from Taiwan that I knew casually, had begun saying that I was a busy man in American society—I sensed their sarcasm. They were probably thinking that I considered it beneath my "dignity" to go out with them. I felt somewhat guilty about this. (p. 168)

Environment

I am a part of all that I have met.

Alfred, Lord Tennyson, *Ulysses*, 1842

Strangers' communication and adaptation in a new cultural environment cannot be fully understood without taking into account the conditions of the environment. To the extent that strangers participate in the social (interpersonal and mass) communication processes of the host environment, they are influenced by that environment. Different conditions of the environment evoke different responses in strangers by serving as the cultural, social, and political forces in accordance to which they must strive to increase their chances for meeting personal and social goals (Murray & Sondhi, 1987). Of particular relevance to the present discussion are those environmental conditions that affect (and are affected by) both the quantity and the quality of strangers' interpersonal and mass communication activities and the development of their host communication competence.

Specifically, three environmental conditions have been identified in the present theory as being most significant to the cross-cultural adaptation process: the receptivity of the host environment toward strangers, the conformity pressure exerted by the host environment on the strangers, and the strength of the strangers' ethnic group within the new environment. It has been theorized that a receptive host environment would facilitate strangers' adaptation to that environment by extending its welcome and support. Such an environment would also facilitate adaptation when it exerts implicit or explicit pressure on strangers to acquire and practice the existing cultural norms and practices. The existence of a resourceful and organized ethnic community, on the other hand, tends to discourage strangers' adaptation, as the availability of a strong ethnic support system tends to perpetuate the long-term maintenance of the original cultural identity and practices.

In examining these environmental factors, we must recognize that the host environment is not a monolithic entity but a multilayered and hierarchically arranged complex social system. The environment includes all levels of the social milieu—from the macro-level societal and intersocietal conditions to the conditions of the mezzo and micro levels of particular regions, local communities, neighborhoods, and workplaces. Although each layer presents characteristics that are unique, it also acts as a metalevel, or context, for the sublevel(s) embedded within it (see Givón, 1989; Kim, 1994, 1997a). This means that the environment at a given level (such as a local community) manifests many of the forces operating in the higher levels of the environment (such as the broad circumstances and events of the society as a whole). The environmental conditions identified in the present theory, therefore, are applicable to the analysis of any one or more levels of the host environment a given researcher deems significant to the scope of a particular investigation. In a study that focuses on strangers' interpersonal communication patterns, for instance, characteristics of the immediate social surroundings (such as the local community, neighborhood, and workplace) would be of primary importance. On the other hand, a more comprehensive examination of multiple layers of the host environment would be necessary to help explain the strangers' overall communication activities, including their exposure to mass media and their psychological experience vis-à-vis the host environment at large.

Host Receptivity

Societies, communities, and groups differ in the degree to which the native population accommodates strangers. *Host receptivity* refers to the natives' openness toward strangers and willingness to accommodate strangers with opportunities to participate in the local social communication processes. From the strangers' perspective, host receptivity means accessibility of the hosts, otherwise referred to as "interaction potential" (Kim, 1976, 1977), "acquaintance potential" (Cook, 1962), "opportunities for contact" (McPherson, 1991), and "communication climate" (Leets & Giles, 1995). The lack of host receptivity, in turn, would mean a constraint in strangers' access to relationship building with local people, as explained by the "contact hypothesis" (Amir, 1969; Amir & Chana, 1977; Worchel, 1979, 1986). In some cases, segregation is forced upon certain groups of strangers but not on others. Generally, however, newly arrived strangers choose to live in close proximity to one another in heavily concentrated ethnic enclaves.

Positive Attitude Toward Strangers

Host receptivity is expressed largely in a continuum of the public and private attitudes of the natives toward strangers—from maximal openness, acceptance, and friendliness to maximal closedness, indifference, rejection, and hostility. Host receptivity is essentially a function of the collective self-confidence of host nationals and the respect, generosity, goodwill, and support they extend to strangers. The overall host receptivity of the United States is shown in the results of the first comprehensive national poll, conducted in 1995, of 732 legal immigrants in the United States (Puente, 1995, p. 1A). Of the survey sample, 90% said that they feel welcome in the United States, and 61% said they have never felt discriminated against as immigrants.

Generally speaking, host receptivity tends to be higher in societies where the government has developed and expanded a variety of policies and programs to provide foreign-born individuals opportunities for participation in the mainstream social processes (Barker, 1994; Kahane, 1986). For example, a small group of countries (e.g., the United States, Canada, France, Great Britain, India, New Zealand, and Spain) grant citizenship based on birthright and long-term residency apart from ethnicity (Ireland, 1994). Many other countries do not grant citizenship to most long-term foreign-born immigrants, such as Gypsies in the Czech Republic and Koreans in Japan (Crossette, 1996; Whitney, 1996). In such restrictive societies, the notion of citizenship is rooted deeply in ethnicity (race, culture, religion, and/or language), and political rights are extended to few foreign-born individuals.

Certain regions or cities within countries are sometimes swept by strong animosity toward people from particular groups of ethnic minorities. In England, for example, negative attitudes have been generated among the public based on that nation's imperial past, as manifested by the mainstream population's discriminatory views of Asians and other Third World migrants (Robinson, 1986). Similar hostility has been observed in Germany toward non-European groups, in Australia toward Asian groups even without the complications of an imperial past, and in the United States toward certain groups from the Middle East. More examples can be found in some local communities in the United States, where Caucasian Canadian visitors arriving in traditional small towns of primarily Caucasian ethnic composition are likely to find relatively high receptivity, whereas visitors from lesser-known and vastly different cultures may not. Also, certain pockets of a host community (e.g., college campuses, churches, workplaces, and neighborhoods) may offer varying degrees of receptivity. Thomas (1991), in a study of the adjustment of Cambodian, Laotian, and Vietnamese refugees since 1978 in the Alabama fishing community of Bayou La Batre, found that local Anglo shrimpers perceived the refugees as threatening the natives' place in the already crowded fishing industry, which was seeing declining profits. On the other hand, fish processors in the same community showed the refugee fishermen greater receptivity, because the processors saw them as much-needed additions to their industry's labor force.

In addition, the receptivity of a host environment may change due to circumstances and shifts in the public mood. Desbarats (1986), for example, has noted that the adaptation of Vietnamese refugees in the United States was significantly facilitated by the post-Vietnam War receptivity of American society. In contrast, lack of host receptivity has been found when a society (or community) is undergoing a stressful period due to high unemployment, political turmoil, or international or domestic conflict (Frey & Tilove, 1995; Worchel, 1979). Increasing discrimination against out-groups, undifferentiated or targeted, is exemplified by the recent political turmoil and economic downturns leading to rising xenophobic "ethnic nationalism" and "hate crimes" in many parts of the world.

Associative Communication Messages

In the everyday lives of strangers, host receptivity (or lack thereof) is manifested in a wide variety of explicit and implicit communication messages in the host environment. The forms such messages take range widely, from public laws, policies, and practices to subtle messages embedded in the communication behaviors of individuals in face-to-face encounters. In the United States, overall receptivity toward immigrants has been increasing over the past decade, according to public opinion polls (Lewin, 1992). Also reflecting this increasing receptivity is the federal law that requires schools to offer immigrant children a bilingual education, and the fact that many large companies now offer "multicultural training" programs for the members of their diverse workforces.

On an interpersonal level, private expressions of host receptivity are witnessed in terms of a bipolar continuum of associative and dissociative behavior (Kim, 1994, 1997a). The continuum incorporates the notions of "accommodation," "maintenance," and "divergence" identified in "speech accommodation theory" (Giles, Bourhis, & Taylor, 1977; Giles, Mulac, Bradac, & Johnson, 1987; Giles & Smith, 1979) and its expanded version, "communication accommodation theory" (Gallois, Franklyn-Stokes, Giles, & Coupland, 1988; Gallois, Giles, Jones, Cargile, & Ota, 1995), as well as other similar concepts such as "communicative distance" (Lambert, 1979; Lukens, 1979; Peng, 1974), "border rituals" (Volkan, 1992), and "prejudiced talk" (van Dijk, 1987).

The associative end of the continuum represents the types of behavior that facilitate the communication process by increasing the likelihood of understanding, acceptance, cooperation, and support for strangers and their inclusion in the daily conversations of the natives. Often such associative behaviors are simply those behaviors we extend to our coworkers, neighbors, friends, and even some strangers. They range from simple expressions of interest and goodwill, such as paying attention, greetings, initiation of small talk, and expressions of regards, to more active expressions, such as offering support and help. Often native speakers accommodate and compensate for the asynchronic behaviors of nonnative speakers through various means such as slowing down, using simplified sentences, and selecting simpler conversation topics that do not require a high level of cultural and linguistic understanding (Miller, 1991; Smith, Scholnick, Crutcher, & Simeone, 1991).

Dissociative behaviors, in particular, have received a great deal of research attention. Among the various dissociative communication behaviors that have been examined are the use of derogatory ethnic jokes and name-calling.[1] Nonverbal codes of distance have also been observed as reflecting and contributing to the psychological barriers between interactants. Employing concepts such as "involvement offenses," "pseudo-conversation," "unfocused interaction," and "forms of alienation," Goffman (1966, 1979) has described a wide range of subtle forms of psychological nonengagement. Also, Lukens (1979) has developed a list of divergent verbal behaviors, including the choice of phonological variants, syntactic structures, idiomatic expressions, discourse structures, and lexical terms. According to Lukens, speakers manipulate linguistic variants either to increase or to decrease the "communicative distance" between one another that stems from the psychological orientations of indifference, avoidance, or disparagement (see also Peng, 1974).

Together, associative and dissociative communication behaviors serve as concrete indications of openness, acceptance, and support of the local people toward strangers, or of the opposite attitudes of closedness, rejection, and discrimination. Messages of varying degrees of receptivity constitute a part of the milieu that strangers must face and cope with if they are to function effectively. The more openness the hosts extend toward strangers, the more opportunities strangers have for new cultural learning and adaptation.

Host Conformity Pressure

Societies and communities vary not only in receptivity but in the degree to which host nationals exert conscious or unconscious pressure on strangers to change their original patterns of behavior and adopt those of the host culture. Conversely, societies and communities differ in the degree to which local people are able or willing to permit, tolerate, accommodate, or appreciate the cultural habits and practices that the strangers bring with them from their original cultures, and to allow them to deviate from the hosts' normative expectations. A local population's expectations for strangers to conform to its prevailing normative communication codes and rules are often expressed in various forms of disapproval, prejudice, and discrimination against those who fail to meet such expectations, even when the natives are not necessarily unreceptive to the presence of strangers around them.

Pressure to conform linguistically and culturally is likely to be more acute for those strangers whose livelihoods are dependent on the natives and host institutions (De Vos & Suárez-Orozco, 1990a, p. 253). Proficiency in the host language and culture is particularly vital for immigrants who are reconstructing their lives and whose success or failure in pursuing personal goals is largely dependent on the acceptance and approval of at least some segments of the host population who constitute the immigrants' immediate social milieu. Even temporary sojourners, such as employees of multinational companies, Peace Corps volunteers, diplomats, and international students, are subject to some degree of conformity pressure from the host environment as they carry out their life activities and develop good relationships with local people. Such is the case, although to a lesser extent, even for sojourners such as American military personnel stationed overseas, whose everyday activities are more or less independent of the workings of the host environment.

A significant factor to be considered in any attempt to understand the degree of host conformity pressure is the prevalence in the environment of an *assimilative (or integrative) ideology* as opposed to a *pluralist ideology*, which encourages ethnic distinctiveness (see Atkinson & Coupland, 1988; Bourhis, Moiese, Perreault, & Senecal, 1997; Kim, 1999; Pettigrew, 1988). In an analysis of "ethnogenesis" in several settings (from the Luba of Kawai in Zaire to the Huron of Canada, who are almost pure white), Roosens (1989) has demonstrated how present-day concepts of ethnicity are significantly motivated by pluralist ideological forces that allow ethnic groups to make significant instrumental as well as expressive gains by insisting on a separate identity. In the United States, an ideological shift from the traditional melting-pot vision to the more recent pluralist ideology has tended to ease the acculturative pressure on new immigrants somewhat. Recent replacement of the melting-pot metaphor with others such as "tossed salad," "quilt," and "mosaic" reflect this ideological shift (Kim, 1999).

Although varied across circumstances, some degree of conformity pressure, no matter how minuscule, exists in almost all cross-cultural situations. One of the most visible aspects of such pressure is found in the official or unofficial language policies and practices of the host society. From the Baltics to Kazakhstan, many people—most but not all of them Russians—are being eliminated from participation in public life and sometimes barred from schools because they do not speak the new official language (Crossette, 1996). Even in the United States, arguably the most tolerant nation toward outsiders, rising legal and illegal immigration has prompted a movement to codify English as the national language. The recent rise in anti-immigration sentiment in the United States, for instance, has led to the passage of laws in a number of states declaring English the official language (Carlson, 1988). In Oklahoma, a law has recently been enacted to allow college students to sue their universities if they find foreign-born instructors' lectures difficult to comprehend. Rising public complaints about difficulty in communicating with some foreign-born taxi drivers in New York City have resulted in an increase in the level of English-language training required of persons applying for cab drivers' licenses in that city (Hevesi, 1991).

Host conformity pressure is not always explicitly codified into official policy. Strangers can more or less sense the presence of the local conformity pressure in public and private debates on issues concerning ethnic minorities. Implicit host conformity pressure is also reflected in the expectations of the natives that strangers ought to learn how to communicate in accordance with the local codes and norms. When such normative expectations are violated, natives are likely to express their discomfort and disapproval in a variety of negative verbal and nonverbal ways.

Homogeneous Ethnic Composition

Few empirical studies have systematically compared societies in regard to cultural conformity pressure, but pluralist societies (in terms of both cultural-political ideology and ethnic composition, such as Australia, Canada, and the United States) appear to manifest a greater tolerance for and accommodation of foreign-born and native-born ethnic minorities. In comparison, stricter imposition of dominant linguistic and cultural patterns on all people can be seen in more traditional and homogeneous societies with authoritarian political systems (e.g., China, Iran, and Saudi Arabia). In such societies, foreign visitors are likely to be subject to greater pressure to follow local beliefs and practices.

Conformity pressure can vary further in different regions or among different groups within a society. Strangers are likely to find that, in general, large urban centers with a heterogeneous and cosmopolitan milieu offer noticeably greater permissiveness than do small rural towns (Boekestijn, 1988). Supermarket price tags, restaurant menus, store signs, and airport public announcement systems often appear in languages other than the dominant host language in large urban centers. Indeed, in urban America today, it is the rare person who feels a clear sense of identification with one and only one group or segment of the community and nation. The typical urban person is a member of many in-groups and may relate him- or herself to many other reference groups (Waterman, 1992). Clément, Noels, and Karine (1994) found that the Francophone students from minority and majority settings attending a bilingual (French-English) university in Canada revealed a link between group status and change in media consumption in a bilingual environment. Students originating from French settings increased significantly in their written and public media consumption in English, whereas students originating from English settings increased in French written media consumption.

Compared with urban areas in the United States, American rural areas draw fewer immigrants or sojourners who are ethnically different, and these areas have shown little room for cultural diversity in schooling and other community affairs. As such, rural communities exert greater pressure on newly arrived strangers to learn English and local customs rapidly (Carlson & Carlson, 1981; Rankin, 1981). A Korean visitor in New York City is unlikely to receive much public attention, as urban residents' social identities are generally relatively diffused and diversified. In contrast with small towns, where the presence of strangers can be a matter of great interest and close scrutiny, the social structures of metropolitan areas exhibit greater tolerance for new and different elements (Laumann, 1973).

Ethnic Group Strength

Both host receptivity and conformity pressure are applied differentially to different ethnic groups, at least partly due to the groups' respective strength. *Ethnic group strength* refers to the relative status and power that membership in an ethnic group accords. In the present theory, three elements are used to assess ethnic group strength: the degree of prestige an ethnic group enjoys in a given society or community, the degree to which the group is institutionalized, and the degree to which the group is engaged in ethnic politics.

Ethnic Prestige

The prestige of an ethnic group is the overall social standing attributed to that group relative to other groups in society. Closely associated with the socioeconomic status of an ethnic group, high ethnic prestige—along with the prestige of ethnic language—serves as a force that helps to increase local people's interest in and acceptance of individual strangers, "softening" the host conformity pressure (Leslie, 1992). Social psychological studies have shown that equal-status contact promotes positive attitudes and behaviors of majority and minority group members and their languages and reduces stereotypes and prejudices (e.g., Amir, 1969; Amir & Chana, 1977; Robinson & Preston, 1976; Sachdev & Wright, 1996; Wood & Sonleitner, 1996). The relative prestige of strangers' ethnic membership is translated into favorable or unfavorable conditions for strangers' communicating with local people.

In the case of Japan, recent studies have found that international sojourners perceive differential degrees of receptivity that Japanese people tend to extend toward Western and non-Western sojourners (e.g., Maruyama, 1998; Maruyama & Kim, 1997; Tanaka, Takai, Kohyama, Fujihara, & Minami, 1994). In the United States, a nationwide poll conducted in 1989 by the National Opinion Research Center shows that European groups with "older" and more-established immigration histories (such as the British, Germans, Irish, and Scandinavians) generally monopolize the top of the ladder of ethnic group prestige, followed by more recent groups such as Italians, Greeks, Poles, Russians, and Jews. Non-European groups, such as Chinese, Mexicans, Africans, African Americans, Puerto Ricans, and Native Americans, on the other hand, are among the lowest ranked in ethnic prestige (Lewin, 1992).

Few strangers needing to function in and benefit from the host environment stand to escape conformity pressure completely. Most of them would do better by becoming more communicatively competent. Daniel Chernin's (1990) personal account of his experiences in Japan illustrate this point. Chernin, an American computer programmer, worked for a large computer manufacturer in Japan for about a year. He tells of the many difficulties with which he was confronted at this company, particularly the difficulties stemming from the strict (although unwritten) company rules his Japanese coworkers expected him to follow. Among other problems, Chernin relates how he received silent gestures of disapproval when he openly disagreed with Ikeda, his Japanese partner, on an existing method of computer programming. Yet, Chernin notes, the subtle but persistent pressure to which he was subjected helped him to realize that he needed to change some of his American ways. This realization, in turn, helped him accept and follow the "company ways" in time. Chernin reflects that, as he became more proficient in following the company rules, his Japanese coworkers' attitudes toward him turned increasingly accepting and appreciative. Toward the end of his sojourn, Chernin writes, he and Ikeda were able to develop a friendship and mutual respect.

Institutional Completeness

The prestige of an ethnic group is closely tied to the objective properties and positions of political and economic "resources" associated with that group. Clarke and Obler (1976) offer a useful model in which ethnic action is argued to evolve in a three-stage developmental process. The first stage is economic adjustment, which occurs upon arrival of the group until group members become an integral part of the permanent economy. The second stage is community building, or the development of community leadership, institutional resources, and communication networks used to assert the ethnic group's interests. This is followed by a third stage, a period of aggressive self-assertion that develops into the group's conventional use of the existing political system.

These stages of ethnic community development—from economic and institutional to political development—are directly linked to the growth in population size and establishment of a group's own institutions. Breton (1964, 1991), in analyzing the strength of different ethnic groups, differentiates ethnic groups in terms of "institutional completeness," that is, the degree to which they are organized and integrated into a collective economic, political, social, and cultural system (see also Goldenberg & Haines, 1992). In an examination of the Chinese community in the Chicago area, for example, Cross (1978) found that the community had set up specific programs to provide various services, including employment services for newcomers, nutrition services for the elderly, and language education for the young.

Corresponding to the sociological concept of institutional completeness is the sociolinguistic and social psychological concept of *ethnolinguistic vitality*. Giles et al. (1977) explain this phenomenon in terms of (a) the status of a language in a community, in terms of the absolute and relative number of its speakers and their distribution within regions and the country as a whole; (b) demographic characteristics, including economic, social, and language status; and (c) the institutional support of the larger society (e.g., government services, schools, mass media) for the language. Throughout Spain, for instance, minority languages such as Castilian, Galician, Catalan, and Basque enjoy healthy vitality due to full institutional support by the Spanish government through its official language policy. The ethnic minorities using these languages demonstrate high levels of competence in their own languages (Rei Doval, 1994).

The notion of ethnolinguistic vitality has been extended to the psychological realm. Terms such as *subjective ethnolinguistic vitality* (Bourhis, Giles, Leyens, & Tajfel, 1979; Bourhis, Giles, & Rosenthal, 1981; Harwood, Giles, & Bourhis, 1994) have been employed to refer to the psychological realm of ethnolinguistic vitality. Specifically, these terms refer to the legitimacy, status, and stability of a group as perceived by its members and have been linked to patterns of language use and speech strategies (such as convergence and divergence) that are used commonly in intergroup encounters. A speaker who perceives his or her group to be weak and subordinate tends to converge upwardly. On the other hand, another speaker who accepts the group's subordinate position to be legitimate tends to employ either the strategy of speech maintenance or downward divergence. In a study of ethnic Chinese communities in London and Taiwan, Yang and Sachdev (1994) have validated the linkage between perceived ethnolinguistic vitality and patterns of language use, suggesting that higher-vitality perceptions are positively related to patterns of ethnic language use and language maintenance. Similar results have been reported by Cenoz and Valencia (1993) in their study of second-language acquisition in the Basque Country in Spain, and by Florack and Piontkowski (1997) in their study among the Dutch and the Germans in the European Union. Subjective ethnolinguistic vitality has also been linked to an individual's ethnic identity (Giles & Viladot, 1994; Hogg & Rigoli, 1996) as well as to "linguistic landscape" (Landry & Bourhis, 1997)—that is, the visibility and salience of languages on public and commercial signs in a given territory or region.

On the other hand, researchers have found a negative relationship between indicators of ethnic group strength and cross-cultural adaptation. Giles and Byrne (1982), for example, found second-language learning to be negatively related to perceived ethnolinguistic vitality. Relatedly, Inglis and Gudykunst (1982) found that the degree of interaction with Americans among Korean immigrants in Hartford, Connecticut, was lower than that among their counterparts in the Chicago area, where the Korean community was considerably larger and better organized. Likewise, McKay (1989) found the Lebanese Christian community in Australia to have limited institutionalization compared with its counterparts in the United States. McKay points to this condition as the main reason (along with the strong conformity pressure of Australian society) for the group's rapid assimilation into the Australian culture (for similar findings, see Herberg, 1989; Shim, 1994).

The adaptation-impeding function of ethnic group strength is further shown in the experiences of different groups of Japanese in the United States, as depicted in the documentary *Between Two Cultures: Japanese in America*, which was broadcast on PBS in August 1994. This film shows two Japanese communities, one in Georgetown, Kentucky, where 70 Japanese families employed at a Japanese company subsidiary reside, and a much larger community of 56,000 Japanese in New York City complete with Japanese grocery stores, shopping centers, clubs, churches, temples, and Japanese-language schools. In the smaller community, the families are shown to interact actively with local Americans. Their New York City counterparts, on the other hand, remain more ethnically isolated from the surrounding population.

Identity Politics

Clearly, the resources, institutions, vitality, and prestige of strangers' ethnic groups influence the overall quality of strangers' contacts with the natives. Almost always, strangers' communication with natives (or, for that matter, all communication events) is influenced not by egalitarian relational norms, but by the norms of power differentials (Cook, 1978; Kramarae, Schulz, & O'Barr, 1984) that influence the nature of stranger-host relationships. Studies have demonstrated the extent to which preexisting status differentials between groups carry over into new situations, making equal-status interaction difficult or impossible. Strangers with strong ethnic group status, therefore, are likely to be less compelled to accommodate the host cultural system (De Vos, 1990a).

Conflict may occur even when two groups are about evenly matched with respect to "objective" properties and positions (Blalock, 1982, p. 101; Brewer & Miller, 1984, p. 291). Such would be the case when other, less-conspicuous power resources are at play, including the forms of psychological posturing derived from the dynamics of "identity politics" (Aronowitz, 1991). Even though objective equality within the contact setting may make group distinctions less salient, systematic attempts to reduce or reverse existing status differentials may threaten members of the initially higher-status group, leading to their active resistance and attempts to reestablish their distinctiveness and positive status differentials. Also, members of a minority group may play up their ethnic identity as a rallying point to assert group members as separate from the identity of the larger society (Rex, Joly, & Wilpert, 1987) and to exert conformity pressure on the group's members. Those in such groups who are successful in their out-group relationships are subtly or explicitly criticized as "deserters" (De Vos & Suárez-Orozco, 1990a, p. 256). Americans who live in Kyoto and are immersed in the local way of life may be seen by other Americans as having "gone native" and being "un-American." Derogatory colloquial terms such as *banana* and *Twinkie* are used among Asian Americans as put-downs of those who act like White Americans. A form of separatist identity politics is also at play in the province of Quebec, Canada, where the Commission de Protection de la Langue Française is so watchful that it forced the removal of a pub sign designed to welcome

English-speaking visitors; the sign advertised in English, "TODAY'S SPECIAL / Ploughman's Lunch" (Richler, 1992).

Thus strangers facing strong in-group political pressure may be discouraged from learning the host language and culture. Research findings support the paradoxical nature of ethnic group strength relative to the long-term adaptation of strangers to the host society at large. Rosenthal and Hrynevich (1985; cited in Phinney & Rosenthal, 1992) found that, in Australia, the Greek immigrant community was more cohesive and organized than was the Italian immigrant community. They also found that, as expected, Greek Australian adolescents placed more emphasis than did Italian Australian adolescents on their ethnic identity and on maintaining their heritage. Further, the Greek Australian adolescents placed less emphasis on adapting to the Australian culture at large. Similarly, Driedger (1976) found that an ethnic group's status in Canada interacted with its institutional completeness, so that groups high on both status and institutional completeness (French and Jews) had the strongest sense of ethnic identity. Driedger also observed the lowest levels of ethnic identity among Germans, Ukranians, and Poles, whose groups had low status and only low-to-moderate levels of institutional completeness.

Linking Factors of Communication and Environment

The three environmental factors examined in this chapter—host receptivity, host conformity pressure, and ethnic group strength—interactively influence the cross-cultural adaptation processes of individual strangers. Like a rider and a horse, a stranger and the receiving environment are engaged in a joint venture. As shown in Figure 8.1, host receptivity and conformity pressure are reciprocally and positively linked with the factors of personal and social communication (Theorems 7, 8, and 9). The receptivity and conformity pressure of the host environment, however, are often at odds with the interest of an ethnic group that aspires to maintain and strengthen its own separate identity. Ethnic group strength serves to interfere with or mediate the stranger's relationship with the host environment. A strong ethnic community that enjoys a significant amount of prestige, economic and political power, and institutional completeness can help facilitate newcomers' adaptation initially. In the long run, however, such ethnic

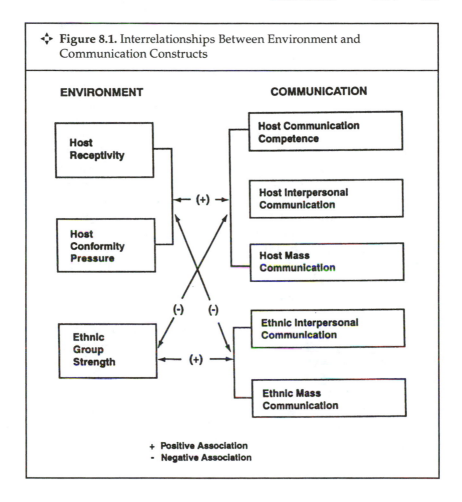

✧ **Figure 8.1.** Interrelationships Between Environment and Communication Constructs

group strength tends to impede individual strangers' development of host communication competence (Theorem 10) and their participation in the host social communication processes (Theorem 11) while facilitating their participation in ethnic social communication processes (Theorem 12). Conversely, the overall strength of a given ethnic group is likely to be diminished by the development of host communication competence and participation in host social communication processes among the individuals affiliated with that group.

As I have argued in Chapter 7, the ethnicity-maintenance roles of ethnic media, ethnic social organizations, and intraethnic interpersonal relationships and communication activities tend to be stronger within newer, less-established ethnic communities and are diminished in older (or more mature) communities whose members have already become well adapted to the mainstream culture (Zubrzycki, 1958). For newer ethnic groups in the United States, such as Koreans and Mexicans, the foreign-language press serves as a powerful and often politically charged force that helps maintain ethnic social cohesion, facilitate interpersonal communication processes, and provide the social controls indispensable to the building of a cohesive ethnic group identity. Ethnic group strength thus serves as a potential source of resistance to the conformity pressures of the dominant forces in the host environment. A strong ethnic community often serves as the "gatekeeper" and "guardian" that mitigates or even replaces much of the direct communication and influence between individual strangers and the host environment. Under such conditions, strangers are unlikely to feel compelled to mainstream themselves into the host society at large. Some immigrant members of strong ethnic groups may even challenge the presumption of their own groups' inferior status. Members of a pluralist multicultural society, likewise, may feel they must not impose their language and culture on other groups.

In contrast, among many successfully mainstreamed immigrant groups (such as Germans, Scandinavians, and Irish in the United States), affiliation and identification with the ethnic group has diminished so that it plays a less active role in individuals' daily lives. The remaining ethnicity-maintenance function of such groups appears to have been reduced to providing a symbolic affirmation and expression of pride in common roots. In the case of Irish Americans, their noticeable presence as a group is conspicuously felt mainly in such symbolic activities as St. Patrick's Day celebrations. Likewise, the successful adaptation of Americans of German descent has confined their ethnic activities largely to informal social celebrations such as Oktoberfest, trips to Germany, and athletic events organized by German American community organizations (Hurst, 1977).

Whether one sees the presence in a society of strong ethnic groups with separatist orientations as good or bad, of course, depends on one's ideological stance. What is important in the present theoretical context is simply the proposition that strong ethnic communities tend to discourage the adaptation of their members to the host environment at large. In the end, most people make pragmatic choices as to the nature of their relationships to their ethnic community and to the larger society. They do so in accordance with what they find useful in pursuing their own self-interests at a given time (Blalock, 1982). They do so by weighing the expected costs and rewards of maintaining their ethnic identity and achieving a better fit into the host society at large, thereby seeking a reasonable balance between the two social orientations.

Predisposition

[We] live in a field that extends into a distant past and into a far
future.

S. E. Asch, *Social Psychology*, 1952

Not all strangers come to a new environment for the same reason or
with the same personal history. Nor are the responses of that environment toward them uniform. Each individual brings his or her own
unique experiential background that serves as a prologue to the subsequent adaptation process. An individual's past history, present action,
and future evolution are linked to the "time-binding" nature of human
"self-reflexivity" (Jantsch, 1980; Korzybski, 1958; Weinberg, 1959/1987).
The past and the future are incorporated into the present realities to
which individual strangers must orient themselves and ground their
aspirations for the future. In Asch's (1952) words: "An integral part of
man's extended horizon is the kind of object he becomes to himself. . . .
Because he is conscious of himself and capable of reflecting on his experiences, he also takes up an attitude to himself and takes measures to
control his own actions and tendencies" (pp. 120-122).

This chapter examines three key aspects of individual strangers'
background characteristics that have significant bearing on their
cross-cultural adaptation processes: their preparedness for change, the
proximity (or distance) of their ethnicity to (or from) that of the host
environment, and their personality attributes. Together, these factors
constitute the overall *adaptation potential* of a given stranger.

Preparedness for Change

Strangers' adaptation potential is directly a function of the degree to which they are prepared for change—that is, their readiness for and understanding of the challenges of crossing cultures and of the particular host culture and its communication system. The greater their preparedness, the more realistic their expectations about their life in the new environment are likely to be, and hence the better their chances are for a smooth transition and adaptation (Black & Gregersen, 1990; Brabant, Palmer, & Gramling, 1990; Searle & Ward, 1990).

On the most general level, strangers' preparedness is enhanced by formal *education*. Schooling, regardless of the specific cultural context, expands learners' overall cognitive capacity for new learning. Often, strangers' formal education may have exposed them to the language, culture, geography, and history of the particular host society or community to which they are migrating. Such premigration familiarity provides added leverage for strangers' building host communication competence and participating in the host social communication processes. Education may also help individuals to be less susceptible to media propaganda and stereotypes about a particular culture and more realistic in their expectations about the new environment (Krau, 1991). This observation helps to explain the finding that male immigrants are significantly more skilled in the host language than are female immigrants, given the same length of time in the new environment (Baldassini & Flaherty, 1982; Furnham, 1988; Kim, 1976; Office of Refugee Resettlement, 1984; Roy, 1987). By itself, gender does not logically explain the observed differences in adaptation, but gender is confounded by other individual background characteristics, particularly education (Kalbach & Richard, 1990; Kim, 1976). Relatedly, more married immigrant women tend not to work outside their homes, whereas their husbands are more actively engaged in the host environment through work (Kim, 1976).

In addition to formal schooling, experiences of *training* in the host language and culture can potentially facilitate adaptation. Recognizing the vital importance of cross-cultural communication and adaptation to success in the global market, many companies and government agencies offer their employees various forms of "culture-general" and "culture-specific" training to prepare their personnel to work in specific target cultures (Brislin & Yoshida, 1994; Landis & Bhagat, 1996). Peace Corps volunteers, for example, go through extensive language and cultural training programs before being sent to their assigned locations. Training programs are also offered to students in missionary preparation programs, businesspeople in multinational corporations, military personnel, diplomats and employees of intergovernmental agencies, and international technical advisers, among others. Language and cultural programs were provided in Southeast Asian refugee camps while the refugees waited to be permitted to enter the United States.

Ample research data demonstrate the contribution of preparedness through education and training to a smoother adaptation overseas. Furnham and Bochner (1982) found that international students who received extensive cultural orientation training prior to coming to the United States were more successful in academic adjustment and had higher satisfaction with the sojourn than did students who did not receive such training. A study of Southeast Asian refugees found that subsequent English acquisition was accelerated by preentry training. The gap in English-language abilities between trained and untrained refugees after 6 months in the United States was particularly great for preliterate individuals (Office of Refugee Resettlement, 1984). Likewise, in a study of Latin American immigrants in Israel, Penalosa (1972) found that prior Zionist education and training was a strong predictor of subsequent assimilation in Israel.

Also influencing strangers' preparedness are their *prior cross-cultural experiences*. Those who have had foreign cultural experiences are better prepared for a new cross-cultural move. Selltiz, Christ, Havel, and Cook (1963) found that foreign students in the United States who had previously been outside their home countries interacted more with Americans during their stay than those who had never before been abroad. Such would also be the case even when the environments of prior sojourns are substantially different from the one to which strangers are headed, or even when they are not in a foreign country but in an unfamiliar environment within their own country. Additional research findings supporting the positive association between prior foreign experience and social participation in a new environment are offered by Church (1982), Furnham and Bochner (1986), and Sewell and Davidsen (1961).

Strangers' adaptation potential is further enhanced when the cross-cultural relocation is *voluntary* rather than involuntary. Unlike those who have had no choice but to move to another culture or subculture, voluntary immigrants or sojourners have freely chosen to join a new social order and are more likely to learn and participate in the host communication processes. Relatedly, strangers' preparedness for a cross-cultural move is influenced by the *abrupt or planned nature of the transition* to a new environment. Abrupt transitions are experienced by refugees around the world who must suddenly leave their homelands involuntarily as a result of wars, natural disasters, or political crises. The abruptness involved in such moves leaves refugees little chance to prepare for life in the new environment. In comparison, people who plan ahead for their moves typically prepare themselves extensively for their new life through reading, studying, personal contacts, and even prior visits. With such preparedness, they can reduce the overall transitional stresses (Taft, 1977, p. 124).

Ethnic Proximity

Ethnicity is both a group-level and an individual-level concept. Traditionally, the term *ethnicity* has been employed by social scientists since the 1930s and 1940s to refer to the group-level concept of a set of "objective" group criteria, such as national, cultural, racial, religious, and linguistic origins (Gordon, 1981; Nash, 1989; Smith, 1981). These criteria have been associated with distinct "ethnic markers" (Nash, 1989) that help distinguish one ethnic group from another, emphasizing the characteristics commonly shared by members of a particular group. Ethnicity is also an individual-level phenomenon in that individual members manifest the group's characteristics to differing degrees. Jewish immigrants in Israel, for example, differ significantly among themselves, from dark-skinned Ethiopians to light-skinned Russians (Abbink, 1984). What is often called the "Hispanic community" in the United States is made up of individuals of widely varying racial, national, linguistic, and cultural backgrounds. In fact, all ethnic groups in the United States are composed of individuals who display a wide range of racial and cultural makeup due to intergroup marriages (Lind, 1995).

Because of the pervasive intraethnic variations, ethnicity is more appropriately examined in the present theory as a set of individual-level background characteristics that bear on the cross-cultural adaptation process. Some of these characteristics are externally discernible physical or material ethnic markers, whereas others are invisible psychological characteristics generally associated with ethnic groups (e.g., thought patterns, values, and social orientations). The term *ethnic proximity* (or *ethnic distance*) is used here to refer broadly to the degree of similarity (or difference) of the stranger's ethnicity-based characteristics relative to the corresponding characteristics predominant in the host environment. A given stranger's low ethnic proximity to (or high ethnic distance from) the mainstream ethnicity dominant among the host population is viewed as a significant handicap in his or her adaptive effort. Conversely, a stranger with many ethnic characteristics that are close to those of the native population is likely to enjoy a smoother transition into the local environment. A case in point is the highly successful assimilation of the Chinese minority in Thailand, partly because of the close racial and cultural proximity that members of this group share with the local people (Kirby, 1989).

More specifically, the ethnic proximity of a given stranger in a particular host environment can be examined in terms of two interrelated factors: the overall *similarity* (or difference) of external ethnic characteristics between the stranger and the natives, and the overall *compatibility* (or incompatibility) of the stranger's internal ethnic characteristics relative to those of the natives.

Ethnic Similarity

Brewer and Miller (1984, p. 285) extend the conceptual domain of social identity to relate to societal environment when they point out that different ethnic individuals are subjected to differential treatment by outside agents. They base this observation on findings from experimental studies with the "minimal intergroup situation" (Brewer, 1979; Tajfel, 1970; Turner, 1978) that attest to the powerful impact that perception by external authorities can have on the formation of subjective group identity on the part of those who are lumped together as a category. Although Brewer and Miller found that mere assignment of individuals to different group labels was not sufficient to create in-group/out-group distinctions, differential treatment of groups by experimenters produced clear disjunctions in perceptions of own-group versus other-group members. The fact that such psychological maneuvering was observed when the subjects themselves had no discernible difference in ethnicity points to the likelihood that strangers must overcome substantial psychological barriers when their ethnicity greatly deviates from the prevailing ethnicity of the local people.

Ethnic markers that most clearly affect the attitudes of the natives are physical or material identifiers commonly associated with particular ethnic groups. Included in such markers are skin color, facial features, and physique as well as dress, food, architectural features, flags, crosses, decorative objects, and certain communication symbols and behaviors, such as anthems, folk songs, unique gestures, and other body movements. Salient ethnic markers also include characteristics in speech patterns when speaking the host language. Different ethnic groups are associated with different paralinguistic patterns of their mother tongues as they speak a new language, including accents, tempos of utterance, intonations, and pitch levels. Anglo-Europeans visiting the United States and Anglo-Americans in Australia, for example, present little physical salience, whereas Asians, Blacks, Latinos, Native Americans, and Asian Indians have physical salience in both those countries. Americans physically stand out in Japan much more than do Chinese or Koreans. In a predominantly Christian community, a Sikh from India wearing a traditional headpiece is likely to be perceived by local people as more "strange" or "foreign" than another Indian without such appearance, even when the two may be similar in most other aspects.

The more easily discernible and distinct the ethnic markers, the more they are likely to exacerbate the psychological posturing of "us versus them" (Kim, 1994, 1997a). External ethnic markers contribute to the "strangeness" or "foreignness" of strangers, adding to the communication barriers that confront all newcomers. As Worchel (1979, p. 272) has observed, sufficient research data are available to show that the simple we/they distinction is all that is necessary to create intergroup (compared to interpersonal) hostility. Gallois and her associates have considered intergroup orientation to be a "situational constraint" influencing the convergent or divergent communication strategies of interactants (see Gallois, Franklyn-Stokes, Giles, & Coupland, 1988; Gallois, Giles, Jones, Cargile, & Ota, 1995). Blalock (1982, p. 15) has further suggested that physical salience is likely to increase the intensity of communication behavior.

An extensive amount of direct and indirect empirical evidence supports the theoretical relationship linking the salience of a stranger's ethnic markers with the difficulty he or she experiences in cross-cultural adaptation. In reviewing the literature on the adaptation of Hispanic adolescents in the United States, Montalvo (1991) found a number of studies that linked darker skin color to greater "phenotyping" and thus greater adaptive stress. Other researchers who have examined the interpersonal relationship patterns of international students have found that European students interacted with Americans more extensively than did students from Asia (Selltiz et al., 1963). Similar results have been seen in studies by Furnham and Bochner (1982) among international students in England; by Stephan and Stephan (1989) among Asian Americans, whose adaptive difficulties were found to be greater than those of Hispanic Americans; by Ward and Kennedy (1994), who found that Malaysian and Singaporean students in New Zealand were experiencing greater sociocultural adjustment problems than Malaysian students in Singapore; and by H. K. Kim (1991), who found that both native and nonnative interaction partners viewed attitudinal similarity derived primarily from ethnic similarity to be a significant predictor of attraction.

Ethnic Compatibility

Frequently, adaptation can be challenged not by different physical appearances but by incompatible *intrinsic markers* of cultural and communication systems. David Mura, a third-generation Japanese American, writes in his book *Turning Japanese: Memoirs of a Sansei* (1991) about the discomfort he experienced when sojourning in Japan, despite his Japanese physical appearance. Research supports the link between the cultural compatibility of strangers and their integration in host social communication networks. Gumperz (1978), for instance, offers insights into communication difficulties that arise in key social situations, such as job interviews and committee meetings, due to incompatible differences in perception and interpretation of verbal and nonverbal behaviors. As long as cultural differences persist, according to Gumperz, there is bound to be a clash between the communication skills and strategies that are effective within the home and friendship circles and those that are effective in public settings where mainstream cultural conventions prevail. Along with goals, values, and attitudes, Gumperz notes, verbal/linguistic patterns of talk serve as the basis for prejudicial judgments about strangers' abilities and attitudes.

Relatedly, studies have demonstrated that various forms of psychological distress (e.g., depression, escapism, neurosis, and psychosis) can be seen among those whose native cultures depart radically from that of the host community (see David, 1969; Kino, 1973; Krau, 1991; Searle & Ward, 1990; Vaz, 1985; Williams & Westermeyer, 1986). Studies of Southeast Asian refugee groups have shown that Vietnamese and Laotian refugees are economically adapting to the American environment more quickly than are Cambodian and Hmong refugees (Goza, 1987; Kim, 1980, 1989, 1990; Ryan, 1987). This differential adaptation is attributed to the cultural backgrounds of the two groups: Vietnamese and Laotian refugees have tended to come from economic backgrounds that are comparable to the mainstream U.S. culture, whereas

Cambodian and Hmong refugees have come from largely agricultural and illiterate backgrounds. Comparable findings have been reported with respect to the value and behavioral conflicts experienced by urban Native Americans with rural backgrounds (Fogelman, 1972; Peck, 1972) and by Asian college students on American campuses experiencing greater adaptation problems than their European counterparts (Lauver & Schram, 1988).[1]

Indeed, compatible areas of ethnicity, such as cultural values and communication patterns, can compensate for the more visible differences in external ethnic markers. Despite salient physical appearances, Vietnamese and other Asian Americans have been able to adapt to the United States more successfully than have some other immigrant groups in socioeconomic spheres (Kim, 1980, 1989, 1990). Their success may be at least partly attributable to certain internalized cultural values (such as a Confucian work ethic, self-discipline, and strong family ties) that are highly compatible with those of mainstream America.

Adaptive Personality

In addition to ethnicity-based similarity/difference and compatibility, the psychological makeup of an individual stranger has an influence on his or her cross-cultural adaptation. Of the many idiosyncrasies that people have, some of the more or less enduring ones are broadly referred to as *personality*—the routinized ways in which individuals respond to environmental stimuli (Horowitz, 1991). Personality attributes such as readiness or capacity for change vary from person to person. As Kagan (1984) observes, about 10% of all babies are born with a biological susceptibility to arousal or anxiety under stress, whereas another 20% are able to "tough it out," may learn to profit by trauma, and are better able to handle later life accidents more effectively. As a set of psychological drives, adaptive personality serves as the power of initiative and being an agent in the living of one's life.

Of particular interest here are those inner resources of personality that differentiate strangers who succumb to intercultural challenges from those who emerge victorious. As Stewart and Healy (1985) note, "New integration takes place within the context of some existing 'personality' " (p. 117). The adaptive drive in an individual's personality channels stress away from debilitating effects and toward learning and growth in a new culture (Walton, 1990, p. 507). It serves as the internal capacity or "survivor merit" (Zurcher, 1977, p. 112) by enabling the individual to "ride" the low points of the adaptation process and to meet new demands again and again (Stewart & Healy, 1985, p. 117). Individuals with adaptive drives have self-propelling, as well as self-constraining, capabilities in an alien milieu. Such capacities, in turn, enable strangers to set goals without being overcome by the challenges of the host environment.

Three facets of adaptive personality are identified in the present theory and are examined in detail here: openness, strength, and positivity. These concepts are employed as high-level abstractions consolidating other similar concepts of greater specificity and frequent semantic redundancy in meaning. Although these three concepts are highly interrelated, each emphasizes a particular personality domain that is somewhat different from the others. Together, the three help construct a profile of the adaptive personality disposition of a stranger in cross-cultural adaptation.

Openness

Openness of personality is the "threshold for receptivity" (Stewart & Healy, 1985, p. 137) toward external stimuli as well as the internal flow of information within the individual (Gendlin, 1962, 1978). Openness is reflected in a tendency to live "without any reserve in the structure of the present, and yet to let go and flow into a new structure when the right time has come" (Jantsch, 1980, p. 255).

Openness is a baseline concept into which can be integrated other similar but more specific variables that are positively correlated with an individual's communication competence. Among such variables are "open-mindedness" (Tamam, 1993), "risk taking" (Fiske & Maddi, 1961), "gregariousness" (Bradburn, 1969), "extroversion" (Stewart & Healy, 1985), "readiness" (Stewart & Healy, 1985), "motivation for self-development" (van den Broucke, de Soete, & Böhrer, 1989), and "willingness to communicate" (McCroskey & Richmond, 1991). By extension, the concept of openness represents other concepts that entail varying degrees of lack of openness, or closedness. Among such concepts that have often been examined in the context of cross-cultural adaptation are "anxiety," "closed-mindedness," "defensiveness," "dogmatism," "rigidity," "reserved personality," "ethnocentrism," and "prejudice." Also included in this group of concepts are "introversion," "shyness," "aloofness," "arrogance," and "lack of interest in new ideas and people." Shyness, in particular, has been found to be associated with spending more time on "self-focusing" and with experiencing more anxious feelings during conversations with strangers (Melchior & Cheek, 1991). In addition, the disposition of high anxiety (Sarason, Sarason, & Pierce, 1991) or "communication apprehension" along with "introversion" has been associated with less "willingness to communicate" (McCroskey & Richmond, 1991).

Clearly, cross-cultural adaptation can only be enhanced by the quality of openness. Openness allows strangers to examine themselves and the environment with a genuine willingness to be transformed as they incorporate new experiences and new learning. Openness affects the quality of communication activities of strangers directly as it promotes their involvement in the host environment by making them more accessible to the local ideas and people. It increases the potential for strangers to assess themselves and the host environment accurately and realistically while discouraging them from making ethnocentric, categorical, and superficial prejudgments of the new milieu. In contrast, strangers with extremely "closed" personalities tend to distort their understanding of the host culture, bitterly denounce it with paranoiac defensiveness in dealing with local people, and engage in excessive glorification of their original cultures. Openness further facilitates flexibility in identity orientation. By its very nature, a strongly maintained ethnic identity puts heavier emphasis on contrastiveness as a mode of social identity—often as a reaction to social discrimination (De Vos & Suárez-Orozco, 1990a, p. 247). Openness allows a stranger to accept the duality of his or her identity, incorporating both the original identity and the new one as a member of the host environment, whereas a closed cognitive style (or defensiveness) that excludes threatening new experiences leads a stranger to maintain a rigid, past-oriented identity.

Some direct and indirect research evidence exists to support the linkage between openness and cross-cultural adaptation. Searle and Ward (1990), in a study of Malaysian and Singaporean students in New Zealand, found that "extroversion" was positively correlated with the students' psychological adjustment. In a study of American managers in Saudi Arabia and French managers in the United States, Dean and Popp (1990) found that the managers assessed the personality attributes associated with tolerance for ambiguity and flexibility to be among the most important individual qualities that helped them to deal with unfamiliar situations and communication misunderstandings.

Openness is a significant factor underlying the common research finding that *age* is inversely associated with cross-cultural adaptation.

Studies of cross-cultural adaptation, particularly those focusing on second-language acquisition, have reported the common finding that the rate of adaptation is inversely associated with advancing age. It has been found, for example, that younger adults tend to acquire English more quickly and attain a higher proficiency in the language than do older adults (Baldassini & Flaherty, 1982; Jones, 1987; Penalosa, 1972; Roy, 1987). Gal (1978) found a strong correlation between an immigrant's age and his or her preference for speaking in the original language. A similar inverse relationship between age and adaptation indicators has been observed among American tourists in Africa during a 6-week tour (Cort & King, 1979) and among Hmong refugees in the United States (Westermeyer, Vang, & Neider, 1986).

Age, however, is not considered a logical and viable "cause" of greater or lesser adaptation in and of itself. Rather, age is a significant factor in cross-cultural adaptation because of its close linkage to openness to change. Older strangers by and large do not have open personality structures due to the fact that their original cultural identities and communication patterns have become solidified. Even when strangers are strongly motivated to learn about and adapt to the host culture, many will find it difficult to do so because of old cultural habits etched into their psyches. The discrepant level of openness between age groups generates the critical issue of the common cultural chasm separating foreign-born parents from their children (Suárez-Orozco, 1990, p. 280). Rather than adapting to the new world around them, many such parents retreat into their own cultures when they face problems with their children. Evidence shows that the primary social identities and attributes of young children are more malleable and are strongly influenced by their peers (other children) and by the host mass media rather than by their parents. Older settlers themselves notice the constraints in new learning associated with their age; this recognition is reflected in the observation of a Hmong refugee in the United States: "Here I'm just starting to learn ABC and 1-2-3. I'm 52 years old, and it is very hard to remember new things. I don't think I'll learn too much. I dream of going back to my village" (quoted in Mullen, 1984, p. 13).

Strength

Along with openness, the strength of personality or "ego strength" (Lazarus, 1966) facilitates cross-cultural adaptation as well. Strangers with varying degrees of personality strength react to stressful situations differently. Some react to difficult situations with composure and clear thinking, whereas others in similar situations "fall apart," unable to collect their resources to manage impending crisis. Strength, as such, is an attribute similar to "coping capacity," the ability to withstand perceived difficulties under duress and to persist in efforts to make things work (Lazarus, 1966; Lifton, 1993). It is the will to bear discomfort, the opposite of extreme ego fragility, or a self-image that can be blown away in the face of a slight challenge by others. At the same time, strength of personality should not be confused with stubbornness, tenseness, or self-centeredness. Strength incorporates in its meaning qualities of flexibility, the ability to "bend" and empathize with others while believing in oneself, and relaxedness, or the ability to "let go" of anxiety and remain integrated (MacKinnon, 1978). Unlike stubbornness, which discourages adaptation, strength of personality helps a stranger to manage stresses and facilitates creative and effective responses to impending problems. It gives the stranger a sense of him- or herself as the main agent of responsibility and the determination to "own" his or her fate (Walton, 1990).

Personality strength, then, is a type of inner resource that enables strangers to face intercultural challenges. Such a trait is seen when Lyfu, a Hmong refugee in the United States, discusses his determination to learn English: "I started reading in English until 3 and 4 in the morning, getting only one or two hours of sleep a night, until my English improved" (quoted in Mullen, 1984, pp. 8, 13). This is an expression of the stranger's resolve to face the difficult challenges of the adaptation process and resilience to learn from each problematic situation. As such, personality strength is a kind of personal power—the capacity to fix one's sights and chart a course without being too dependent on, or blaming, external forces. As a theoretical concept, strength serves as a higher-level abstraction of other concepts that have been employed previously. These include "tolerance for ambiguity" (Dean & Popp, 1990), "risk taking" (Fiske & Maddi, 1961), "hardiness" (Quisumbing, 1982; Walton, 1990), "resilience" (Quisumbing, 1982), "internal locus of control" (Lefcourt, 1984; Padilla, Wagatsuma, & Lindholm, 1985; Rotter, 1990; Yum, 1986), and related concepts such as "ego strength" (Lazarus, 1966), "self-confidence/assertiveness" (van den Broucke et al., 1989), and "self-esteem" (Padilla et al., 1985).

Research has provided some evidence for the linking of personality strength to adaptation. Brown (1991), for example, has observed a relationship between the capacity to tolerate mistakes and breaking language barriers. Yum (1986) found a positive correlation between immigrants' internal locus of control (defined as the tendency to place the responsibility for events within oneself) and the extent to which the immigrants develop native-born acquaintances and friends. Walton (1990) has observed the hardiness of sojourners to be a factor in their greater knowledge of a new culture. Other studies of sojourners have reported a clear linkage between sojourners' self-confidence or self-esteem and their motivation for, and actual participation in, personal relationships with host nationals (e.g., Morris, 1960; Ota & Gudykunst, 1994; Selltiz et al., 1963; Sewell & Davidsen, 1961). Studies of Southeast Asian refugees in the United States have also demonstrated the importance of refugees' positive self-image in their social and economic adaptation (e.g., Office of Refugee Resettlement, 1984). Discussions with teachers and students in English-as-a-second-language classes have further indicated that depression and lack of self-confidence impede refugees' learning. In addition, behavioral characteristics of personality strength, such as extroversion, tolerance for ambiguity, and self-control, have been identified as contributing to effective psychological and functional adjustment in the new culture (Dean & Popp, 1990; Ruben & Kealey, 1979; Searle & Ward, 1990).

Positivity

The personality attributes discussed above, openness and strength, are closely related to yet another attribute: positivity, or an affirmative and optimistic mental outlook. Unlike blind romanticism or far-fetched idealism, positivity is the enduring tendency to see bright and hopeful sides to all things *despite* their dark shades. Among the terms in semantic opposition to *positivity* are *negativity, cynicism, pessimism, hostility, competitiveness, fearfulness, suspicion, bitterness,* and *hypercriticalness.* Positivity helps to defy negative prediction (Dean & Popp, 1990): If one believes that change is not only possible but rewarding as well, that becomes the source of personal power or "general self-efficacy" (Harrison, Chadwick, & Scales, 1996). A positive person tends to experience more joy and satisfaction in life activities in general (Seligman & Weiss, 1980). Positivity is similar to what Maslow (1969) refers to as "metamotivation," that is, a drive beyond mere desire to survive physically and socially. Even somewhat unrealistic positivity has been shown to perform a more practical adaptive role than realistic pessimism (Seligman & Weiss, 1980; Taylor, 1991).

Positivity facilitates strangers' engagement with local social processes. As positive-minded strangers tend to reach out to members of the local community for engagement, their efforts are likely to be reciprocated by the natives in the form of greater receptivity. As Worchel

(1979) observes: "Cooperation could be induced by having each side set aside its weapons or reduce its potential to threaten or harm the other. The less the two parties fear each other, the greater should be the likelihood that they will cooperate" (p. 266). The basic requirement for a cooperative situation is that when individuals behave in a way that increases their own chances of goal attainment, they also increase the chances that the others will attain their goals. Worchel (1986) has proposed that fear and perceived threat can be minimized through the dissemination of positive information, which eases negative perceptions and tension and increases the attractiveness of the out-group.

When directed inwardly, positivity is linked to "self-esteem," an affirmative acceptance and evaluation of each component of self. This positivity is not narcissism or blind self-glorification, as it acknowledges weaknesses and limitations (Zurcher, 1977). A positive person believes, however, that one can overcome one's weaknesses and does not allow such weaknesses to cripple him or her with feelings of inferiority or worthlessness (Maslow, 1969, p. 35). The link between optimism and performance is basically persistence. Optimists keep at it; pessimists give up and fail, even if they have equal talent. And because optimists are always hopeful about outcomes, they tend to take more risks and try more new things. Horst Bienek (1990), a Polish émigré in exile in Germany, exemplifies positive personality when he states: "I do not believe in impoverishment which supposedly occurs when one moves from one language to another. I regard it even as an enrichment" (p. 46). An underlying positive outlook such as this reflects the kind of idealism—a belief in possibilities in life and a faith in the goodness of people—that the Peace Corps reportedly looks for in prospective members (Collin, 1978).

A Profile of Adaptive Personality

These three attributes—openness, strength, and positivity—are the mutually reinforcing hallmarks and pillars of adaptive personality. They are inseparably intertwined facets of personality: One cannot be strong and positive as long as one is closed-minded, and vice versa. Together, these three attributes help strangers to absorb culture shocks and manage the challenges of cross-cultural adaptation. When armed with these internal resources, strangers are able to maintain sufficient "give" in their personality structures to withstand the often stormy challenges of the unfamiliar environment. The combination of openness, strength, and positivity constitutes more than mere "coping capacity" (Lazarus, 1966, p. 225); it projects a kind of personality that acts to forge a gallant stand even against seemingly insurmountable odds, remaining resourceful, imaginative, and in good spirits for the future.

Rooted in a fundamental sense of self-trust, adaptive personality manifests itself in social ease, a sense of humor, the ability to imagine, and the perspective to understand that one's plight may not be unique or permanent. Exuding such inner resources is Edward Limonov (1990), an exile from the former Soviet Union who emigrated to New York City in 1975 and then moved to France. Limonov reflects on his life in the West:

> Life abroad is a lot more interesting than in the country where you were born and grew up, if only because the newness is so stimulating. If I had my druthers, I would like to live many lives, each in a different country. Despite the petty inconveniences involved, I am fascinated by the process of getting to know a new country, its ways, language, mores. . . . And having lived now in three countries—the USSR, the USA and France—I really am unable to answer the question: "Which is best?" All of them have become part and parcel of my own personal history. (p. 50)

Mohm, a Cambodian refugee described by Gail Sheehy in her book *Spirit of Survival* (1987), is another person who exemplifies a highly adaptive personality. Mohm was one of the first Cambodian refugees to be settled in New York City in 1982. Having lived through the genocidal regime of Pol Pot—during which her entire family, with the possible exception of a brother, was killed—Mohm became Sheehy's adopted daughter at the age of 12. Mohm's diary during her first 2 years in the United States is interspersed with Sheehy's reflections throughout the book. In describing Mohm's spirit, Sheehy points out Mohm's adaptive personality as follows, reflecting the profile of adaptive personality—its openness, strength, and positivity:

> Already I could see in Mohm one of the hallmarks of the victorious personality. Despite the unfamiliarity or chaos of the conditions she found herself in, no matter how distressed or disoriented she was, she had a knack for making the other person feel comfortable. . . . Mohm extended herself to people whose goodwill she needed. Standing before a doctor who had offended her sense of modesty, Mohm, instead of sulking or becoming hostile, had disarmed the doctor. . . . Using whatever she had to work with, she touched people. (pp. 223-224)

Yet another example of adaptive personality is found in the story of Sam Baraker, an immigrant from Ukraine living in Brooklyn, New York. Baraker spent five mornings a week in an English class for immigrants and was determined to find people with whom to practice his English and develop friendships. After failing to find anyone with whom he could speak regularly, Baraker, with his resourceful mind, hit upon an ingenious solution: He began calling the toll-free ordering numbers in various retail catalogs—from Tiffany & Company, L. L. Bean, and J. Crew to American Express and the Metropolitan Museum of Art (Rimer, 1991).

Linking Factors of Communication and Predisposition

The basic personality dispositions, along with the overall preparedness for a new life and the proximity (or distance) of visible and invisible ethnic characteristics to (or from) those of the natives, constitute a stranger's overall individual potential for adaptation in the host environment. Figure 9.1 summarizes the relationship between each of the three predispositional factors and the development of host communication competence and host social communication practices. To the extent that strangers are prepared for cross-cultural adaptation (educated, trained, cross-culturally experienced, and voluntarily relocating), they are more likely to be successful in their personal and social communication practices in the new environment (Theorems 13 and 14) and less likely to be engaged in extensive and prolonged ethnic social communication activities (Theorem 15). Strangers' chances for successful cross-cultural adaptation are greater when their ethnic (linguistic, national, cultural, religious, and otherwise) backgrounds are similar to and compatible with the mainstream ethnicity of the host environment (Theorems 16 and 17), whereas vastly different and incompatible ethnic backgrounds tend to encourage greater ethnic involvements (Theorem 18). In addition, strangers' possession of the three interrelated traits of adaptive personality—openness, strength, and positivity—is likely to facilitate their development of host communication competence and participation in host social communication processes (Theorems 19-21).

The predispositional factors discussed so far in this chapter serve as a more or less enduring internal adaptive apparatus, the personal

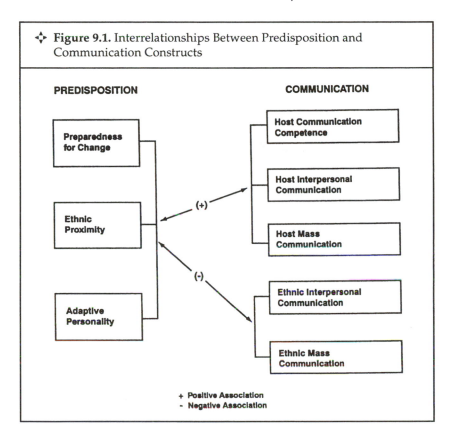

✧ **Figure 9.1.** Interrelationships Between Predisposition and Communication Constructs

capital for adaptive change. At the same time, at least some of the predispositional characteristics of strangers in turn undergo change. Extensive research findings in personality have documented, for example, that exposure to strong environmental influences can change even genetically "fixed" temperaments such as shyness (Gallagher, 1996; Wrightsman, 1994). Similar changes are expected in some ethnic traits, such as cultural values and aesthetic/emotional sensibilities (including tastes for food, clothing, music, and sense of humor). A stranger's adaptive apparatus works as a variation of "self-fulfilling prophecy," helping to shape the subsequent unfolding of an adaptive journey. Conversely, the progression of adaptation affects the stranger's predisposition as well, even as we recognize the enduring nature of ascribed ethnicity and basic personality characteristics.

Intercultural Transformation

At the end of this gradual evolution my inner universe reaches homogeneity in which not forms but the opposition of forms is abolished. Everything is equalised.

Hubert Benoit, *The Supreme Doctrine*, 1955

When strangers enter a new culture, the process of cross-cultural adaptation is set in motion. The process continues as long as the strangers maintain some form of communication with the host milieu. Throughout this process, individuals undergo a degree of intercultural transformation corresponding to the extent of their communicative interface with the host milieu. Adaptation occurs naturally and inevitably even when strangers do not plan or actively seek for it to happen, have no intention of participating fully in host social communication activities, and confine themselves to mostly superficial relationships with the natives. Even in extreme adversarial situations, such as those experienced by hostages and war refugees, individuals returning home are no longer the same persons they were before they left.

As explained in Chapter 4, adaptive changes occur gradually, almost imperceptibly, with each stage of change serving as a necessary result of the preceding condition of adaptation. Cross-cultural adaptation, then, may be seen as a continuum along which individual strangers show differential rates or levels of intercultural transformation, from minimal to maximal. The accompanying changes are a cumulative result of all conceivable communication activities—conscious or

183

unconscious, instrumental or noninstrumental. Although strangers' motivations will potentially influence the distances they will travel in their adaptation process, some change will inevitably occur. Very gradually, through the processes of acculturation and deculturation, some of the old cultural habits are replaced by new ones, so as to move the individual in the direction of a state of assimilation, the highest possible theoretical level of acculturation.

The process of intercultural transformation rides on the stress-adaptation-growth dynamic (Figure 4.3), which is filled with a continual resolution of difficulties and produces setbacks of temporary disintegration, or even "breakdown" in some extreme cases, of the internal psyche. When successfully managed, the "old" person breaks up and a "new" person emerges at a higher level of integration (Kim, 1988, 1995b, 1997b; Kim & Ruben, 1988). Large and sudden modifications are likely during the initial phase of adaptation, when strangers are least prepared to cope with the challenges. Large changes are themselves indicative of difficulties and disruptions, as has been demonstrated amply in culture-shock studies, followed by subsiding intensities in fluctuations of stress, adaptation, and growth (Figure 4.4). An individual can halt the process by leaving a particular host environment, only to begin again when he or she faces a new set of challenges upon returning home. This intrapsychic phenomenon echoes the dynamic nature of "ego identity" and its evolution throughout life, as articulated by personality theorists such as Csikszentmihalyi (1993), Erikson (1959, 1969), Grotevant (1992, 1993), Kroger (1993), and Wrightsman (1994).[1]

The present theory has depicted intercultural transformation in terms of its three specific facets: an increased functional fitness in the host environment, an increased psychological health vis-à-vis the host environment, and an emergence of an intercultural identity that reaches beyond the perimeters of the original cultural identity. As depicted in Figure 10.1, the gradual and largely unconscious process of intercultural transformation is the chief outcome of, as well as a contributing factor in, strangers' development of host communication competence (Theorem 3) and participation in host social communication activities (Theorem 5). At the same time, strangers' active and prolonged involvement in ethnic social communication processes is likely to impede long-term intercultural transformation (Theorem 6).

We now take a closer look at each of the three facets of intercultural transformation and the nature of an "intercultural personhood," an emerging state of a person's changed outlook and behavior accompanying a substantial amount of cross-cultural adaptation experience. An

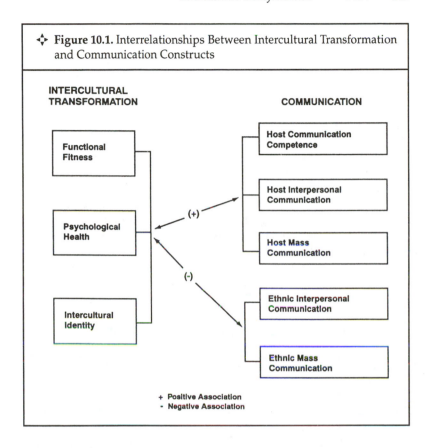

◆ **Figure 10.1.** Interrelationships Between Intercultural Transformation and Communication Constructs

illustration of this special form of human development is offered at the end of this chapter.

Functional Fitness

Strangers in an unfamiliar environment instinctively strive to "know their way around," so as to control their own behavior and the behavior of others. Functional fitness represents an outcome of such effort, manifested in the suitability of strangers' internal capabilities to meet the external challenges of the environment (Brody, 1969; French, Rodger, & Cobb, 1974; Taft, 1977). The notion of functional fitness is consistent with what is commonly understood when we say that a person is "well adapted"—that is, this person is capable of carrying out everyday-life activities smoothly and feeling comfortable in a particular environment. It is mainly this ideal that the family, the school, and other social institutions have in mind when they concern themselves with children's socialization. In the case of cultural strangers, functional fitness is linked directly with host communication competence and participation in host social communication processes. After all, competence is an individual's ability to respond "in a way that optimally satisfies and integrates the demands of the environment" (Heath, 1977, p. 37).

An increase in functional fitness is reflected, in turn, in increased *congruence of subjective meaning systems* between strangers and their hosts. Functionally fit individuals have developed a broadened, clearer, more objective, and more differentiating perception of the host cultural and communication patterns. Closely accompanying the perceptual refinement is the increasing capacity to participate in the emotional and aesthetic experiences of the natives and the resourcefulness and synchrony to make appropriate behavioral adjustments to specific situations and to manage them effectively and creatively. As Ruesch (1957/1972) states, "One of the criteria for successful communication is the mutual fit of over-all patterns and constituent parts, integration, synchrony, smoothness so that no particular person is overburdened with or completely relieved of work, and thus the exchange of messages becomes efficient, clear, economical, and well timed" (p. 34).

One method of assessing strangers' meaning congruence is to observe them as they interact with local people, assess the smoothness of the interaction patterns, and obtain the opinions of both the strangers and their native partners to test the *mutuality of perceptions* (Kim, 1979c). Tamam (1993) conducted a study that assessed such perceptual mutuality and found a high degree of correspondence between international students' assessments of their own host communication competence and assessments of the same by their American professors and fellow graduate students. Similarly, Szalay and Inn (1988) measured functional fitness in terms of the subjective meaning systems of Mexican Americans and Puerto Ricans from New York. As noted in Chapter 5, these investigators compared the data with the meaning systems of Anglo-Americans in New York and of Puerto Ricans in San Juan. Findings from this study demonstrate a general progression of the meaning systems of Puerto Ricans in New York toward the Anglo-American meaning system. A further indication of increasing functional fitness is the finding that the meaning systems of Puerto Ricans in New York were located between those of their San Juan Puerto Rican and Anglo-American counterparts.

Researchers have examined a lack of functional fitness in terms of *social alienation*, a sense of "being left out." The experience of alienation is the self-consciousness that strangers derive from their inability to communicate and empathize with the emotional experiences of the natives (De Vos, 1990b). Conversely, the lack of alienation experience is indicative of satisfaction and other positive feelings toward the host environment. Also associated with functional fitness is an enhancement in *socioeconomic status indices* such as income, occupational status, housing status, and other tangible achievement indices, such as academic and job-related successes. All of these variables have been documented to be positively correlated with other adaptation indicators, such as the level of involvement in host interpersonal and mass communication activities (e.g., Kim, 1976, 1990; Kim, Lujan, & Dixon, 1998a, 1998b; Shah, 1991).

An advanced state of achieved functional fitness further reflects what Harris (1979) refers to as "optimal communication competence"—the maximum capacity to communicate with the natives and make deliberate choices of actions in specific situations, rather than simply following the dictated normative courses of action in a given culture. A high level of functional fitness is evident in this self-reflection of Jeanne Wakatsuki Houston (1981), a Japanese American writer:

> Now I entertain according to how I feel that day. If my Japanese sensibility is stronger, I act accordingly and feel okay. If I feel like going all-American, I can do that too and feel okay. I've come to accept the cultural hybrid of my personality and recognize it as a strength, not as a weakness. Because I am culturally neither pure Japanese nor pure American . . . does not mean that I am less of a person. It seems that I have been enriched by the heritages of both.

Psychological Health

An increase in functional fitness is accompanied by an increase in psychological integration and health—a state in which the individual's cognitive, affective, and operational tendencies work in harmony. Psychological health is a phenomenon that is difficult to observe concretely because it reflects a normal, taken-for-granted state of being. On the other hand, symptoms of psychological illness are readily identifiable, as they deviate from normalcy. Among the common manifestations of psychological illness are the frequently investigated culture-shock symptoms, which include negative self-image, low self-esteem, low morale, social isolation, dissatisfaction with life in general, a bitter attitude of being a helpless victim of circumstance, and related distresses such as depression (Berry, 1990; Dyal & Dyal, 1981; Furnham & Bochner, 1986; Hurh & K. C. Kim, 1990; Searle & Ward, 1990). Such symptoms of dysfunction reflect some level of communication breakdown between a stranger and the environment and a serious disequilibrium within the stranger's psyche (Taft, 1977).

In addition, strangers' experience of psychic disintegration is often manifested in the form of *hostility or aggression toward the host environment*. As suggested in the "frustration-aggression hypothesis" (Zajonc, 1952), the stranger who experiences a need to conform and cannot do so owing to lack of host communication competence is subject to frustration (that is, the blockage of a goal). Such frustration, in turn, serves to reduce the stranger's need to adapt by devaluing the need for it. Frustration is always followed by some form of aggression, which is not always directed toward the actual source of frustration. In many instances, the causes of goal blockage may be highly complex, may not be due to any single person, or may be poorly understood by the individual concerned. The cause of goal blockage may also be a specific but powerful force capable of inflicting severe punishment for aggression. In such instances, the aggression may be displaced, taking a more subtle, indirect, or delayed form.

Psychiatry has concerned itself for the past several decades with the clinical description of mental illnesses among immigrants and refugees. The unsettling condition of "uprootedness" has been linked with "identity crisis" and associated symptoms (Erikson, 1968, 1969), "paranoid syndrome" (Meznaric, 1984), and schizophrenia (Sauna, 1969). As Ruesch (1957/1972) explains, the condition that the psychiatrist labels "psychosis" can be interpreted to be the result of the patient's misinterpretation of messages received due to a cognitive structure that lacks the ability to differentiate and selectively integrate the information received from the environment. Also, the condition commonly labeled "neurosis" can be a result of the unfortunate attempts of a patient to convey messages to others in social situations without success. Likewise, schizophrenic individuals can be those whose cognitive structure is incapable of discerning the multiplicity of messages.

The development of mental and behavioral disorders in immigrants is due not so much to innate characteristics as to a severely poor fit between the stranger and the receiving milieu. Stress seems particularly acute among those whose native cultures differ radically from the culture of the host community. Also, stress can be intensified even further when there is strong pressure for rapid assimilation and the stranger is unable or unwilling to join a familiar group that might offer tension reduction and flexibility in coping with cultural change (David, 1969; Kleiner & Parker, 1969). Kino (1973) describes this situation succinctly based on psychiatric case studies of Polish men in England voluntarily admitted to mental hospitals:

> The change [toward illness] occurred with their transfer to workshops or pits, where they found themselves isolated in a foreign environment whose language and habits were unknown to them, making every attempt at interpersonal approach very difficult. Being accustomed at home to lively and voluble companionship, the impossibility of making conversation and friendly contact with their new companions left them emotionally upset. Misunderstandings and misapprehensions unavoidable in such a situation evoked their suspicion and mistrust. Harmless talks or remarks of their fellow workers to one another were interpreted as hostile observations, though they were unable to understand the language. Gradually this morbid state of mind grew to such intensity that a rational appreciation of the environment became quite impossible. (p. 63)

A healthy psychological state is a dynamic fit between parts of the internal system and external realities—that is, an attainment of internal coherence and meaningful relationship to the outside world. Such internal and external congruence is difficult for newcomers to achieve initially, when they are least equipped with a cohesively developed system of host communication competence: One or more of the dimensions or elements of host communication competence may be lacking, whereas others may be strong. A stranger may be quite knowledgeable about the host culture and yet may find it almost impossible to understand and share many of the culture's aesthetic sensibilities. Another stranger may be adequately skilled in performing social roles, but may find some of the operant values in the role performance disagreeable. Yet another stranger may be sufficiently capable of participating in the emotional and aesthetic experiences of the natives, but may be unable to express such experiences adequately through verbal and nonverbal performances. The lack of host communication competence thus accounts for many of the psychological problems associated with strangers' maladaptation. A negative self-image, low self-esteem, low morale, social isolation, dissatisfaction with life in general, and a bitter attitude of being a helpless victim of circumstance—all of these phenomena can be traced to internal imbalance. Persistence of the imbalanced internal state contributes to what is called psychotic or neurotic behavior or thought (De Vos, 1990c, p. 62).

Paradoxically, the experience of internal disintegration, more commonly called *culture shock*, serves as a transformative force for individuals. The inherent "homeostatic" tendency toward achieving internal equilibrium allows the integration of the cognitive, affective, and operational capacities. This internal healing is owed to what Jantsch (1980) calls the "self-organizing" human capacity—the capacity to endure the broken intra-psychic and person-environment symmetry. Such a capacity and the resulting personal growth can be witnessed not only among those crossing cultures but more generally among those who have experienced the aftermath of traumatic events in their lives (Moos, 1976, 1986). The cognitive, affective, and operational capabilities that constitute host communication competence influence and reinforce each other to achieve a balance. As Maslow (1970) observes: "What had been considered in the past to be polarities or opposites or dichotomies were so only in unhealthy people. In healthy people, these dichotomies were resolved, the polarities disappeared, and many oppositions thought to be intrinsic merged and coalesced with each other to form unities" (p. 232).

In contrast to psychological illness, achievement of psychological health is a direct response to increased host communication competence that enables strangers to be effective in their dealings with the host environment. As Erikson (1969) notes, a "healthy personality" requires that the person have the ability "to perceive the world and himself correctly" (p. 31). This means that if strangers are to be psychologically healthy, they must concentrate on improving their host communication competence and participate in local interpersonal and mass communication processes. Studies of immigrants and sojourners have documented close links among indicators of strangers' psychological health (such as satisfaction and happiness) and stress (such as alienation), their host communication competence, and their social communication activities, particularly those within interpersonal networks (e.g., Arevalo, 1987; Nishida, 1985; Searle & Ward, 1990; van Oudenhoven & Eisses, 1998; Ward, Okura, Kennedy, & Kojima, 1998).[2]

Intercultural Identity

Increased functional fitness and psychological health of the stranger in the host environment are accompanied by emergence of an identity that is increasingly richer in content and more complex in structure. The singular identity of a stranger shaped and conditioned by the original cultural milieu, along with the singular identification with and loyalty to that group, is expanded beyond the perimeters of the original cultural conditioning. The term *intercultural identity* thus refers to an acquired identity constructed after the early childhood enculturation process through the individual's communicative interactions with a new cultural environment. It is consistent with Grotevant's (1992) notion of "adopted" identity as well as Phinney's (1993) notion of "achieved" identity (in contrast to "assigned" or "ascribed" identity).

Whereas these and related concepts point to the notion that identity is shaped not only by influences of the culture of childhood but also by contacts with new cultural elements, they also suggest that the identity of an individual is not an either/or state; rather, it is a continuum or an evolutionary process moving in the direction of fuller psychological integration and health (Jahoda, 1958; Waterman, 1992, p. 50). In Adler's (1982) words, the development of an intercultural identity places the stranger in the position of continually "negotiating ever new formations of reality" (p. 391). Internalizing new cultural elements lies at the core of a person's development from a passive self based on ascription to an actively constructed and achieved self based on learning—from a cultural identity to an intercultural identity in which previously unknown life patterns are etched. The impressions received from surroundings, from others, and from the self, as well as the retention of these impressions for future reference—all become integral parts of an evolving person. Such development is far from smooth, as has been shown in the upward-downward-forward-backward movement of the stress-adaptation-growth dynamic depicted in Figures 4.3 and 4.4. Intense stress can reverse the process at any time, and strangers may indeed "regress" toward reaffirming and reidentifying with their ethnic origins, having found the alienation and malaise involved in maintaining a new identity too much of a strain (De Vos & Suárez-Orozco, 1990a, p. 254). As such, the development of an intercultural identity is grounded in the situation of "marginality"—the state in which a stranger is "poised in uncertainty between two or more social worlds" and characteristically experiences an acute sense of self-doubt, loneliness, isolation, hypersensitivity, and restlessness (Stonequist, 1937, 1964; Taft, 1977).

Although these psychological conflicts are an integral part of the process of intercultural identity development, the process moves beyond them. Just as cultural identity links a person to a specific culture, intercultural identity links a person to more than one culture and, ultimately, to humanity itself. Having internalized an increasing level of host communication competence and integration into the host social communication processes, strangers are better able to manage the dynamic and dialogical interaction between the original culture and the new culture. They are also better able to experience different cultural worlds with increasing ease, with a greater capacity to make deliberate choices of actions in specific situations rather than simply following the dictates of the prevailing norms of the culture of childhood.

Individualization

An important element of intercultural identity development is an emerging self—other orientation that is individualized. Individualization allows strangers to practice life that comes without being rigidly constrained by conventional categories. Individualization of one's self-other orientation involves a clear self-definition and definition of the other that reflects a capacity to see one's connectedness to humanity without being restricted by categories of social grouping. The resulting selfhood generates a heightened self-awareness and self-identity—an epoche, authenticity, and a feeling of certainty about one's place in the world. It establishes a foundation for mutuality with respect to people in general (Adler, 1982; Seelye & Wasilewski, 1996). With this capacity, one can see oneself and others on the basis of individual uniquenesses rather than as social stereotypes, reflecting a mental outlook that exhibits greater cognitive differentiation and particularization (see Amerikaner, 1978; Billig, 1987; Boekestijn, 1988; Hansel, 1993; Oddou & Mendenhall, 1984).

An individualized intercultural identity entails a clearer sense of selfhood and well-being in the form of self-acceptance and self-esteem and the relative absence of malice and other debilitating emotional states such as anxiety and depression. An individualized identity is manifested in the enactment and pursuit of socially constructive ends in terms of the attitudes of tolerance, acceptance, and cooperation, helping, and seeking of intimate personal relationships (Waterman, 1992). Individualized orientation is expressed in a sense of oneself as the main agent of action and responsibility and in the determination to "own" one's fate. Research findings provide some direct and indirect evidence for the individualization of self-other orientation among those who are successfully adapted in new cultural or subcultural environments. Amerikaner (1978) found in a study of military cadets, seminarians, and college fraternity members that subjects of a high degree of personality integration (measured by the ability "to deal effectively with everyday tensions and anxieties") exhibited greater cognitive differentiation and integration, less categorical and simplistic self-identity, and greater openness to new social experiences (Oddou & Mendenhall, 1984). Murphy-Shigematsu (1987) found that Amerasians with first-generation Japanese mothers and White American fathers had a clear desire to learn about their Japanese cultural heritage as a growing and powerful influence in their lives and a need to connect their struggles with others involved in similar issues and conflicts. The form of resolution involved accepting and asserting their authentic self-image in society through their unique experience of racial and cultural conditions. In a study of Asian Indian immigrants in the United States, Dasgupta (1983) found that the immigrants were able to resolve the conflict between their traditional value of holism and ascription and American values of individualism, achievement, and competition by dichotomizing and attaining a healthy balance between primary in-group relationships and achievement in their occupational lives in the larger society.[3]

Universalization

Accompanying the individualization of self-other orientation is a parallel development of a universalistic mental outlook—a synergistic cognition "of a new consciousness, born out of an awareness of the relative nature of values and of the universal aspect of human nature" (Yoshikawa, 1978, p. 220). As people advance in their intercultural transformation process, they are better able to see the oneness and unity of humanity, feel greater compassion and sensitivity toward others who are different, and locate the points of consent and complementarity beyond the points of difference and contention. As such, they are on the way to overcoming cultural parochialism and forming a wider circle of identification. Like hikers climbing a high mountain who finally see that all paths below ultimately lead to the same summit, with each path presenting unique scenery, becoming intercultural is a gradual process of freeing one's mind from an exclusive parochial viewpoint so as to attain a greater perspective on the more inclusive whole. A universalistic outlook reflects a nondualistic, metacontextual, and synergistic attitude through which one experiences the humanness in all people beyond apparent differences.

Universalization of identity serves as a mind-set that integrates, rather than separates, all the perspectives represented in a communication transaction. It accentuates a cognitive orientation based on an understanding of profound differences between and among human groups and, at the same time, of profound similarities in human conditions. It further suggests a vital component of an individual's emotional, aesthetic, attitudinal, and moral identity that is not limited to his or her ascribed culture but embraces other cultures (or subcultures) as well. In becoming intercultural, then, we rise above the hidden grip of culture and discover that there are many ways to be "good," "true," and "beautiful." Such an outlook allows what Bakhtin (1990) describes as "a simultaneous exercise of empathy (entering into the other's world) and 'outsidedness' (viewing the other from the perspective of my own world)" (p. 11). The universalized identity orientation thus cultivates what has been called a "third-culture" perspective (Gudykunst, Wiseman, & Hammer, 1977; Mendenhall & Oddou, 1985; Useem, 1963), an orientation toward overcoming the "paradigmatic barriers" between divergent philosophical traditions (Bennett, 1986). Intercultural persons display a greater empathy, or the capacity to "step into and imaginatively participate in the other's world view" (Bennett, 1977, p. 49). They can make value judgments with fewer ethnocentric biases and better connect to people everywhere based on basic human conditions and their variations.

Emergence of Intercultural Personhood

Becoming intercultural, then, is a continuous process of psychic transformation in which the person "brings all parts within himself together into a complete and harmonious whole that is organically in order" (Kao, 1975, p. 33). Research has begun to document this process. In a study of Native Americans in Oklahoma, a positive correlation was found between and among indicators of the three facets of intercultural transformation: functional fitness, psychological health, and intercultural identity (Kim et al., 1998a, 1998b). Ethnic minorities in Canada (including Indians) favoring integration have been found to experience the least psychological stress, whereas those preferring ethnic separation have been found to experience the most (Berry, U. Kim, & Boski, 1988). Szapocznik and Kurtines (1980), in a study of Eastern

European immigrants in the United States, found that "bicultural" identity orientation contributed to greater adaptation. Studies of reservation Indians and structurally isolated ethnic minorities have also documented close links among separation identity, lack of out-group communication activities, and various psychological and social ills. It has been shown, for instance, that separatist identity and social isolation are associated with lack of economic upward mobility (e.g., Berreman, 1964/1972), "social polarization" (Lanigan, 1988), and regressive and dysfunctional personality and behavior characteristics (e.g., Berlin, 1986; Holmgren, Fitzgerald, & Carman, 1983).

The simultaneous development of individualization and universalization of identity, as discussed above, endows individuals with a special kind of freedom and creativity—an ability to make deliberate choices for actions in specific situations rather than simply being restricted by conventions. Intercultural identity development is consistent with two main characteristics of human "maturity," namely, psychic integration and objectivity (Heath, 1965, 1977; Kao, 1975). Mature persons manifest a high degree of internal harmony and of detachment from themselves. This is illustrated by George's (1985) finding in a study of Hindu Indian nationals in the Washington, D.C., metropolitan area that many of these immigrants no longer held the strict belief in a caste system that they had held previously (for similar findings, see Hansel, 1993).

The quiet evolution of intercultural transformation allows strangers to free themselves from and grow out of the hidden grip of parochialism. The process of intercultural transformation is filled with challenges; intercultural personhood is hard-won through many moments of inner crisis, large and small. Once attained, it is not the product of marginality but represents a high degree of psychic evolution. It is a process in which ordinary people struggle and triumph in the act of "stretching" themselves out of the biological and social categorization of themselves and others. As individuals become increasingly proficient in two or more languages and cultures and move toward a more inclusive group identity that embraces many groups, they are better able to make rational comparisons among different philosophical and ideological systems, as well as identify with the experiences of all parties involved.

Cross-cultural adaptation, then, is a personal journey that ultimately leads to a transcendence of cultural categories in individual consciousness. The emerging intercultural personhood is a special kind of orientation toward self, other, and, indeed, the world (see Csikszentmihalyi, 1993). It is a way of life that projects a high level of personal development through extensive and cumulative experiences of acculturation and deculturation, and of stress, adaptation, and growth. Indeed, the emergence of an intercultural personhood involves a continuous struggle of searching for the authenticity in self and others across group boundaries. The process of becoming intercultural is not one of having to replace one culture with another. It is, instead, a "working through" of all cultural experiences, so as to create new constructs—that is, constructs that did not exist previously (Belay, 1993).

The concept of intercultural personhood integrates and represents a number of other similar concepts, such as "multicultural man" (Adler, 1982), "universal man" (Tagore, 1961; Walsh, 1973), "cultural hybrid" (Park, 1939), "international man" (Lutzker, 1960), "species identity" (Boulding, 1988), "cosmopolitan communicator" (Pearce, 1989), and "mediating person" (Bochner, 1981). Walsh's (1973) concept of the universal person, for instance, emphasizes three aspects of a "cosmopolitan" viewpoint: (a) respect for all cultures; (b) understanding of what individuals in other cultures think, feel, and believe; and (c) appreciation for differences among cultures. Although all of these concepts project similar images of personhood, with varying degrees of descriptive and explanatory value, I prefer to use the term *intercultural personhood* because it is more generic, broader, more inclusive, and more flexible in meaning than other terms without implying any specific cultural attributes. It depicts personal characteristics that transcend any given cultural group. Unlike the term *multicultural person*, it does not imply that the individual necessarily "possesses" characteristics of more than one culture. Unlike the term *universal person*, it does not suggest an awareness and identification with all groups of the world. Instead, the notion of intercultural personhood focuses on the expanded psychological orientation beyond national and ethnic boundaries, but it does not emphasize numerous subcultural groups within a society.

This kind of human development echoes one of the highest aims of humans in the spiritual traditions of the Eastern cultures. Suzuki (1968) notes, "The fundamental idea of Buddhism is to pass beyond the world of opposites, a world built up by intellectual distinctions and emotional defilements, and to realize the spiritual world of non-distinction, which involves achieving an absolute point of view" (p. 18). A virtuous person in this philosophical tradition is not one who undertakes the impossible task of striving for the good and eliminating the bad, but rather one who is able to maintain a dynamic balance between good and bad. This Eastern notion of dynamic balance is reflected in the symbolic use by Chinese sages of the archetypal poles of yin and yang. These sages call the unity lying beyond yin and yang the Tao and see it as a process that brings about the interplay of the two poles. Yoshikawa (1986) describes this development as a stage of "double-swing" or "transcendence of binary opposites" (p. 146). Likewise, novelist Salman Rushdie (1992) characterizes his own intercultural transformation in terms of "double perspective" and "stereoscopic vision" (p. 19). With this transcendental understanding, intercultural persons can better reconcile seemingly contradictory elements and transform them into complementary, interacting parts of a single whole.

Through individualization and universalization in self-other orientation, intercultural persons possess an element of increased mental and emotional refinement toward greater realism, comprehensiveness, and objectivity. This development corresponds to an achievement of "cultural reflexibility" (Roosens, 1989), "cultural relativistic insight" (Roosens, 1989), and "moral inclusiveness" (Opotow, 1990). These concepts characteristically show an increased self-knowledge free from the hidden grip of culture and noncategorical perceptions, but allow the intercultural person to empathize with all kinds of people. Such identity orientation is consistent with Erikson's (1969) notion of "transcendence" in characterizing "self-actualizing" people and Ricoeur's (1992) idea of a "transcendental ego." Both highlight the idea of a noncategorical, noncultural, and universalistic orientation as a higher-level self-integration and can be witnessed in the testimonial of Edward Limonov (1990), a Russian exile who reflects on his own cross-cultural journey after having lived in Paris and in New York:

> Having been through the struggle for existence in three countries (and not in the form of package tours or diplomatic junketing), I do not share the multiplicity of prejudices, phobias, and myths extant in the world. I do not, for example, perceive a great difference in the life of ordinary people in most countries. Under any political system the working man . . . puts in his eight hours a day. The social system has yet to be invented which will free him from these eight unpleasant hours of daily slavery. Both in the USSR and in the USA, people wolf down their breakfasts and rush off to work. Perhaps the Soviet worker is more poorly dressed and his breakfast less nutritious than that of his alter ego in the USA, and perhaps he travels to work in a bus rather than in his own car, but such differences are hardly sufficient cause for two peoples to fling atom bombs at each other. (pp. 51-52)

One of the most succinct and eloquent testimonials to the present conception of intercultural personhood is offered by Yoshikawa (1978). As someone who has lived in Japan and in the United States, Yoshikawa offers the following insight into his own psychic transformation—an insight that captures the very essence of what it means to be an intercultural person:

> I am now able to look at both cultures with objectivity as well as subjectivity; I am able to move in both cultures, back and forth without any apparent conflict. . . . I think that something beyond the sum of each [cultural] identification took place, and that it became something akin to the concept of "synergy"—when one adds 1 and 1, one gets three, or a little more. This something extra is not culture-specific but something unique of its own, probably the emergence of a new attribute or a new self-awareness, born out of an awareness of the relative nature of values and of the universal aspect of human nature. . . . I really am not concerned whether others take me as a Japanese or an American; I can accept myself as I am. I feel I am much freer than ever before, not only in the cognitive domain (perception, thoughts, etc.), but also in the affective (feeling, attitudes, etc.) and behavioral domains. (p. 220)

An additional illustration of intercultural synthesis is provided by Duane Elgin, who was born and raised in the United States as a Christian and later studied Buddhism in Tibet and Japan for many years. In his book *Voluntary Simplicity* (1981), Elgin integrates the philosophical ideas of Eastern and Western civilizations. He presents the idea of voluntary simplicity as "global common sense" and as a practical lifestyle to reconcile the willful, rational approach to life of the West and the holistic, spiritual orientation of the East. Examining historical trends, cycles of civilizations, and related ecological concerns, Elgin proposes voluntary simplicity as a goal for all of humanity. The main issue he addresses is how humans can find ways to remove, as much as possible, the nonessential "clutter" of life. He suggests, for example, that we should own or buy things based on real need, and that we should consider the impact of our consumption patterns on other people and on the earth. Before purchasing nonessential items, Elgin suggests, we should ask ourselves if these items promote or cloud the quality of our nonmaterial life. We can also consciously simplify communication activities by making them clearer, more direct, and more honest, without idle, wasteful, and manipulative speech, and by respecting the value of silence and nonverbal actions.

All in all, the present theory presents an alternative to the conventional view of identity and selfhood. The psychological health of a stranger resides not only in a positive sense of cultural identity but in the integration of the cultural identity with a new, alternative identity that is broader than the individual's ascribed cultural membership. Rigid adherence to the original identity without the ability to transcend it is counterproductive to the stranger's psychological health as long as the stranger lives in a new milieu and is functionally dependent on it. In the words of Muruddin Farah (1990), a Somali exile in London who has visited Cairo, Budapest, and the Soviet Union, "One of the pleasures of living away from home is that you become the master of your destiny, you avoid the constraints and limitations of your past and, if need be, create an alternative life for yourself. That way everybody else becomes *the other*, and you the center of the universe" (p. 65).

Numerous other firsthand accounts and stories bear witness to the idea of intercultural personhood projected in the present theory as an ultimate outcome of the cross-cultural adaptation process. These personal accounts are found in case histories, memoirs, biographies, and essays of self-reflection and self-analysis in various forms—popular books, newspaper and magazine articles, and radio and television programs. Such accounts often present vivid testimonials and offer special insights into the emotional ebb and flow and the progressive and eventual realization of intercultural transformation.[4] From these accounts, we learn that no two strangers travel the same path at the same speed and that each must find his or her own path. Through it all, we recognize that the intense experiences of crossing cultures offer everyone opportunities for the full blossoming of the uniquely human capacity to face challenges, learn from them, and grow into a greater self-integration—a state in which all aspects of adaptive change cohere in harmony and readiness for further change yet to come.

Part IV

The Theory and the Reality

Research Considerations

> *The arbitrary structural and dimensional categories are not inde-*
> *pendent of each other. . . . Each is one facet on a multifaceted, com-*
> *plexly organized, and, let us say, living crystal. Each is intrinsic to*
> *the unity of the crystal. Alteration in one facet affects the struc-*
> *tural relations of the entire crystal.*
>
> Douglas Heath, *Maturity and Competence:*
> *A Transcultural View,* 1977

Throughout this volume, I have made an effort to achieve a balance between what Dubin (1978) identifies as the two distinct goals for social science: understanding and prediction. I have sought to promote understanding through a detailed description of the complex and dynamic nature of cross-cultural adaptation as an evolutionary process of intercultural transformation (Figures 4.3 and 4.4). I have sought a degree of predictive precision by introducing theorems specifying the interrelationships between and among the constructs that facilitate (or impede) the adaptation process (Figure 5.1). The theorizing process itself has taken the form of back-and-forth movement between the conceptual realm of reasoning and logical deduction and the empirical realm of proofs available through research evidence. Juxtaposing the deductive and inductive processes, I have substantiated patterns of interrelationship among theoretical constructs to the extent possible. I have used personal testimonials and anecdotes obtained from various sources to provide concrete illustrations of theoretical ideas.

This chapter highlights the key features of the theory before addressing a number of research considerations that are suggested by the dynamic, multidimensional conception of cross-cultural adaptation. Some of the theoretical dimensions and concepts that have received insufficient research attention in the past are identified.

The Theory: Principal Features

By the logic of theorizing, the present account of cross-cultural adaptation offers a particular way of comprehending the phenomenon and the principal patterns in which it occurs. By identifying and formulating the uniformity and regularity in what are infinitely varied individual experiences of cross-cultural adaptation, the theory serves as an abstraction and simplification of the reality it depicts. The theory is integrative in nature, bringing together various disciplinary perspectives and approaches to cross-cultural adaptation to form a more comprehensive and general system of description and explanation. The often divergent sets of more restrictive factors previously seen as influencing the adaptive experiences of individuals have been consolidated into a set of higher-level constructs. Some of the conceptual domains that have been investigated separately across the social sciences have been consolidated, and their interrelatedness has been clarified.

This interdisciplinary integration has been achieved through the use of constructs that are broad and general enough to represent various narrower concepts. To begin with, the concept of *strangers* represents all individuals who find themselves in a cultural or subcultural milieu for varied time periods under varied circumstances. Likewise, *cross-cultural adaptation* incorporates a number of other more restrictive concepts, such as acculturation, psychological adjustment, assimilation, and integration. Given these concepts, the *domain* of the present theory is broad, limited by three *boundary conditions:*

1. The strangers have had a primary socialization in one culture (or subculture) and have moved into a different and unfamiliar culture (or subculture).

2. The strangers are at least minimally dependent on the host environment for meeting their personal and social needs.

3. The strangers are at least minimally engaged in firsthand communication experiences with that environment.

The theory is grounded in three open-systems *assumptions* about the nature of human adaptation (Chapter 3). These assumptions characterize cross-cultural adaptation not as a distinct phenomenon but as a fundamental life activity of all humans, an activity that expresses individuals' inherent drive to maximize the "fit" between their internal conditions and the conditions of the environment in which they live. Driving this struggle is the give-and-take of communication—a multidimensional and multifaceted process of person-environment interface that, over time, leads to the gradual psychic growth of an individual. These foundational assumptions (or premises) are taken as "givens," based on which cross-cultural adaptation is conceived of as a *process* of psychic evolution toward increased functional fitness and psychological health, as well as increased intercultural identity. This evolutionary process is characterized as being punctuated by the dialectics of change and stability, engagement and disengagement, acculturation and deculturation. These "opposing" forces underlie the *stress-adaptation-growth dynamic*, a psychological movement that is central to the cross-cultural adaptation process (Figure 4.3). The movement resembles that of a wheel, in which the downward-backward pull of adaptive stress serves to compel the subsequent forward-upward push for adaptation and growth. Except for a minority who fail in this personal evolution, most strangers are able to overcome many temporary setbacks along the path of gradual intercultural transformation—a process of qualitative change toward their becoming no longer cultural outsiders. This process of personal evolution is marked by diminished severity of fluctuation in the stress-adaptation-growth dynamic (Figure 4.4).

Merged within this conception are the view of cross-cultural adaptation as a problem and the more positive view of such adaptation that emphasizes learning and growth. It reconciles the assimilationist and pluralist views that have divided the field. Both new cultural learning (acculturation) and unlearning of some of the old cultural elements (deculturation) are incorporated. The theory further bridges the two seemingly divergent value premises by treating them as important environmental conditions reflected in the receptivity and conformity pressure the host environment exerts on strangers and the overall strength of their ethnic groups. On the individual level, the differing ideological stances are viewed as a foundational element of host communication competence, reflected in a given stranger's adaptation motivation.

Building on this evolutionary conception of cross-cultural adaptation, the theory proceeds to identifying its *structure* (Figure 5.1). With its six dimensions of constructs, this structural model depicts the reciprocal, interdependent relationships among the constructs and serves as a template for explaining the differential rates (or speeds) at which the adaptation process unfolds over time. The dimension of *personal communication* (Dimension 1) is seen as the intrapersonal system of *host communication competence* that serves as the engine that pushes a given stranger along the adaptation process. Inseparably linked with host communication competence is participation in the *interpersonal and mass communication* activities of *host social communication* (Dimension 2). At the same time, the strangers' *ethnic social communication* activities (Dimension 3) add complexity by impeding long-term adaptation to the host environment at large.

Interfacing with the personal and social (host and ethnic) communication dimensions are the three conditions of the *environment* (Dimension 4): the degree of *host receptivity, host conformity pressure,* and the stranger's *ethnic group strength.* Also affecting the stranger's adaptation are three aspects of the stranger's own *predisposition* (Dimension 5): *preparedness* for life in the host environment, the degree of the stranger's *ethnic proximity* to the dominant ethnicity of the host environment, and the degree of openness, strength, and positivity in his or her *personality.* Together, these dimensions of factors influence (facilitate or impede) the stranger's *intercultural transformation* (Dimension 6)— internal changes embodied in increased *functional fitness, psychological health,* and *intercultural identity.*

Ten axioms summarize the general principles that define the nature of the process and the structure of cross-cultural adaptation derived from the open-systems perspective. These axioms are presented as lawlike statements that collectively help us understand the nature of cross-cultural adaptation, its evolutionary process, and its constituent factors. From the axioms, *23 theorems* are extrapolated. These theorems specify the functional linkages between/among the key constructs (Chapter 5) and, together, form the structural model (Figure 5.1), which consists of six interrelated dimensions of constructs. Macro-level constructs (such as the conditions of the host environment, ethnic community, and ethnic background of the stranger) are incorporated into this structural model along with the micro-level factors of personal and social communication. Long-term immigrant adaptation and short-term sojourner adaptation, commonly treated as two separate phenomena, are fused.

Because of the general nature of the constructs, simple operationalizations may not be adequate to ensure the reliability and validity of the data. In elaborating each of the theoretical constructs in Chapters 6 through 10, I have discussed a number of *empirical indicators* for each construct. Table 11.1 lists these indicators. Each indicator serves as a potential research variable for which specific operational definitions

TABLE 11.1   Indicators for Constructs

Dimensions	Constructs	Indicators
Personal communication	Host communication competence	*Cognitive* Knowledge of host communication system Cultural understanding Cognitive complexity
		Affective Adaptation motivation Identity flexibility Aesthetic coorientation
		Operational Technical skills Synchrony Resourcefulness
Host social communication	Host interpersonal communication	Size/proportion of host ties Strength (intimacy, centrality) of host ties
	Host mass communication	Amount of host media use Information-oriented use of host media
Ethnic social communication	Ethnic interpersonal communication	Size/proportion of ethnic ties Strength (intimacy, centrality) of ethnic ties
	Ethnic mass communication	Amount of ethnic media use Information-oriented use of ethnic media
Environment	Host receptivity	Positive attitude toward strangers Inclusive/associative communication messages
	Host conformity pressure	Assimilative ideologies, norms, policies Homogeneous ethnic compostion
	Ethnic group strength	Ethnic prestige Institutional completeness Identity politics

(continued)

TABLE 11.1 Continued

Dimensions	Constructs	Indicators
Predisposition	Preparedness for change	Education/training Prior cross-cultural experience Voluntary/planned relocation
	Ethnic proximity	Ethnic similarity Ethnic compatibility
	Adaptive personality	Openness Strength Positivity
Intercultural transformation	Functional fitness	Perceptual mutuality (Lack of) psychological alienation Socioeconomic status
	Psychological health	(Lack of) hostility toward host environment (Lack of) mental illnesses (Lack of) culture-shock symptoms
	Intercultural identity	Individualization of identity Universalization of identity

for empirical observation may be devised. Indicators for host communication competence, for example, include knowledge of the host communication system (language, verbal and nonverbal patterns, communication rules), cognitive complexity (differentiation, integration, flexibility), affective coorientation (affirmative attitude, aesthetic participation), and operational (verbal, nonverbal, interactional) proficiency. Likewise, host interpersonal communication can be assessed using the heterogeneity of the stranger's relational network and the strength (intimacy and centrality) of relational ties involving members of the host environment.

Theory-Research Correspondence

For the most part, empirical validation of the present theory would involve testing the validity of the 23 theorems. Through validation of these theorems, the basic assumptions and axioms from which they are derived can be indirectly tested as well (see Figure 3.2). The following discussion examines four key research issues for the design and implementation of research in consonance with the present theoretical conception of cross-cultural adaptation.

Previously Neglected Constructs

Of the six dimensions of constructs from predispositional characteristics to environmental conditions, some have been underinvestigated and others have been investigated more extensively. Among the most neglected constructs is *intercultural identity*, one of the three facets of gradual transformation (along with functional fitness and psychological health). Little research attention has been given to this phenomenon, presenting a stark contrast with the abundance of research activities on cultural identity. The dearth of research on the phenomenon of intercultural identity development reflects the prevailing conception of cultural identity as an a priori, immutable, nonnegotiable, and inherently moral entity. In emphasizing the importance of positive cultural identity to psychological health and social functioning, social scientists in general have tended to obscure cultural identity's complex and evolutionary nature.

What is needed is a series of detailed and systematic investigations focusing on the dynamic, evolving nature of cultural identity articulated in the present theory. Only recently has attention been given to the ways individuals reconcile and integrate multiple identities as they struggle to form a personhood capable of moving beyond parochial interests. My colleagues and I, for example, have examined how Oklahoma Indians reconcile the duality in their identity experience and how such experience is linked with other facets of their lives, including interpersonal relationships (Kim, Lujan, & Dixon, 1998a). Utilizing both numerical and verbal data obtained through one-on-one interviews, we found a preponderance of intercultural identity among the Indians in our sample, mixed with varying degrees of separation orientation.

Along with intercultural identity development, greater research attention is needed concerning the three conditions of the receiving environment: *host receptivity, host conformity pressure,* and *ethnic group strength.* Few studies of culture shock and immigrant acculturation have incorporated environmental factors in examining personal and social aspects of adaptation, such as psychological adjustment, interpersonal communication, and mass-media use. Most social psychological studies of cross-cultural adaptation and interethnic relations have taken a variable-analytic approach, focusing exclusively on micro-level (intrapersonal or interpersonal) factors without taking the surrounding milieu into consideration (see Singelis, 1996). Systematic and detailed future investigations of how the three environmental factors and the interrelationships among them influence the personal and social communication patterns of individual strangers can help verify and elaborate on the present theory (Theorems 7 through 12; Figure 8.1). In particular, we need to develop a more refined understanding of the relationship between host receptivity and host conformity pressure— the two forces that often appear to be at odds with the third environmental condition, ethnic group strength. Further research can ascertain the complex ways in which forces of the host environment and of the ethnic group work simultaneously on the individual stranger's communication behaviors and intercultural transformation (or lack of it).

Broadening the Conceptual Base of Research

In the field of cross-cultural adaptation, various narrowly conceived studies have been conducted to generate varied and inconsistent models, indices, and scales that are often at odds with one another. The variables in one model often do not add up or bear coherent relationships to the variables in other models. Researchers studying limited domains have interpreted their findings in terms of only those variables that they regard as important, without mention of the excluded factors. Such studies have been atheoretical, with their primary interest focused on specific sets of variables that have been chosen largely for practical (rather than theoretical) reasons. Often, such variables belong to a single level of dimension (psychological or social), leading to a tendency toward "premature closure" and fragmentation of knowledge. Future studies need to be grounded in an expanded conceptual domain whenever possible. Instead of focusing on a narrowly drawn domain with only a small number of variables, researchers must make an effort to provide data that inform more of the phenomenon of cross-cultural adaptation (Marshall & Rossman, 1989, p. 17). Anchoring research in a broader domain allows us to seek a greater conceptual correspondence between the findings of given studies and the multidimensional and multifaceted reality of cross-cultural adaptation depicted in the present theory. As Fielding and Fielding (1986) have pointed out, there needs to be "a greater empirical and conceptual accountability on the part of the research" (p. 90).

A particularly important way in which we can broaden the conceptual horizon is by conducting "multilevel research" (DiPrete & Forristal, 1994) that tests the relationships between/among more than one level of theoretical units at once and bridges the gap between traditionally sociological or group-level units and those at the individual (psychological) level. The present theory rejects the rigid dichotomy between atomistic and holistic strategies of explanation. It views cross-cultural adaptation as a unitary psychosocial process in which all of the elements work together in a reciprocal manner. This systemic conception of cross-cultural adaptation encourages "vertical integration" (as well as "horizontal integration") in empirical research—that is, the linking of micro-level analysis of intrapersonal variables (host communication competence, personality factors, predisposition factors), intermediary-level analysis of the factors of the social context (interpersonal and mass communication activities both within and outside the ethnic community), and macro-level analysis of the larger environmental factors (including the ethnic community factors and host society at large). Thus the conceptual scheme guiding our research should be aimed at illuminating the interactions within and between these layers of variables rather than taking individuals apart from their social milieu. This approach necessitates the reframing of distinctions such as those between the individual and the collectivity, between action and structure, between small-scale uniformity and large-scale complexity.

Ideally, a given researcher would accommodate all of the six dimensions of constructs previously identified. However, there are numerous difficulties and constraints inherent in the undertaking of a research project with such a broad and complex conceptual domain. Additional difficulties often stem from limited time, financial resources, and access to subjects. The specialized interests of individual investigators and their discipline-based perspectives place additional constraints on those who would attempt to test a broad-based, interdisciplinary theory (see Blalock, 1984). It is nonetheless critical that we consider the elements required for an ideal (or best possible) research project, so that we may readily discern the limitations imposed on a given study and clearly identify the extent to which the research findings compare to the overall structure and its constituent elements of cross-cultural adaptation. Ultimately, such a larger perspective makes it possible for independent investigators to compare their own work with that of others and to integrate one another's research findings in a cohesive manner within a common conceptual framework.

Striving for Longitudinal Research

As we strive to increase the conceptual domains of individual studies, we also need to move toward conducting longitudinal research whenever possible (Krull & Paulson, 1977; Menard, 1991; Ostrom, 1978). Such research requires sets of observations of some variables of cross-cultural adaptation for the same unit of analysis over a series of time points (days, months, years). For example, data may be obtained on the evolutionary process of change in individual strangers over time through repeated measures of key variables such as host communication competence and relational network compositions. Critical to the task of tracing this process is either a "panel" sample consisting of the same individuals repeatedly investigated or "cohort" samples consisting of different but equivalent individuals (Glenn, 1977). By following either type of sample throughout a given time period (such as the entire duration of a sojourn or the initial several years after immigration), researchers can gather information about changing patterns of one or more aspects of cross-cultural adaptation identified in the present theory. These methods clearly demand the investment of substantial amounts of time, resources, and commitment on the part of both researchers and subjects. Yet it is through such longitudinal studies that we can accurately document the changes in the lives of strangers.[1]

One way to reduce the necessary challenges associated with time-series panel or cohort studies is to limit either the sample size or the number of variables. In doing so, the researcher must maintain control over the excluded dimensions of variables throughout the phases, thereby keeping the overall conceptual scheme intact while making each phase simple enough to manage. For instance, a researcher can limit the number of variables to three adaptive predisposition factors (preparedness, ethnic proximity, and adaptive personality) and three types of host communication competence (cognitive, affective, and behavioral). On the other hand, the researcher may keep a larger number of variables and reduce the sample size. If a given sample cannot be studied repeatedly in more than one phase, the researcher can use cohorts, or samples drawn from equivalent populations across phases.

Yet another alternative to time-series longitudinal studies is the employment of cross-sectional or "synchronic" analysis based on comparison groups (Rosenthal & Rosnow, 1991, pp. 144-146). Given the substantial constraints involved in implementing time-series panel studies, a more feasible design can be developed that uses two or more comparison groups whose members are estimated to be at differing stages of the adaptation process based on their length of residence in the host environment. Indeed, most of the research findings cited throughout this book indicating the overall upward-forward movement of adaptive change over time come from studies based on such a synchronic cross-sectional design. An example of such cross-sectional analysis is offered by a series of studies that Taft conducted in Australia in the 1950s and 1960s (see Taft, 1986). Taft examined changes in immigrants to Australia in some of the cognitive, affective, and operational components of host communication competence (e.g., cultural learning, language skills, attitudes toward the host environment, and self-concept). He assessed change in these variables through cross-sectional analyses of immigrants with different lengths of time in Australia and across two generations in the same immigrant families. Gebart-Eaglemont (1994) also employed cross-sectional analysis in testing the relationship between stress and adaptation based on cross-sectional data collected from Polish immigrants in Australia. Results showed a significant negative correlation between the two factors, indicating that as the immigrants achieve greater adaptation, they experience less stress.[2]

Toward Methodological Integration

As we broaden the conceptual base for research and thereby increase theory-research correspondence, we also need to broaden the range of research methods derived from different methodological traditions (Fielding & Fielding, 1986; Lincoln & Guba, 1985; Strauss & Corbin, 1990). Given the abstract and general constructs employed in the present theory, the dynamic and evolutionary nature of the cross-cultural adaptation process, and its multidimensional/multifaceted structural model, the present theory lends itself to the utilization of research methods that reflect both *emic* (insider) and *etic* (outsider) methodological perspectives.

Although the objective-quantitative etic approach and the subjective-qualitative emic approach are polar opposites, the approaches complement each other and may be integrated in practice (Becker, 1970; Ellis & Flaherty, 1992b; Hall, 1986; Headland, Pike, & Harris, 1990). Whereas building or testing broad-based theories requires a set of etic measures that transcend subjective perspectives, emic methods allow researchers to capture the complexity of given phenomena through "thick description." As McGrath (1982) notes:

"One must use multiple methods, selected from different classes of methods with different vulnerabilities. . . . knowledge requires convergence of substantive findings derived from a diversity of methods of study" (p. 99). Likewise, Miles and Huberman (1994) observe, "We have to face the fact that numbers and words are both needed if we are to understand the world" (p. 207).[3]

In the study of cross-cultural adaptation, emic descriptions can help to illuminate the details of the ways in which groups of strangers experience an alien milieu.[4] Emic-qualitative methods can be particularly useful for improving our understanding of the previously underinvestigated aspects of cross-cultural adaptation, environmental conditions and identity transformation, and their relationships to personal and social communication patterns articulated in the present theory. Emic methods can further help researchers to operationalize theoretical constructs in ways that maximally reflect the actual experiences of strangers in alien environments and the strangers' own interpretations of their experiences. In assessing host communication competence, for example, a researcher might employ a theory-derived objective-quantitative scale as well as obtain the subjects' self-assessments of their own host communication competence and experiences in communicating with the natives and in using host mass media. The investigator might also obtain the opinions of those natives who regularly interact with the strangers about the strangers' host communication competence. When there is a convergence of assessments between these two sets of data, the investigator can achieve a methodological "triangulation" (Campbell & Fiske, 1959; Crano, 1981)—that is, he or she can attain increased confidence in the research outcomes through the confrontation of two or more different but complementary methods of testing a hypothesis.

One way to integrate the etic-quantitative and emic-qualitative methods is to combine a large-sample quantitative survey study with a series of in-depth, qualitative case studies of one or more individual cases selected from the original sample (see Dyal & Dyal, 1981, p. 320; Stake, 1995). As Taft (1986) notes, carefully selected case studies add qualitative insights to the patterns observed in statistical analyses. In other words, qualitative insights gained from case studies help identify, define, and operationalize quantitative variables that can subsequently be analyzed statistically. A researcher may begin with small-scale in-depth interviews and then proceed to a large-scale quantitative assessment, or may reverse the sequence. The case study represents an unparalleled means for communicating contextual information that is grounded in the particular setting studied (Crawford, 1996; Jones, 1979).

Cross-cultural adaptation research that has employed the case study method includes Ainslie's (1994) study of the acculturative psychodynamics of a single Mexican American family, Wade and Souter's (1992) study of British Asian girls' adaptation and identity experience, and McEvoy-Jamil's (1996) study of one international student's coping strategies and acculturation. The primary research tool utilized in such case studies is *ethnographic interviewing* (Marshall & Rossman, 1989, pp. 93-94), or *qualitative interviewing* (Rubin & Rubin, 1995). In this method, the researcher employs open-ended questions to encourage subjects to expand on their responses in one-on-one interviews. Interviews can also be conducted in *focus groups,* an efficient format when it appears that respondents will be more forthcoming if they have the stimulus or the safety of a group of fellow respondents (Krueger, 1988; Morgan, 1988; Stewart & Shamdasani, 1990).

Research objectives may also call for other less commonly used emic methods, including analysis of documents, personal memoirs, stories, literature records, and public and private records (McCracken, 1988, p. 28; Runyan, 1982). The method of "interpretive biography"—the "studied use and collection of the documents, or documents of life . . . which describe turning point moments in individuals' lives" (Denzin, 1989, p. 7)—may also be used. According to Denzin (1989), the biographical method "rests on subjective and intersubjectively gained knowledge and understanding of the life experiences of individuals, including one's own life" (pp. 27-28). Denzin particularly emphasizes the identification of "epiphanies," or "moments of revelation in a person's life" (p. 33), in which individual character is revealed as a crisis or other significant event is confronted and experienced. Through epiphanies, experiences are given expression in a variety of ways, including rituals, diaries, routines, myths, novels, films, dramas, songs, and biographies. Biographical sources are the basis of Abramson's (1992) case study of a diary written over a 12-year period by a Russian Jewish immigrant. In analyzing this diary, Abramson argues that such a case study may lead to insights into the actual experiences of a person while effectively portraying the social and historical world in which the person has lived. Also, Stewart and Healy (1984; Healy & Stewart, 1984) illustrate how autobiographical accounts of the periods after major life changes may yield knowledge into individual differences as well as common themes, based on the autobiographies of Leonard Woolf, Malcolm X, Vera Brittain, and Bernard Baruch. Such life histories reveal the sequence of emotional adjustment and qualitative transformation that follows such life changes.

Among other naturalistic sources for emic analysis of cross-cultural adaptation are unsolicited personal anecdotes, essays of reflection, and testimonials that are available in the print and electronic media (books, magazines, newspapers, reports, videotapes, television programs, radio programs, computer and Internet sources). Even though sources such as these do not allow for systematic gathering of data, they can supplement conventional interviews and observations by providing anecdotal evidence for the ways in which some of the theoretical ideas play out in specific situations (Strauss & Corbin, 1990, p. 51).

Exploring Creative Hybrid Methods

It is complicated and time-consuming for researchers to carry out in-depth case studies in conjunction with large-scale surveys. Thus we need to find creative ways of blending qualitative and quantitative assessment methods into a single method. To this end, a number of "hybrid" or "mixed" assessment methods have been developed (Fielding & Fielding, 1986, p. 25) whereby initial qualitative data are utilized to generate quantitative data (Strauss & Corbin, 1990, p. 18). As Yin (1994) notes, a hybrid method using case studies can systematize assessments, maximizing reliability and validity, which are often difficult to establish in naturalistic, qualitative case studies. In the development of theory, case studies can supplement conventional surveys. Data thus obtained can be analyzed using "ethnostatistics" (Gephart, 1988), which helps to bridge the gap between qualitative and quantitative research by examining the qualitative aspects of doing statistical analyses.

These research techniques are often found in *standardized interview methods* (Weller & Romney, 1988) or *focused semistructured interviews* (Moos, 1974). Employing rank-order data for statistical analysis, these techniques complement the traditional ethnographic practice of using open-ended questions. Fowler and Mangione (1990) elaborate on the various practices of standardized interviewing, including standardization of question wording, the positions of questions in an interview schedule, the ethnicity of the interviewer, the interviewer's reading of the questions exactly as worded, standardization of nondirective probes for clarification and elaboration, verbatim recording and transcribing, and the interviewer's neutral stance with respect to the substance of answers. Such systematized techniques help to increase efficiency and reliability and to decrease interviewer bias, and they enable the investigator to code the data in a manner that allows statistical analysis (Moos, 1974). A similar hybrid method called the *long interview* has been proposed by McCracken (1988), who describes it as a sharply focused and streamlined interview process that seeks to diminish the indeterminacy and redundancy that attend unstructured research processes.

Other hybrid methods include techniques such as *ethnographic content analysis* (Altheide, 1987) and the *reflexive analysis of documents* (Plummer, 1983). Such techniques are less than widely recognized as distinct methods, although their various facets have been utilized in document analyses by historians, literary scholars, and social scientists. Relying on the reflexive nature of the investigator as well as drawing on numerical and narrative data, the hybrid methods are oriented toward the checking, supplementing, and supplanting of theoretical claims through the simultaneous gathering of categorical and unique data for every case studied. The investigator can count items and topics and put them into emergent categories while also gaining good descriptive information from them. Another hybrid research method is the *Q-technique* (or Q-sort technique), which is used in interviews and allows factor analysis (McKeown & Thomas, 1988; Stephenson, 1953). The Q-technique allows subjects to construct their own reality through indirect construction of the research content. As McKeown and Thomas (1988) describe it, this self-reference technique allows the person's internal frame of reference (emic) to be employed in quantitative measurements.

The benefit of integrating objective and subjective aspects of an object of inquiry is exemplified by Kemnitzer's (1973) study of Dakota Indians in the San Francisco Bay Area. Kemnitzer found the following method to be effective for assessing subjects' value hierarchies. First, the researcher hands the subject a deck of cards representing 36 different situations and asks the subject to rank the cards in order of preference "if the world were just the way you wanted it." Then the researcher gives the subject a new deck of cards and asks the subject to rank the situations they represent according to "the most important things to get along in the city." The results are an ideal value hierarchy and a hierarchy of values perceived as necessary to live. Discrepancies between the two hierarchies, then, are interpreted as the sources of value conflict or "dissonance" experienced by the subject.

Whichever integrative method a researcher uses, some form of compromise will result. The methods discussed above are some of the promising forms of compromise between the relatively real but less rigorous feature of qualitative approaches and the efficient and rigorous but less in-depth feature of quantitative approaches. Hybrid methods such as the ones examined above can be fruitfully applied to the study of cross-cultural adaptation. Examples include recent studies of Native Americans' adaptation to the mainstream culture (Kim et al., 1998a) and studies of American and Japanese coworkers in Japanese subsidiaries in Oklahoma (Kim & Paulk, 1994a, 1994b). These studies employed a series of loosely structured one-on-one interviews or focus group interviews to explore the subjects' experiences and insights into the changes that have taken place in their own intercultural understanding. Standardized questions can be used to solicit metaphors for subjects' views on life in the host environment; for example, a subject may be asked to complete the sentence "If I say to you, 'Life in this country is like _____,' how would you fill in the blank?" Questions such as this allow, in effect, quantification of qualitative data for systematic analysis. This type of hybrid method can help to situate quantitative information on strangers' adaptation experiences in a fuller historical, social, and cultural context, as called for by the present theory.

So far in this chapter, I have made a case for a number of research considerations that are consistent with the theoretical formulation. First, some of the previously underinvestigated theoretical constructs, such as the conditions of the host environment, need to be taken more seriously in future studies. Second, the conceptual base of a research design needs to include more than a single dimension of factors linking individual-level and group-level factors. Third, longitudinal analyses need to be undertaken so that researchers can assess the dynamic and evolving nature of the cross-cultural adaptation process over time. Fourth, researchers need to strive to employ multiple and hybrid research methods combining etic-quantitative and emic-qualitative research approaches. These methodological considerations are aimed at investigating the complex and dynamic cross-cultural adaptation phenomenon with maximum theory-research correspondence as well as maximum reliability and validity. The integrative methodological approach offers a way to overcome each method's weaknesses and limitations by deliberately combining different types of methods within an investigation. The methods used in multimethod studies are, for the most part, the standard practices employed in contemporary social research. In this regard, there is little new in the multimethod approach. What is new, however, is the planned and systematic synthesis of these different research styles, purposefully aimed at improving the correspondence to the dynamic and transformative process of cross-cultural adaptation as articulated in the present theory.

The achievement of true methodological integration is easier said than done, of course. Yet, as Ellis and Flaherty (1992a) note, such integration offers us a way to clarify "the ways in which our knowledge is grounded in our practical, personal, and participatory experience in the field as much as our detached [theoretical] observations" (p. 6).

Practical Insights

When the skies grow dark, the stars begin to shine.

Charles Austin Beard

In the midst of winter, I found there was within me, an invincible summer.

Albert Camus, *Summer*, 1954

In the end, the viability of any theory about cross-cultural adaptation rests on the very reality to which it is directed, that is, the unfolding of experiences and accompanying changes in the individuals who, at this very moment and in all corners of the world, are striving to forge new lives away from familiar ground. There is no denying that cross-cultural adaptation does occur in these individuals as they struggle with the continual challenges of new learning. The theory presented in this volume affirms this reality. It recognizes that most people possess the drive and capacity to accommodate to change in favor of survival and continued evolution even when they resist it. The Amish in North America are a case in point. Although traditional Amish communities have remained largely sealed from the influence of the larger cultural milieu, many Amish have moved from farming into cottage industries involving crafts, cabinetmaking, construction, steel fabrication, and carpentry (Brooke, 1996; Janofsky, 1997; Kraybill, 1995).

Once strangers understand the unavoidable and undeniable reality of cross-cultural adaptation, the only real choice left for them concerns the *degree* of change they hope to accomplish during their sojourn or resettlement. By refusing to change, they can minimize the change. By accelerating their adaptive efforts, they can facilitate their own inter-cultural transformation. While recognizing the important role of the host environment, they need to place the primary locus of responsibility within themselves, as they are the ones who shoulder the bulk of the "burdens" and "rewards" of adaptive change. It would be neither reasonable nor practical to expect any large population to modify its cultural habits significantly and with the sense of urgency required of newcomers. The main source of power for change has to reside in individual strangers. In the end, they stand with their own psychological and social welfare. Even during the colonial days when cultural practices of the occupying outsiders were forced on indigenous peoples' folkways, the colonists had to make at least some adjustments in themselves in order to under-stand and deal with the local people effectively.

The question, then, is no longer whether cross-cultural adaptation occurs; rather, at issue is how individuals can help themselves to accomplish their own adaptive ends. In this final chapter, we will put ourselves in the position of strangers in an unfamiliar environment and deliberate on the question of self-facilitation of adaptation. We will do so by examining some of the more transparent practical insights ema-nating from the theory developed in the preceding chapters. It is at this pragmatic juncture that the theory moves beyond a logical realm of interconnected propositions and begins to serve the reality it purports to help us understand.

Understanding Adaptation Potential

To an extent, successful adaptation hinges on conditions established even prior to our embarking on a cross-cultural move. We must care-fully and realistically evaluate whether to relocate and the goal of the relocation based on an equally careful understanding of the adaptation potential in our predispositions. How similar or compatible is my eth-nicity (culture, language, race, and national origin) to the dominant ethnicity of the host environment? How does it fare in the minds of the natives? Is my country of origin (or ethnic group) in a friendly or adversarial relationship with the host country? How thoroughly am I motivated and prepared for the move psychologically? How well equipped am I with knowledge and understanding of the host culture and communication system, particularly its language? How strongly am I committed to learning about them? How willing and capable am I to undertake necessary and appropriate changes in my old cultural habits? Am I flexible enough to assimilate new learning? How resilient am I? Am I sufficiently tolerant of uncertainty? Do I have a positive and respectful attitude toward the host society and its people?

We must take the answers to these and related questions into account in estimating the enormity of challenges we are likely to face once we move to the host culture, particularly if we are going to stay in the host environment over an extended period. These predispositional factors can help us select a host country or the community to which we migrate, or at least help us to decide whether we should be taking the risk of a potentially strenuous start in the prospective new environment. We must realize that our background characteristics constitute much of who we are and what we are, and cannot easily be changed. What is important is that we become aware of the potential positive or negative implications that our background characteristics have for the adaptation process and that we make a rational decision as to whether we are able and willing to take on the challenges that lie ahead.

As we make an honest self-appraisal on these and related issues, we can estimate our likelihood of successful adaptation. We can find ways to better prepare ourselves to embark on a smoother transition to the new environment. We may, for instance, study the culture at a distance and familiarize ourselves with the host environment and its communication systems (particularly language). Organizations take into consideration some of the predispositional factors identified here in screening personnel for basic qualifications and fitness in prospective host environments. An increasing number of companies and international organizations offer orientation and training programs to employees who are to be sent overseas. Some offer short briefings on historical and cultural differences, whereas others, most notably the Peace Corps, offer more extensive training programs on wider ranges of topics, from language and culture to communication practices (see Bhawuk, 1990; Landis & Bhagat, 1996).

Host Environment as Partner

Along with making an honest self-appraisal of our individual adaptation potential, we need to recognize the vital role that host environment plays in the adaptive journey. If we are to adapt well, we need to choose an affirmative attitude that lends itself to working with the host environment, not against it. This means that we strive to minimize the us-versus-them psychological orientation—a fundamental aspect of intercultural training, as Cargile and Giles (1996) point out. From neighbors to public institutions, the host environment is an integral part of our new lives. As long as we remain in it, every facet of our lives is affected by and dependent on it, directly or indirectly. Coming to grips with this reality enables us to view the adaptation process as a joint, collaborative partnership—one in which our personal well-being is also in the interest of the overall cohesiveness of the host sociocultural system. This understanding of person-environment interdependence engenders a spirit of cooperation and self-responsibility, as it helps us not to blame the host environment for all our cross-cultural predicaments. Doing so would ultimately be counterproductive to our own adaptive self-interest. We can also better appreciate the fact that all societies and communities assert their sociocultural integrity and justifiably exert some degree of conformity pressure on strangers, subtly or explicitly.

This is not to suggest that we "go native" or blindly accommodate the local cultural norms and practices. Rather, it is to recognize the fact that, for the most part, local cultural norms and practices, even those that are incompatible with our core values, are upheld by local people for a reason. We, as strangers, need to respect the basic integrity of the local culture—just as we would expect strangers coming to our own community to do the same. The acceptance of ethnic difference is the hallmark of a free individual, just as it is of a free society. It is also bound up with an understanding of natural human prejudices that exist in all peoples. Such an affirmative outlook on the receiving group serves as a foundation on which to build a new life, if only temporarily. Even when such an attitude is not reciprocated by the natives and our sojourn is only for a short duration, we can certainly try to build reasonably harmonious relationships with the natives while there. Such an effort begins with our affirmation of the existing community we have entered and helps to avoid self-indulgence in unfair and biased criticisms. Indeed, affirmative attitude is a basic prerequisite of active and cooperative engagement.

We can help our own adaptation by seeking out those elements within the host environment that are most receptive toward us. Recognizing that not all layers and facets of the environment are equally receptive toward us, we may look for and reach out to those places, groups, and individuals that are particularly open and accessible. We may find concrete forms and expressions of host receptivity, for example, at local colleges, schools, businesses, civic organizations, churches, and other public and private entities. There may be ongoing programs such as "host families" and "buddy systems" that provide strangers and natives opportunities to interact and engage in interpersonal relationships. Some towns and cities may have voluntary organizations dedicated to serving newcomers' resettlement needs. There may be language and cultural programs available for new arrivals. We may initiate conversations with those neighbors or coworkers who are willing to offer us opportunities to participate in the local social processes.

As new arrivals, we may also benefit from seeking support from fellow coethnics or other ethnics who share some of our cross-cultural predicaments. On college campuses, for example, we may be able to find technical, informational, and emotional support in international student organizations. There may be formal or informal ethnic community organizations such as church programs and social clubs available to assist us. Sometimes, the host community may offer physical and mental health services for new arrivals through ethnic support systems. We can benefit from utilizing such programs when available, as long as we do not lose sight of the importance of direct communicative interactions with the host environment itself.

Willingness to Be Changed

As we regard the host environment as a partner and engage ourselves in that environment, we need to be prepared to accept the likelihood that a part of who we are and what we are may be changed by our new experiences, at least temporarily. This willingness to be changed is vital if we are to attain a degree of functional fitness in the new sociocultural system. Some change in our original cultural habits is necessary for almost all strangers as long as our success in life activities in the host environment depends on our capacity to understand, and practice in accordance with, the local cultural system. Temporary sojourners, such as diplomats, international students, and employees of multinational corporations, are also dependent for successful sojourns on their capacity to understand relevant local standards and practices.

Our willingness to be changed by the cross-cultural experience should increase when we clearly understand that most, if not all, of us are capable of absorbing and integrating at least some of the new and even incompatible elements into our existing psychic systems without being destroyed by them. We need to recognize, further, that we, not the local people, are the ones who are expected to make adaptive self-corrections. This simple understanding echoes the time-honored folk wisdom, "When in Rome, do as the Romans do." Most of us certainly understand and accept this commonsense principle as part and parcel of living in an alien milieu. This understanding of the adaptive capacity within ourselves brings hope and strength even in the midst of severe culture-shock experiences. Such has certainly been the experience of many Peace Corps volunteers, missionaries, and exchange students, not to mention the numerous immigrants and refugees who have ventured through new experiential territories they seldom thought possible or even desirable. In a 1995 national poll of immigrants in the United States, 6 out of 10 of those surveyed agreed with the statement, "It's better for immigrants to blend into American culture, even if that means giving up some aspects of their own background" (Puente, 1995, p. 5A).

In accepting change, we may also recognize the fact that our basic cultural programming endures even as it is changed by new experiences. Our willingness to undergo personal transformation is in no way an expression of denial of our original cultural identity. It is simply a recognition that we need to be open to new experiences that may transform us. The principle of the simultaneous interplay of new learning (acculturation) and loss of old habits (deculturation) makes it plain that as strangers we cannot realistically choose between keeping our original identity intact and adapting to the new environment successfully. Once we understand this principle, we can see that it would be illogical to say that there is an "either/or" choice between the two ways of life—a choice between clinging to our original cultural habits in fruitless panic and having our eyes opened to the new world. Being unwilling to commit to new learning while insisting on maintaining the old ways inevitably impedes our successful engagement and functioning in the new environment. As Anderson Cooper, a foreign correspondent for ABC Television News, has insightfully pointed out: "I think it's important to allow things to change you either positively or negatively. . . . if you're not willing to be changed by a place, there's no point going" (quoted in Mifflin, 1996, p. H32).

Embracing the idea that new experiences will change us somewhat becomes easier if we can foresee that at the end of our wanderings in crossing cultural boundaries await our larger, reconstituted selves. This insight serves as a guiding vision that can help us to face some of our short-term stresses with optimism and resolve. It is in this sense that the ongoing ideological debate between assimilationists and pluralists loses its logical as well as its pragmatic relevance. Of course, in a free society, each of us should be entitled to an ideological choice concerning his or her own relationship to the host environment. At the same time, however, we need to recognize that such ideologies are accompanied by "blind spots" that inhibit our ability to see clearly the inherent duality of acculturation and deculturation that always inhabits the process of cross-cultural adaptation. Whereas the aim and the substance of either ideology serves a political purpose, in defining the way things *ought to be* in interethnic relations, neither ideology accurately shows the way things really *are* in cross-cultural situations. Both ideologies fail to affirm the consistent research evidence that both convergent (assimilative) and divergent (pluralist) tendencies play out simultaneously whenever differing cultural (or subcultural) systems interface for prolonged periods. Individuals with rigid ideological beliefs fail to see that adaptive changes are an inevitable part of the dialectics of give-and-take, or "push and pull."

As strangers wanting to be successful in our journey of cross-cultural adaptation, then, we need to put aside the ideology-laden question of whether adaptive changes are good or bad. Instead, we need to accept a seeming paradox—that we may lose some of what can be lost but that, in losing, we gain self-renewal. Our focus needs to be placed on the vital issues of pragmatism and functionality—that is, concerns about how the changes taking place in ourselves serve our own adaptive ends and the integrity of the host sociocultural system. As we come to grips with the duality of the adaptation process, we can make a conscious decision to be changed by the acculturative forces of the host milieu, so as to maximize our functional fitness and psychological health in relation to that milieu.

Managing Stress

No matter how willing and prepared we are to be changed by our new cultural experiences, the cross-cultural journey is seldom smooth. Life in an unfamiliar milieu entails some of the most stressful experiences we may ever face. Acute stress necessarily occurs as long as we are engaged in the life of the new cultural milieu. Our experiences of adaptive stress will tend to be particularly acute during the initial phase, when rapid learning is taking place. We are bound to encounter many moments of self-doubt and self-inquiry—a kind of existential despair that grows out of the restless inner spirit that seeks the known and the constant when familiar relationships and routines are broken.

Interestingly, a basic means we have for managing adaptive stress and countering its potential ill effects is to accept stress and stop fighting it. As Moustakas (1977) observes, we need to see "that there is no escape from the pain," yield our minds to it, absorb it, and become conscious of it without resisting it (p. 98). For most of us, of course, our natural instinct is to avoid stress by separating ourselves from what we see as its source, the host environment itself. However, each time we withdraw, we pass up opportunities for new cultural learning and instead engage in fearful clinging to the past. It is like what happens when we try to learn to swim for the first time: "If you try to stay on the surface of the water, you sink; but when you try to sink you float. When you hold your breath, you lose it" (Watts, 1951, p. 9).

Our facing adaptive stress further means that we recognize that stress is not only part and parcel of our adaptation experiences but, more important, a necessary condition for our adaptation. It helps to know that in the most frustrating moments new awareness arises, and that the darker the frustration, the deeper and more acute the awakening of the mind and its sensibilities for new formulation of self. As Atwater (1983) puts it: "Growth involves stepping into unfamiliar and potentially dangerous situations that often leave us more vulnerable to hurt and disappointment. Each step forward may result in a step backward. . . . The willingness to take risks is a key to personal growth" (p. 14). Stress is, indeed, an integral part of the internal dynamics that help us mobilize for our adaptation and growth. To experience growth we must go through stressful experiences, not avoid them. The challenged life leads to a maturity that enables us to reconcile contradictions and achieve a synthesis of the old and the new.

Facing up to adaptive stress also means that we need to recognize that our individual capacity to absorb stress and instability is not limitless. We need to appreciate the fact that some of us, owing to innate temperament or circumstance, may be extremely susceptible to ill effects from trauma. We must understand the differing limits of personal capacity to endure stress so as to find ways not to be seriously damaged by it. We can increase our ability to manage adaptive stress by developing a habit of relaxation. In Watts's (1951) words:

> One who falls from a height with stiff limbs will break them, but if he relaxes like a cat he will fall safely. A building without "give" in its structure will easily collapse in storm or earthquake, and a car without the cushioning of tires and springs will soon come apart on the

road. The mind has just the same powers, for it has *give* and can *absorb* shocks like water or a cushion. (p. 96)

Relaxation tends to bring about a state of self-reflection—or what Moustakas (1977, p. 96) calls a "silence" for self-discovery. Self-reflection as a quiet, fully engaged state of mind involves a form of self-dialogue, self-learning, and self-integration. Particularly in times of crisis, self-reflection helps us to understand how we are doing, how we are feeling, and in what direction we need to move. New perspectives arise, new feelings that awaken us to new insights into ourselves and our milieu.

Focusing on Communicative Engagement

Successful management of adaptive stress, in turn, enables us to confront problematic encounters in the host environment. Whenever opportunities for communication with the natives present themselves, we need to try to participate. Better yet, we need to seek out such opportunities and not just wait for them to occur. It is true that, more often than not, ethnic support systems are among the more common, more accessible sources of help for releasing our adaptive stress (Walton, 1990). Many of us prefer to settle at least initially near where we have access to coethnics. New international students often choose universities where they know some of their fellow countrymen and -women are enrolled; immigrants often settle near where relatives and other coethnics live.

In time, however, we facilitate our own successful adaptation by going beyond our ethnic community and reaching out for opportunities to participate in the interpersonal and mass communication processes of the host milieu. We cannot truly learn to communicate without communicating, just as we cannot learn to swim without actually plunging into the water. As host communication competence serves as the internal resource that fosters cross-cultural adaptation, participation via interpersonal and mass communication channels serves as the "social capital" that provides information, resources, and emotional support. Through active social engagements, we learn how to communicate better. As Jantsch (1980) notes, "True learning is never rote learning, but always stimulated experience by oneself" (p. 205). Arrangements such as enrolling in an academic program of a local university would provide intensive interpersonal contact situations that would offer challenging environments in which we could cultivate our host communication competence. By actively engaging ourselves in the host social processes, we are, in fact, facilitating the development of our host communication competence.

Host communication competence, indeed, is a sine qua non of successful adaptation. It is the very force that "brings the soloists to sing in the choir" (Grotevant, 1993, p. 121), serving as the fundamental nexus of human groups on all levels. The entire dynamic of our cross-cultural adaptation hinges on our ability to communicate with the host milieu. Specifically, becoming competent in the host communication system entails learning all facets of that communication system, including formal and informal usages of the host language and nonverbal patterns (knowledge of the host communication system). We need to cultivate a more refined perception and understanding of the host communication system (cognitive complexity) and be motivated to participate in the host social processes (adaptive motivation). We need to hold an attitude that affirms the existing host sociocultural system (affirmative attitude) and appreciate the local affective sensibilities (aesthetic/emotional appreciation). We need to cultivate an operational competence that allows us to be in tune with the local communicative styles (synchrony) and find creative ways to manage situations in which cultural differences play out (resourcefulness).

Of these various facets of host communication competence, the ability to understand and use the host language is of central importance, particularly for long-term resettlers such as immigrants. Language competence serves us as the primary instrument in promoting our social power and credibility, whereas its lack becomes a salient deprivation. Acquiring language competence allows us access to many of the benefits that native speakers enjoy. Exceptions to this observation can be made, of course; for example, a minority population in a given society may gain enough social and political power to claim special language rights, ranging from local tolerance for limited purposes to universal and equal status for all purposes under the jurisdiction of the state. Afrikaans in South Africa, Flemish in Belgium, French in Canada, and, more recently, Basque and Catalan in Spain are examples of minority languages that have gained official status within bilingual states (Mackey, 1979). Except for these special circumstances of multilingual nations, our mastery of the host language is critical to our becoming fully functional and gaining opportunities for full participation in the mainstream social processes.

Cultivating Adaptive Personality

The challenge of developing our host communication competence and participating in the host social communication processes is profoundly affected by our own individual personality dispositions. Some of us are more open, stronger, and positive than others in basic psychological tendencies. Even though our personality differences are difficult to change once we reach adulthood, all of us can strive to raise our levels of openness, strength, and positivity if we can find in ourselves sufficient will and determination for cross-cultural adaptation.

Openness allows us to be more receptive to new learning. Like a clear window, it helps us to face reality with clarity and accuracy and without prejudice, enabling us to be fully engaged in and sensitive to the new information the host environment reveals. It is as though openness in our personality works as an inner posture of being ready to cease fighting for or against change and being willing to let go of some of our existing presumptions. In Moustakas's (1977) words, openness is "an attitude, a receptiveness, a willingness to go wide open, to see what there is, to hear all that is available, to feel and know what is in me and before me" (p. 96). Thus cultivating openness in our personality is not merely an intellectual exercise. It requires a formation in our basic and stable psychological orientation that is less self-centered and judgmental and more altruistic and accepting of those who are alien to us. But it is essential that we try to cultivate within ourselves a sufficient level of openness, so that we can accept, appreciate, and participate meaningfully in the subtleties of local mind-sets and their emotional and aesthetic idiosyncrasies, which often elude casual observers.

Openness works side by side with *strength*—the personality resource that enables us to absorb life's stresses and strife. Strength represents the quality of resilience rather than volatility, commitment rather than wishful illusion, and confidence rather than false pride. The workings of personality strength resemble the situation in which we sink when we try to stay on the surface of the water, but float when we let our bodies go. Instead of resisting, a strong personality enables us to "ride with" what comes our way, with a spirit of exploration. Temporarily, at least, we can suspend our preconceived notions about the way things ought to be and experience the place as it reveals itself. If and when benevolent circumstances are restored, inner strength leads to a kind of self-trust that allows us to understand that making adaptive changes is not at all the same as denying our past experiences.

The openness and strength of personality fosters, and is fostered by, yet another psychological orientation, *positivity*. A positive outlook on life and in our basic self-other orientation encourages realistic optimism and discourages false illusions, destructive anger, and bitter cynicism, which, in the end, are self-belittling and self-destructive. Negativity often reflects inner weakness and our struggle to free ourselves from stress. Not only will an affirmative orientation enhance the supportive climate, providing us strangers with a needed environmental "pull," it will affect those who come into contact with us. By being positive, we can help the natives develop their own communication competence, only this time, interculturally. Through such opportunities, they are able to increase their knowledge and understanding of some of our own cultural communication practices. Experiences of dealing with differences potentially challenge their cultural habits and facilitate their ability to communicate interculturally—just as we strangers become increasingly competent in communicating with the natives.

Forging a Path of Intercultural Personhood

As we strive to become more open, strong, and positive in our basic disposition, and as we undergo the stressful experiences of cross-cultural adaptation, we grow and mature as humans. In this unique developmental process, we experience a gradual psychic transformation—a subtle and often unconscious change that leads to an increasingly intercultural personhood. Of particular importance in this growth process is the development of a perceptual and emotional maturity and a deepened understanding of human differences. Despite, and because of, the many unpredictable vicissitudes of the new milieu, we are challenged to integrate new experiences into a new form of life. The key is understanding that human growth involves stepping into unfamiliar and even potentially dangerous situations and that, even though taking such steps may result in some backward steps of "regression," refusing to accept that risk is detrimental to successful adaptation to changed circumstances.

Growth beyond the original cultural perimeters means forging an identity and selfhood that is at once individualized and universalized. We achieve psychological health not by rigidly adhering to our original identity but by forging a new, alternative identity that is broader, more inclusive, more intercultural. It may be comforting to know that in this process of intercultural development, our old identity is never completely replaced by a new one. Instead, our identity is transformed into something that will always contain the old and the new side by side to form "a third kind"—a kind that allows more openness and acceptance of differences in people. With these developments comes a creative self with an individualized definition of self and others and a universalized perspective that reaches beyond the conventional categories of "us" and "them."

Modern history presents many examples of successful immigrants and sojourners who have demonstrated extraordinary openness and resilience. From them, we learn that experiences of going through adaptive challenges bring about a special privilege and freedom—to think, feel, and act beyond the boundaries of any single culture and beyond "either/or" categorization. Revealed in this perspective is an understanding of "both/and" and an increased capacity to participate in the depths of the aesthetic and emotional experience of others. Salman Rushdie (1994) has written about this transcendence of categories in the voice of his narrator: "I, too, have ropes around my neck, I have them to this day, pulling me this way and that, East and West, the nooses tightening, commanding, *choose, choose*. . . . Ropes, I do not choose between you. . . . I choose neither of you, and both. Do you hear? I refuse to choose" (p. 211).

Most of us in most circumstances—to the extent that we are willing—are capable of finding ways to face and overcome intercultural challenges, of exploring a trajectory of intercultural growth. The experiences of others have shown us that we need not be locked in a single identity, and that we can incorporate into our psyches new cultural elements without "throwing away" or "being disloyal to" our original cultural groups. In becoming intercultural, we develop a more progressive orientation toward life, with new roles for our individual selves in this increasingly integrated world. Rigid and exclusive adherence to any single identity, even that of childhood, reflects a posture that clings to a past-oriented self and forgoes an openness to meeting a new reality with confidence and optimism. In the words of Russian exile Nedim Gursel, crossing cultures is "an enriching experience, one which can lead to greater openness. People come to know other countries, other cultures. And in this process humanity is enriched" (in Brodsky, 1990, p. 111). It is in this light that international exchange programs for college students offer opportunities for personal development (Gmelch, 1997; Kauffmann, Martin, & Weaver, 1992). Likewise, the true meaning of the Peace Corps's familiar slogan, "The toughest job you'll ever love," is revealed in this intangible yet undeniable transformative cross-cultural adaptation process.

In coping with the unfamiliar domains of life, we affirm and reaffirm the human capacity to adapt and forge a new selfhood. Our true strength is no longer found in our rigid insistence on who we were in the past and who we are at the moment, but in our affirmation of our "uncommitted potentiality for change" (Bateson, 1951/1972, p. 49) and in our embracing what we may yet become. In moments of inner calm, our victorious personality springs forward, accompanying altered perceptions and flashes of insight. These transformative experiences of immigrants and sojourners foster our capacity to meet one of the significant challenges of our time, that is, the need to develop what Toffler (1980) calls a "personality of transcendence":

> [The individual] must reach out in totally new ways to anchor himself, for all the old groups—religion, nation, community, family or profession—are now shaking under the hurricane impact of the accelerative thrust of change. . . . Each time we make a life-style choice, a super decision, each time we link up with some particular subcultural group or groups, we make some change in our self image. . . . what is there of self or personality in the sense of a continuous, durable internal structure? For some the answer is very little . . . a new serial personality that takes into account the discontinuities in many lives, as well as the continuity. (pp. 121-123)

The idea of intercultural personhood has profound relevance for our time of great uncertainty. People the world over are being challenged to adapt to an unprecedented acceleration of technological, social, and cultural change and to discover ways to live more cooperatively together. The individuals, social organizations, communities, and nations that are unable to adapt to these changing forces will eventually alienate themselves from the world. Cross-cultural adaptation, indeed, has come to be the essential business of our time. As Lifton (1993) proposes in his book *The Protean Self,* we need to draw a line between multiplicity and fragmentation. To those who are nostalgic for the age of certainty, permanence, and the fixed and unitary identity, Lifton's message is that it is better to be fluid, resilient, affirmative, and on the move, and that discontinuity can be a mirror of reality and the standard for a reasonable life. We can refuse to admit this, but only at the cost of the immense and futile effort of spending our whole lives resisting the inevitable. Once we understand this, we can see how misguided it is to say that there is a choice or an alternative between the two ways of life—between resisting the stream in fruitless panic and having our eyes opened to a new world.

The concept of intercultural personhood further holds significance in light of rising nationalism and ethnic clashes around the world. The boundaries of cultural or ethnic identity have too often become international as well as domestic battle lines drawn over economic, political, and social issues. The present conception of identity development offers a viable vision of personhood, one that is no less genuine and far more adaptable than the conventional practice of exclusive ethnic loyalty. This point was eloquently made by the president of the Czech Republic, Vaclav Havel, in his remarks on July 4, 1994, on the occasion of his receiving the Philadelphia Liberty Medal:

> It logically follows that, in today's multicultural world, the truly reliable path to coexistence, to peaceful coexistence and creative cooperation, must start from what is at the root of all cultures and what lies infinitely deeper in human hearts and minds than political opinion. It must be rooted in self-transcendence. Transcendence as a hand reached out to those close to us, to foreigners, to the human community, to all living creatures, to nature, to the universe, transcendence as a deeply and joyously experienced need to be in harmony even with what we ourselves are not, what we do not understand, what seems distant from us in time and space, but with which we are nevertheless mysteriously linked because, together with us, all this constitutes a single world. Transcendence as the only real alternative to extinction. (Havel, 1995, p. 113)

Although the process of becoming intercultural is never complete, each step on this path brings a new formation of life. This accomplishment is not one that only extraordinary people can attain. Rather, it is an instance of the normal human mutability manifesting itself in the work of ordinary people stretching themselves out of the old and familiar. The transformative experiences of intercultural persons around the world bear witness to the remarkable human spirit and capacity for self-renewal beyond the constraints of a single culture. Their struggles, as well as their triumphs, hold out wisdom and promise for us as we walk through our own intercultural journeys.

Notes

---

1. Introduction

1. Further discussions of various contexts of cross-cultural adaptation are offered by Berry (1990), Bochner (1982), Furnham (1988), Furnham and Bochner (1986), and Volkan (1993).

2. Existing Approaches to Cross-Cultural Adaptation

1. Bentley (1981) and Shibutani and Kwan (1965) present further examples of sociological studies concerning ethnicity and interethnic relations.

2. Berry (1976, 1980) and De Vos (1990c, 1993) present additional arguments for the integration of environmental and individual factors in cross-cultural adaptation and interethnic relations.

3. For reviews of studies on sojourner effectiveness, see Church (1982), Furnham (1988), Furnham and Bochner (1986), and Torbiorn (1982).

4. For additional writings on culture shock and related psychological problems, see Adler (1975), Barna (1983), Furnham (1988), Furnham and Bochner (1986), and Torbiorn (1982, 1988).

5. Brein and David (1971), Church (1982), and Klineberg and Hull (1979) offer extensive discussions on the U-curve and W-curve processes.

6. In the interest of avoiding confusion and for greater efficiency, I cite my own work throughout this book using only my last name. Citations to other investigators with the same last name include their initials.

7. Similar explanations for the overseas effectiveness of sojourners are offered by Coelho (1958), Furnham (1988), Klineberg and Hull (1979), Selltiz, Christ, Havel, and Cook (1963), and Torbiorn (1982, 1988).

8. Other models for predicting acculturation rates are offered by Nagata (1969), Szalay and Inn (1988), Szapocznik, Scopetta, Kurtines, and Aranalde (1978), and Taft (1988).

9. Additional multivariate models of psychological adaptation have been proposed by Benson (1978), De Vos (1990c), Padilla (1980a), and Szapocznik et al. (1978), among others.

10. For detailed historical accounts of ideologies of intercultural/
interethnic relations, see Bentley (1981), Feagin (1984), and Postiglione (1983).

3. Organizing Principles

1. For additional information on various uses of these terms, see
Amersfoort (1972/1984), Berry and Sam (1997), Dyal and Dyal (1981), and
Shibutani and Kwan (1965).

2. Gudykunst and Kim (1997), Levine (1979/1992), and Rogers (1999)
provide recent overviews of the concept of the stranger.

3. For writings on open systems, see Boulding (1975), Davidson (1983),
Laszlo (1972), Rapoport (1986), Ruben (1972, 1975, 1983), and von Bertalanffy
(1968). Open-systems approaches to human communication and psychology
are presented by Allport (1960), Bateson (1951/1972), Fogel (1993), Ford and
Lerner (1992), Grotevant (1993), Ruesch and Bateson (1951/1968), and
Watzlawick, Beavin, and Jackson (1967).

4. See Strauss and Corbin (1990) for an argument concerning the utilization of information available in nontechnical, nonacademic sources.

4. The Process of Cross-Cultural Adaptation

1. Additional sources on intergroup communication and group identity
include Tajfel and Turner (1986), Turner (1987), and Turner and Giles (1981).

2. For additional research data indicating the assimilative trend, see
Caselli (1973), Connor (1977), Kincaid, Yum, Woelfel, and Barnett (1983),
Namazi (1984), Neidert and Farley (1985), Szalay and Inn (1988), Taft (1966),
and Zenner (1991).

3. Among other fictional and nonfictional first-person accounts and
ethnographic essays are the contributions to volumes edited by Friedlander
(1988), Kennedy (1991b), and Lewis and Jungman (1986), as well as the writings of Gehl (1984), Karl (1984), and Salzman (1986).

4. Additional sources that address the phenomenon of psychic integration and transformation include Allport (1955), Atwater (1983),
Csikszentmihalyi (1993), Cypser and Cypser (1989), Erikson (1969), Grotevant
(1992, 1993), Hettema (1979), Sarter (1988), Slavin and Kriegman (1992), White
(1991), and Zurcher (1977).

5. Other research has further documented the trend of increasing psychological well-being of immigrants and sojourners; see, for example, Deutsch
and Won (1963), Kim (1976, 1977, 1978b, 1980, 1989, 1990), and Wong-Rieger
(1984, 1987).

6. The flexibility/complexity of cultural identity has also been
addressed by Collier and Thomas (1988), Cupach and Imahori (1993), and
Ethier and Deaux (1994).

5. The Structure of Cross-Cultural Adaptation

1. Additional arguments for conceptualizing communication competence in terms of cognitive, affective, and operational components are offered

by Barker, Barker, and Hauser (1988), Hammer (1989), Imahori and Lanigan (1989), and Kim (1991).

6. Personal Communication

1. Additional data indicating a positive association between host language competence and psychological/social adaptation are reported by Chance (1965/1972), Dorais (1987), Graves (1967), Kim (1976, 1977, 1978a, 1978b, 1978c, 1980, 1989, 1990), Price (1968), and Richmond (1967).

2. For further empirical support for the role of motivation in cross-cultural adaptation, see Kantima (1982), Kim (1976, 1977, 1978b, 1980, 1989, 1990), and Maruyama and Kim (1997).

7. Social Communication

1. Discussions on the support functions of relational networks are also presented by Eckenrode and Gore (1981), Gore (1984), Gottlieb (1981), Hirsch (1981), Moos and Mitchell (1982), Pescosolido (1992), Pogrebin (1987), Takai (1991), Terry, Rawle, and Callan (1995), Vaz (1985), and Wellman (1992).

2. Methods of investigating relational networks are elaborated further by Knoke and Kuklinski (1982), Marsden (1993), Mitchell (1994), Monge and Contractor (1988), Rogers and Kincaid (1981), Scott (1991), van der Poel (1993), Weimann (1983, 1989), and Yum (1988).

3. Research findings linking host interpersonal contact/relationship to psychological adaptation are also reported by Hong (1976), Kapoor and Williams (1979), J. Kim, Lee, and Jeong (1982), Oehlkers (1991), Walker (1993), and Yang (1981), among others.

4. Among other researchers who have provided evidence for a positive relationship between indicators of host (out-group) interpersonal involvement and psychological health are Hamers (1994) and Kamali (1987).

5. Additional findings linking host (out-group) interpersonal ties and indicators of functional fitness (such as socioeconomic status/mobility) are reported by Kim (1976, 1977, 1978b, 1978c, 1979a, 1980, 1989, 1990), Kim, Lujan, and Dixon (1998a, 1998b), Oehlkers (1991), Searle and Ward (1990), and Zimmermann (1995).

6. Other studies of Asian immigrants in the United States, including those conducted by J. Kim (1980), Kim (1976, 1977, 1978a, 1978b, 1979a, 1980, 1989, 1990), and Mirowsky and Ross (1983), have also shown the same trend of diminishing involvement in coethnic relationships.

7. For further elaboration on the centrality of relational ties, see Friedkin (1991) and Kim (1986, 1987).

8. The correlation between the use of host mass media and other aspects of cross-cultural adaptation has been further observed by Chaffee and Mutz (1988), Dong and Tan (1996), Kim (1976, 1977, 1978b, 1979b, 1980, 1989, 1990), and Lam (1980).

9. The essentially stereotypical nature of mass-media messages is discussed further by Chaffee and Mutz (1988), Haslett and Alexander (1988), and Lam (1980).

10. Additional research data and anecdotal evidence for immigrants' reliance on ethnic ties for mental health and the problems associated with such reliance are offered by Chan and Lam (1987a), King (1984), Krause (1978), Mullen (1984), Sherman (1988), Silverman (1979), Snyder (1976), Valdéz (1979), and Yum (1983).

11. I employ the term *ethnic media* broadly here to include what Constantakis-Valdés (1992) refers to as "immigrant media." The role of ethnic media in providing new arrivals with information about the host environment is also noted by Hunter (1960), Jaret (1979), Jeffres and Hur (1981), Marzolf (1979), Park (1922), Subervi-Velez (1986), and Zubrzycki (1958).

12. More research evidence for a negative association between the extent of ethnic communication and the development of host language competence is offered by the contributors to Ferguson and Heath's (1981) edited volume as well as by Mercer, Mead, and Mears (1979) and Robinson (1985).

13. Similar patterns of relationships between ethnic/host communication and various other aspects of adaptation have been identified by Chang (1972), Kim (1976, 1977, 1980, 1990, 1991), Kim et al. (1998a, 1998b), Nagata (1969), Pedone (1980), Richmond (1967), Selltiz, Christ, Havel, and Cook (1963), Sewell and Davidsen (1961), Shim (1994), and Yum (1982).

14. The inverse relationship between ethnic involvement and psychological and communication indicators of cross-cultural adaptation is also reported by Anderson and Christie (1978), J. Kim (1980), Kim (1976, 1977, 1978b, 1978c, 1980, 1989, 1990), Kim et al. (1998a, 1998b), Maruyama (1998), Maruyama and Kim (1997), Ryu (1978), Shah (1991), Subervi-Velez (1986), Walker (1993), and Yang (1988).

15. Other researchers who have reported a positive association between ethnic media use and ethnicity and a negative association between ethnic media use and participation in host interpersonal and mass communication activities include J. Kim (1980) and Ryu (1978).

16. Findings on the trend toward increasing self-sufficiency are also reported by Chang (1972), Jeffres and Hur (1981), Kim (1976, 1977, 1980, 1989, 1990), Nagata (1969), Richmond (1967), and Yum (1982).

8. Environment

1. Researchers who have documented derogatory and other discriminatory language behaviors directed toward out-groups include Allen (1983), Gadfields, Giles, Bourhis, and Tajfel (1979), Kirkland, Greenberg, and Pysczynski (1987), McConahay and Hough (1976), and van Dijk (1987).

9. Predisposition

1. The problem of cultural value conflict has been documented extensively by such researchers as Berry and Sam (1997), Church (1982), Dyal and Dyal (1981), Furnham and Bochner (1986), Goza (1987), Kemnitzer (1973), Lauver and Schram (1988), Ryan (1987), Vaz (1985), and Weinberg (1973).

10. Intercultural Transformation

1. Additional personality theorists whose conceptions of identity are dynamic and evolutionary include Allport (1955, 1960), Atwater (1983), Cypser and Cypser (1989), Graafsma, Bosma, Grotevant, and de Levita (1994), Slavin and Kriegman (1992), and Zurcher (1977).

2. Other researchers who have found positive associations between psychological health and various personal, interpersonal, and mass communication factors include Cho (1982), Church (1982), Deutsch and Won (1963), Kim (1976, 1977, 1978b, 1978c, 1979a, 1980, 1989, 1990), Kim, Lujan, and Dixon (1998a, 1998b), Maruyama (1998), and Maruyama and Kim (1997).

3. For additional research findings and theoretical discussions concerning the patterns of coping and successful resolution of value conflicts among immigrants and ethnic minorities, see Boekestijn (1988), Earlum (1980), Hutnik (1986), and Hutnik and Bhola (1994).

4. Such individual stories and testimonials are found in volumes edited by Eddy (1996) and Glad (1990) as well as in the writings of Ainslie (1994), Coffee (1990), Copelman (1993), Davis (1990), Dublin (1993), Hansel (1993), Keene (1994), Miller (1988), Murphy-Shigematsu (1987), O'Halloran (1994), Parks (1992), Rodriguez (1981), and Sheehy (1987), among others.

11. Research Considerations

1. Longitudinal research methods are also discussed by Bailar (1989), Lehnen and Koch (1974), Lepkowski (1989), and Little and Su (1989).

2. On the utilization of cross-sectional analysis to make indirect estimates of the patterns of change in adaptation variables, see also Kim (1976, 1977, 1978b, 1980, 1989, 1990) and Maruyama (1998).

3. Other advocates of multimethod research include Brewer and Hunter (1989), Cahn and Hanford (1984), Fielding and Fielding (1986), Hall (1986), Jones (1979), and Strauss and Corbin (1990).

4. Further arguments in support of the use of verbatim quotations in qualitative studies are made by the contributors to Ellis and Flaherty's (1992b) edited volume as well as by Altheide (1987), McCracken (1988), Miles and Huberman (1994), and Strauss and Corbin (1990).

References

Aames, J., Aames, R., Jung, J., & Karabenick, E. (1977, September 30). *Indochinese refugee self-sufficiency in California.* Report submitted to the California State Department of Health.

Abbink, J. (1984). The changing identity of Ethiopian immigrants (Falashas) in Israel. *Anthropological Quarterly, 57*(4), 139-153.

Abramson, P. (1992). *A case for case studies: An immigrant's journal.* Newbury Park, CA: Sage.

Adams, B. N. (1971). *The American family: A sociological interpretation.* Chicago: Markham.

Adelman, M. (1988). Cross-cultural adjustment: A theoretical perspective on social support. *International Journal of Intercultural Relations, 12,* 183-204.

Adkins-Hutchison, C. (1996). Social support and adjustment among Black psychology graduate students (Doctoral dissertation, Rutgers State University, 1996) [Abstract]. *Connections, 20*(1), 56.

Adler, N. (1981). Reentry: Managing cross-cultural transitions. *Group & Organization Studies, 6,* 341-356.

Adler, P. (1975). The transnational experience: An alternative view of culture shock. *Journal of Humanistic Psychology, 15*(4), 13-23.

Adler, P. (1982). Beyond cultural identity: Reflections on cultural and multicultural man. In L. A. Samovar & R. E. Porter (Eds.), *Intercultural communication: A reader* (3rd ed., pp. 389-408). Belmont, CA: Wadsworth.

Adler, P. (1987). Culture shock and the cross-cultural learning experience. In L. F. Luce & E. C. Smith (Eds.), *Toward internationalism: Readings in cross-cultural communication* (pp. 24-35). Cambridge, MA: Newbury. (Original work published 1972)

Ady, J. (1995). Toward a differential demand model of sojourner adjustment. In R. L. Wiseman (Ed.), *Intercultural communication theory* (pp. 92-114). Thousand Oaks, CA: Sage.

Ainslie, R. (1994). Notes on the psychodynamics of acculturation: A Mexican-American experience. *Mind and Human Interaction, 5*(2), 60-67.

Aitken, T. (1973). *The multinational man: The role of the manager abroad.* New York: John Wiley.

Alba, R. D. (1976). Social assimilation among American Catholic national origin groups. *American Sociological Review, 41,* 1030-1046.

Alba, R. D. (1978). Ethnic networks and tolerant attitudes. *Public Opinion Quarterly, 42,* 1-16.

Alba, R. D. (1990). *Ethnic identity: The transformation of white America.* New Haven, CT: Yale University Press.

Alba, R. D., & Chamlin, M. (1983). A preliminary examination of ethnic identification among whites. *American Sociological Review, 48,* 240-247.

Albrecht, T. L., & Adelman, M. B. (1984). Social support and life stress: New directions for communication research. *Human Communication Research, 11,* 3-32.

Allen, I. L. (1983). *The language of ethnic conflict: Social organization and lexical culture.* New York: Columbia University Press.

Allport, G. W. (1954). *The nature of prejudice.* Reading, MA: Addison-Wesley.

Allport, G. W. (1955). *Becoming: Basic consideration for a psychology of personality.* New Haven, CT: Yale University Press.

Allport, G. W. (1960). The open systems in personality theory. *Journal of Abnormal and Social Psychology, 61,* 301-311.

Altheide, D. L. (1987). Ethnographic content analysis. *Qualitative Sociology, 10,* 65-77.

Altman, I., & Taylor, D. (1973). *Social penetration: The development of interpersonal relationships.* New York: Holt, Rinehart & Winston.

Amerikaner, M. (1978). *Personality integration and the theory of open systems: A cross-subcultural approach.* Unpublished doctoral dissertation, University of Florida, Gainesville.

Amersfoort, H. (1984). *Immigration and the formation of minority groups: The Dutch experience 1945-1975* (R. Lyng, Trans.). New York: Cambridge University Press. (Original work published 1972)

Amir, Y. (1969). Contact hypothesis in ethnic relations. *Psychological Bulletin, 7,* 319-342.

Amir, Y., & Chana, G. (1977). Personal influence on attitude change following ethnic contact. *International Journal of Intercultural Relations, 1,* 58-75.

Anderson, G., & Christie, T. (1978). Ethnic networks: North American perspectives. *Connections, 2*(1), 25-34.

Anderson, L. (1994). A new look at an old construct: Cross-cultural adaptation. *International Journal of Intercultural Relations, 18,* 293-328.

Anderson, R., & Saenz, R. (1994). Structural determinants of Mexican American intermarriage, 1975-1980. *Social Science Quarterly, 75,* 414-430.

Anderson, T. (1993). *Den of lions: Memoirs of seven years.* New York: Crown.

Ansari, A. (1988). *Iranian immigrants in the United States: A case study of dual marginality.* Millwood, NY: Associated Faculty.

Applegate, J. L., & Delia, J. G. (1980). Person-centered speech, psychological development, and the contexts of language usage. In R. St. Clair & H. Giles (Eds.), *The social and psychological contexts of language* (pp. 245-282). Hillsdale, NJ: Lawrence Erlbaum.

Applegate, J. L., & Leichty, G. (1984). Managing interpersonal relationships: Social cognitive and strategic determinants of competence. In R. N. Bostrom (Ed.), *Competence in communication: A multidisciplinary approach* (pp. 33-55). Beverly Hills, CA: Sage.

Applegate, J. L., & Sypher, H. E. (1988). A constructivist theory of communication and culture. In Y. Y. Kim & W. B. Gudykunst (Eds.), *Theories in intercultural communication* (pp. 41-65). Newbury Park, CA: Sage.

Arevalo, L. (1987). Psychological distress and its relationship to acculturation among Mexican-Americans. *Dissertation Abstracts International, 48*(06), 1842B. (University Microfilms No. AAC87-20973)

Argyle, M. (1975). *Bodily communication.* New York: International University Press.

Arnberg, L. (1987). *Raising children bilingually: The pre-school years.* Clevedon, England: Multilingual Matters.

Aronowitz, S. (1991). *The politics of identity: Class, culture, social movements.* New York: Routledge.

Asch, S. E. (1952). *Social psychology.* Englewood Cliffs, NJ: Prentice Hall.

Atkinson, K., & Coupland, N. (1988). Accommodation as ideology. *Language and Communication, 8,* 321-328.

Atwater, E. (1983). *Psychology of adjustment: Personal growth in a changing world* (2nd ed.). Englewood Cliffs, NJ: Prentice Hall.

Austin, C. (1983). *Cross-cultural reentry: An annotated bibliography.* Abilene, TX: Abilene Christian University Press.

Austin, C. (Ed.). (1986). *Cross-cultural reentry: A book of readings.* Abilene, TX: Abilene Christian University Press.

Bailar, B. (1989). Information needs, surveys, and measurement errors. In D. Kasprzyk, G. Duncan, G. Kalton, & M. Singh (Eds.), *Panel surveys* (pp. 1-24). New York: John Wiley.

Bakhtin, M. M. (1990). *Art and answerability* (M. Holquist & V. Liapunov, Eds.; V. Liapunov, Trans.). Austin: University of Texas Press.

Baldassini, J., & Flaherty, V. (1982). Acculturation process of Colombian immigrants into the American culture in Bergen County, New Jersey. *International Journal of Intercultural Relations, 6,* 127-135.

Banks, S. P., Gao G., & Baker, J. (1991). Intercultural encounters and miscommunication. In N. Coupland, H. Giles, & J. M. Wiemann (Eds.),

"Miscommunication" and problematic talk (pp. 103-120). Newbury Park, CA: Sage.

Banton, M. (1961). The restructuring of social relationships. In A. Southall (Ed.), *Social change in modern Africa* (pp. 113-125). London: Oxford University Press.

Barker, D., Barker, L., & Hauser, M. (1988). Origins, evolution, and development of a systems-based model of intra-personal processes: A holistic view of man as information processor. In B. D. Ruben (Ed.), *Information and behavior* (Vol. 2, pp. 197-215). New Brunswick, NJ: Transaction.

Barker, M. (1994, July). *English for all! A second language for all! An analysis of language policy for Australia.* Paper presented at the Fifth International Conference on Language and Social Psychology, Brisbane, Queensland.

Barna, L. (1983). The stress factor in intercultural relations. In D. Landis & R. W. Brislin (Eds.), *Handbook of intercultural training: Vol. 2. Issues in training methodology* (pp. 19-49). New York: Pergamon.

Barnlund, D. (1994). Communication in a global village. In L. A. Samovar & R. E. Porter (Eds.), *Intercultural communication: A reader* (7th ed., pp. 26-36). Belmont, CA: Wadsworth.

Barona, A., & Miller, J. (1994). Short acculturation scale for Hispanic youth: A preliminary report. *Hispanic Journal of Behavioral Sciences, 16,* 155-162.

Bar-Yosef, R. (1968). Desocialization and resocialization: The adjustment process of immigrants. *International Migration Review, 2,* 27-42.

Bates, T. (1994). Social resources generated by group support networks may not be beneficial to Asian immigrant-owned small businesses. *Social Forces, 72,* 671-689.

Bateson, G. (1972). *Steps to an ecology of mind: Collected essays in anthropology, psychiatry, evolution, and epistemology.* New York: Ballantine. (Original work published 1951)

Bateson, M. C. (1989). *Composing a life: Life as a work in progress.* New York: Penguin.

Beardsmore, H. (1986). *Bilingualism: Basic principles* (2nd ed.). Clevedon, England: Multilingual Matters.

Becker, H. (1970). Which side are we on? In W. Filstead (Ed.), *Qualitative methodology: Firsthand involvement with the social world* (pp. 15-26). Chicago: Markham.

Belay, G. (1993). Toward a paradigm shift for intercultural and international communication: New research directions. In S. A. Deetz (Ed.), *Communication yearbook 16* (pp. 437-457). Newbury Park, CA: Sage.

Bennett, J. (1977). Transition shock: Putting culture shock in perspective. In N. Jain (Ed.), *International intercultural communication annual* (Vol. 4, pp. 45-52). Falls Church, VA: Speech Communication Association.

Bennett, M. (1986). A developmental approach to training for intercultural sensitivity. *International Journal of Intercultural Relations, 10,* 179-196.

Benson, P. (1978). Measuring cross-cultural adjustment: The problem of criteria. *International Journal of Intercultural Relations, 2,* 21-37.

Bentley, G. (1981). *Ethnicity and nationality: A bibliographic guide.* Seattle: University of Washington Press.

Berger, C. R. (1979). Beyond initial interaction: Uncertainty, understanding, and the development of interpersonal relationships. In H. Giles & R. St. Clair (Eds.), *Language and social psychology* (pp. 122-144). Baltimore: University Park Press.

Berger, C. R., & Bradac, J. J. (1982). *Language and social knowledge.* London: Edward Arnold.

Berger, C. R., & Calabrese, R. J. (1975). Some explorations in initial interactions and beyond: Toward a developmental theory of interpersonal communication. *Human Communication Research, 1,* 99-112.

Berkowitz, L. (1962). *Aggression: A social psychological analysis.* New York: McGraw-Hill.

Berkowitz, S. (1982). *An introduction to structural analysis: The network approach to social research.* Toronto: Butterworth.

Berlin, I. (1986). Psychopathology and its antecedents among American Indian adolescents. *Advances in Clinical Psychology, 9,* 125-152.

Bernstein, B. (1975). *Class, codes, and control: Theoretical studies toward a sociology of language* (Rev. ed.). New York: Schocken.

Berreman, G. (1972). Aleut reference group alienation, mobility, and acculturation. In D. Walker (Ed.), *The emergent Native Americans: A reader in culture contact* (pp. 533-549). Boston: Little, Brown. (Original work published 1964)

Berry, J. W. (1970). Marginality stress and ethnic identification in an acculturated aboriginal community. *Journal of Cross-Cultural Psychology, 1,* 239-252.

Berry, J. W. (1975). Ecology, cultural adaptation, and psychological differentiation: Traditional patterning and acculturative stress. In R. W. Brislin, S. Bochner, & W. J. Lonner (Eds.), *Cross-cultural perspectives on learning* (pp. 207-228). Beverly Hills, CA: Sage.

Berry, J. W. (1976). *Human ecology and cognitive style: Comparative studies in cultural and psychological adaptation.* New York: Halsted.

Berry, J. W. (1980). Acculturation as varieties of adaptation. In A. Padilla (Ed.), *Acculturation: Theory, models and some new findings* (pp. 9-25). Boulder, CO: Westview.

Berry, J. W. (1990). Psychology of acculturation: Understanding individuals moving between cultures. In R. W. Brislin (Ed.), *Applied cross-cultural psychology* (pp. 232-253). Newbury Park, CA: Sage.

Berry, J. W., & Annis, R. C. (1974). Acculturative stress: The role of ecology, culture, and differentiation. *Journal of Cross-Cultural Psychology, 5,* 382-406.

Berry, J. W., & Kim, U. (1987). Acculturation and mental health. In P. Dasen, J. W. Berry, & N. Sartorius (Eds.), *Health and cross-cultural psychology* (pp. 207-236). Newbury Park, CA: Sage.

Berry, J. W., Kim, U., & Boski, P. (1988). Psychological acculturation of immigrants. In Y. Y. Kim & W. B. Gudykunst (Eds.), *Cross-cultural adaptation: Current approaches* (pp. 62-89). Newbury Park, CA: Sage.

Berry, J. W., Kim, U., Minde, T., & Mok, D. (1987). Comparative studies of acculturative stress. *International Migration Review, 21,* 491-511.

Berry, J. W., & Sam, D. (1997). Acculturation and adaptation. In J. W. Berry, M. H. Segall, & Ç. Kagitçibasi (Eds.), *Handbook of cross-cultural psychology* (pp. 291-326). Boston: Allyn & Bacon.

Bharati, A. (1972). *The Asians in East Africa.* Chicago: Nelson-Hall.

Bhawuk, D. (1990). Cross-cultural orientation programs. In R. W. Brislin (Ed.), *Applied cross-cultural psychology* (pp. 325-346). Newbury Park, CA: Sage.

Bienek, H. (1990). Exile is rebellion. In J. Glad (Ed.), *Literature in exile* (pp. 41-48). Durham, NC: Duke University Press.

Billig, M. (1987). *Arguing and thinking: A rhetorical approach to social psychology.* New York: Cambridge University Press.

Billig, M., Condon, S., Edwards, D., Gane, M., Middleton, D., & Radley, A. (1988). *Ideological dilemmas.* London: Sage.

Black, J., & Gregersen, H. (1990). Expectations, satisfaction, and intention to leave of American expatriate managers in Japan. *International Journal of Intercultural Relations, 14,* 485-506.

Blalock, H. M., Jr. (1969). *Theory construction: From verbal to mathematical formulations.* Englewood Cliffs, NJ: Prentice Hall.

Blalock, H. M., Jr. (1982). *Race and ethnic relations.* Englewood Cliffs, NJ: Prentice Hall.

Blalock, H. M., Jr. (1984). *Basic dilemmas in the social sciences.* Beverly Hills, CA: Sage.

Blalock, H. M., Jr. (1989). *Power and conflict: Toward a general theory.* Newbury Park, CA: Sage.

Bochner, S. (Ed.). (1981). *The mediating person: Bridges between cultures.* Cambridge, MA: Schenkman.

Bochner, S. (1982). The social psychology of cross-cultural relations. In S. Bochner (Ed.), *Cultures in contact: Studies in cross-cultural interaction* (pp. 5-44). New York: Pergamon.

Boekestijn, C. (1988). Intercultural migration and the development of personal identity: The dilemma between identity maintenance and cultural adaptation. *International Journal of Intercultural Relations, 12,* 83-105.

Booth-Butterfield, M. (Ed.). (1991). *Communication, cognition, and anxiety.* Newbury Park, CA: Sage.

Boulding, E. (1988). *Building a global civic culture.* New York: Teachers College Press.

Boulding, K. (1975). General systems theory: The skeleton of science. In B. D. Ruben & J. Y. Kim (Eds.), *General systems theory and human communication* (pp. 21-32). Rochelle Park, NJ: Hayden.

Boulding, K. (1977). *The image: Knowledge in life and society.* Ann Arbor: University of Michigan Press. (Original work published 1956)

Bourhis, R. Y., Giles, H., Leyens, J., & Tajfel, H. (1979). Psychological distinctiveness: Language divergence in Belgium. In H. Giles & R. St. Clair (Eds.), *Language and social psychology* (pp. 158-185). Baltimore: University Park Press.

Bourhis, R. Y., Giles, H., & Rosenthal, D. (1981). Notes on the construction of a "subjective vitality questionnaire" for ethnolinguistic groups. *Journal of Multilingual and Multicultural Development, 2,* 145-155.

Bourhis, R. Y., Moiese, L., Perreault, S., & Senecal, S. (1997). Towards an interactive acculturation model: A social psychological approach. *International Journal of Psychology, 32,* 369-386.

Brabant, S., Palmer, C., & Gramling, R. (1990). Returning home: An empirical investigation of cross-cultural reentry. *International Journal of Intercultural Relations, 14,* 387-404.

Bradburn, N. (1969). *The structure of psychological wellbeing.* Chicago: Aldine.

Brein, M., & David, K. (1971). Intercultural communication and the adjustment of the sojourner. *Psychological Bulletin, 76,* 215-230.

Breton, R. (1964). Institutional completeness of ethnic communities and the personal relations of immigrants. *American Journal of Sociology, 70,* 193-205.

Breton, R. (1991). *The governance of ethnic communities: Political structures and processes in Canada.* Westport, CT: Greenwood.

Breton, R., Isajiw, W., Kalbach, W., & Reitz, J. (1990). *Ethnic identity and equality: Varieties of experience in a Canadian city.* Toronto: University of Toronto Press.

Brewer, D. (1992). A note on the relationship between centrality and cultural knowledge in a professional network. *Connections, 15*(1-2), 21-28.

Brewer, J., & Hunter, A. (1989). *Multimethod research: A synthesis of styles.* Newbury Park, CA: Sage.

Brewer, M. (1979). In-group bias in the minimal intergroup situation: A cognitive-motivational analysis. *Psychological Bulletin, 86,* 307-324.

Brewer, M. (1986). The role of ethnocentrism in intergroup conflict. In S. Worchel & W. G. Austin (Eds.), *Psychology of intergroup relations* (2nd ed., pp. 288-304). Chicago: Nelson-Hall.

Brewer, M., & Campbell, D. (1976). *Ethnocentrism and intergroup attitudes: East African evidence.* New York: John Wiley.

Brewer, M., & Gardner, W. (1996). Who is this "we"? Levels of collective identity and self-representations. *Journal of Personality and Social Psychology, 71,* 83-93.

Brewer, M., & Miller, N. (1984). Beyond the contact hypothesis: Theoretical perspective on desegregation. In N. Miller & M. Brewer (Eds.), *Groups in contact: The psychology of desegregation* (pp. 281-302). New York: Academic Press.

Brislin, R. W., Landis, D., & Brandt, M. (1983). Conceptualizations of intercultural behavior and training. In D. Landis & R. W. Brislin (Eds.), *Handbook of intercultural training: Vol. 1. Issues in theory and design* (pp. 1-35). New York: Pergamon.

Brislin, R. W., & Yoshida, T. (1994). *Intercultural communication training: An introduction.* Thousand Oaks, CA: Sage.

Brodsky, J. (1990). The condition we call "exile." In J. Glad (Ed.), *Literature in exile* (pp. 100-130). Durham, NC: Duke University Press.

Brody, E. (1969). Migration and adaptation: The nature of the problem. In E. Brody (Ed.), *Behavior in new environments: Adaptation of migrant populations* (pp. 13-21). Beverly Hills, CA: Sage.

Brooke, J. (1996, August 11). Amish going modern, sort of, about skating. *New York Times,* p. A10.

Broom, L., & Kitsuse, J. (1955). The validation of acculturation: A condition to ethnic assimilation. *American Anthropologist, 57,* 44-48.

Brown, H. (1991). *Breaking the language barrier.* Yarmouth, ME: Intercultural Press.

Bruner, J. (1957). On perceptual readiness. *Psychological Review, 64,* 123-151.

Bryce, R. (1995, August 6). The American dream glitters still—in foreign countries. *New York Times,* p. F10.

Buck, R. (1984). *The communication of emotion.* New York: Guilford.

Burgess, M. (1978). The resurgence of ethnicity: Myth or reality? *Ethnic and Racial Studies, 1,* 265-285.

Burgoon, J. K., Dillman, L., & Stern, L. (1993). Adaptation in dyadic interaction: Defining and operationalizing patterns of reciprocity and compensation. *Communication Theory, 3,* 295-316.

Burleson, B. R. (1983). Social cognition, empathic motivation, and adults' comforting strategies. *Human Communication Research, 10,* 295-304.

Cahn, D., & Hanford, J. (1984). Perspectives on human communication research: Behaviorism, phenomenology, and an integrated view. *Western Journal of Speech Communication, 48,* 277-292.

Campbell, D. T., & Fiske, D. W. (1959). Convergent and discriminant validation by the multitrait-multimethod matrix. *Psychological Bulletin, 56,* 81-105.

Cargile, A. C., & Giles, H. (1996). Intercultural communication training: Review, critique, and a new theoretical perspective. In B. R. Burleson (Ed.), *Communication yearbook 19* (pp. 385-423). Thousand Oaks, CA: Sage.

Carley, K. (1991). A theory of group solidarity. *American Sociological Review, 56,* 331-354.

Carlson, M. (1988, December 5). Only English spoken here. *Time,* p. 29.

Carlson, M., & Carlson, R. (1981). *The country school and the Americanization of ethnic groups in North Dakota.* Silt, CO: Country School Legacy Project. (ERIC Document Reproduction Service No. ED 211 250)

Caselli, R. (1973). Making it in America: The Italian experience. *Social Studies, 64*(4), 147-153.

Castles, S. (1986). The guest-worker in Western Europe: An obituary. *International Migration Review, 20,* 761-778.

Cegala, D. (1981). Interaction involvement: A cognitive dimension of communicative competence. *Communication Education, 30,* 109-121.

Cegala, D. (1984). Affective and cognitive manifestations of interaction involvement during unstructured and competitive interactions. *Communication Monographs, 51,* 320-338.

Cenoz, J., & Valencia, J. F. (1993). Ethnolinguistic vitality, social networks and motivation in second language acquisition: Some data from the Basque country. *Language, Culture and Curriculum, 6,* 113-127.

Chaffee, S. H., & Mutz, D. (1988). Comparing mediated and interpersonal communication data. In R. Hawkins, J. M. Wiemann, & S. Pingree (Eds.), *Advancing communication science: Merging mass and interpersonal processes* (pp. 19-43). Newbury Park, CA: Sage.

Chaffee, S. H., Nass, C., & Yang, S. (1989, November). *The bridging role of television in immigrant political socialization.* Paper presented at the annual meeting of the Speech Communication Association, Chicago.

Chan, K., & Lam, L. (1987a). Community, kinship and family in the Chinese Vietnamese community: Some enduring values and patterns of interaction. In K. Chan & D. Indra (Eds.), *Uprooting, loss and adaptation: The resettlement of Indochinese refugees in Canada* (pp. 15-26). Ottawa: Canadian Public Health Association.

Chan, K., & Lam, L. (1987b). Psychological problems of Chinese Vietnamese refugees resettling in Quebec. In K. Chan & D. Indra (Eds.), *Uprooting, loss and adaptation: The resettlement of Indochinese refugees in Canada* (pp. 27-41). Ottawa: Canadian Public Health Association.

Chance, N. (1972). Acculturation, self-identification and personality adjustment. In D. Walker (Ed.), *The emergent Native Americans: A reader in culture contact* (pp. 513-532). Boston: Little, Brown. (Original work published 1965)

Chang, W. (1972). *Communication and acculturation: A case study of Korean ethnic groups in Los Angeles.* Unpublished doctoral dissertation, University of Iowa, Ames.

Chen, G. (1990, November). *Communication adaptability and interaction involvement as predictors of cross-cultural adjustment.* Paper presented at the annual meeting of the Speech Communication Association, Chicago.

Chernin, D. (1990, July). An American learns to work in Japan. *World Monitor*, pp. 50-56.

Cho, C. (1982). Communication modes in adaptation process: A case of Korean immigrants. *Dissertation Abstracts International, 43*(06), 1885A. (University Microfilms No. DA82-24926)

Chodoff, P. (1976). The German concentration camp as a psychological stress. In R. Moos (Ed.), *Human adaptation: Coping with life crises* (pp. 337-349). Lexington, MA: D. C. Heath.

Chomsky, N. (1968). *Language and mind.* New York: Harcourt, Brace & World.

Chomsky, N. (1986). *Knowledge of language: Its nature, origin, and use.* New York: Praeger.

Christie, T. (1976). *Reverse colonialism and sociocultural change: A case study.* Unpublished doctoral dissertation, University of Toronto.

Church, A. (1982). Sojourner adjustment. *Psychological Bulletin, 91*, 540-572.

Clachar, A. (1997). Students' reflections on the social, political, and ideological role of English in Puerto Rico. *Hispanic Journal of Behavioral Sciences, 19*, 461-478.

Clark, M. (1985). Social stereotypes and self-concept in black and white college students. *Journal of Social Psychology, 125*, 753-760.

Clarke, S., & Obler, J. (1976). Ethnic conflict, community-building, and the emergence of ethnic political traditions in the United States. In S. Clarke & J. Obler (Eds.), *Urban ethnic conflicts: A comparative perspective* (pp. 1-34). Chapel Hill: University of North Carolina Press.

Clément, R., Noels, K., & Karine, G. (1994, July). *Media influence in minority group acculturation.* Paper presented at the Fifth International Conference on Language and Social Psychology, Brisbane, Queensland.

Coelho, G. (1958). *Changing images of America: A study of Indian students perceptions.* New York: Free Press.

Coffee, G. (1990). *Beyond survival: A POW's inspiring lesson in living.* New York: Berkeley.

Cohen, Y. (1968). *Man in adaptation.* Chicago: Aldine.

Cohn, S., & Wood, R. (1982, July). Peace Corps volunteers and host country nationals: Determinants of variations in social interaction. *Journal of Developing Areas*, pp. 543-560.

Coleman, D. (1987). U.K. statistics on immigration: Development and limitations. *International Migration Review, 21*, 1138-1169.

Collier, M., & Thomas, M. (1988). Cultural identity: An interpretive perspective. In Y. Y. Kim & W. B. Gudykunst (Eds.), *Theories in intercultural communication* (pp. 99-120). Newbury Park, CA: Sage.

Collin, D. (1978, February 5). New Peace Corps—a shot of idealism. *Chicago Tribune*, sec. 1, p. 33.

Connor, J. (1977). *Tradition and change in three generations of Japanese-Americans.* Chicago: Nelson-Hall.

Conroy, H., & Miyakawa, T. (Eds.). (1972). *East across the Pacific: Historical and sociological studies of Japanese immigration and assimilation.* Santa Barbara, CA: ABC-Clio.

Constantakis-Valdés, P. (1992, May). *Toward a theory of "immigrant" and "ethnic" media: The case of Spanish-language television.* Paper presented at the annual meeting of the International Communication Association, Miami, FL.

Cook, S. W. (1962). The systematic analysis of socially significant events: A strategy for social research. *Journal of Social Issues, 18*(2), 66-84.

Cook, S. W. (1978). Interpersonal and attitudinal outcomes in cooperating interracial groups. *Journal of Research and Development in Education, 12,* 97-113.

Coombs, G. (1979). Opportunities, information networks and the migration-distance relationship. *Social Networks, 1,* 257-276.

Copelman, D. (1993). The immigrant experience: Margin notes. *Mind and Human Interaction, 4*(2), 76-82.

Cort, D., & King, M. (1979). Some correlates of culture shock among American tourists in Africa. *International Journal of Intercultural Relations, 3,* 211-225.

Crano, W. (1981). Triangulation and cross-cultural research. In M. Brewer & B. Collins (Eds.), *Scientific inquiry and the social sciences* (pp. 317-344). San Francisco: Jossey-Bass.

Crawford, L. (1996). Personal ethnography. *Communication Monographs, 63,* 158-170.

Cross, R. (1978, February 5). That world we call Chinatown. *Chicago Tribune Magazine,* pp. 16-21, 23.

Crossette, B. (1996, August 18). Citizenship is a malleable concept. *New York Times,* p. E3.

Crossley, N. (1996). *Intersubjectivity: The fabric of social becoming.* Thousand Oaks, CA: Sage.

Crowe, P. (1991, May-June). *Sociocultural units in progress.* Paper presented at the annual meeting of the International Society for the Comparative Study of Civilizations, Santo Domingo, Dominican Republic.

Csikszentmihalyi, M. (1993). *The evolving self: A psychology for the third millennium.* New York: HarperCollins.

Cuéllar, I., & Roberts, R. (1997). Relations of depression, acculturation, and socioeconomic status in a Latino sample. *Hispanic Journal of Behavioral Sciences, 19,* 230-238.

Cupach, W. R., & Imahori, T. T. (1993). Identity management theory: Communication competence in intercultural episodes and relationships. In R. L. Wiseman & J. Koester (Eds.), *Intercultural communication competence* (pp. 121-131). Newbury Park, CA: Sage.

Cypser, R. J., & Cypser, C. E. (1989). *The process of becoming: A guide to personal fulfillment.* Katonah, NY: Kim Pathways.

Dabrowski, K. (1964). *Positive disintegration.* Boston: Little, Brown.

Dance, F., & Larson, C. (1976). *The function of human communication: A theoretical approach.* New York: Holt, Rinehart & Winston.

Dasgupta, S. (1983). *Indian immigrants: The evolution of an ethnic group.* Unpublished doctoral dissertation, University of Delaware, Newark.

David, H. (1969). Involuntary international migration: Adaptation of refugees. In E. Brody (Ed.), *Behavior in new environments: Adaptation of migrant populations* (pp. 73-95). Beverly Hills, CA: Sage.

Davidson, M. (1983). *Uncommon sense: The life and thought of Ludwig von Bertalanffy, father of general systems theory.* Los Angeles: J. P. Tarcher.

Davis, M. (1990). *Mexican voices/American dreams: An oral history of Mexican immigrants to the United States.* New York: Henry Holt.

Dawson, E., Crano, W., & Burgoon, M. (1996). Refining the meaning and measurement of acculturation: Revising a novel methodological approach. *International Journal of Intercultural Relations, 20,* 97-114.

Dean, O., & Popp, G. (1990). Intercultural communication effectiveness as perceived by American managers in Saudi Arabia and French managers in the U.S. *International Journal of Intercultural Relations, 14,* 405-424.

Deaux, K., Reid, A., Mizrahi, K., & Ethier, K. (1995). Parameters of social identity. *Journal of Personality and Social Psychology, 68,* 280-291.

DeCocq, G. (1976). European and North American self-help movements: Some contrasts. In A. Katz & E. Bender (Eds.), *The strength in us: Self-help groups in the modern world* (pp. 202-208). New York: New Viewpoint.

DeFleur, M., & Cho, C. (1957). Assimilation of Japanese-born women in an American city. *Social Problems, 4,* 244-257.

Denzin, N. K. (1989). *Interpretive biography.* Newbury Park, CA: Sage.

Der-Karabetian, A. (1980). Relation of two cultural identities of Armenian-Americans. *Psychological Reports, 47,* 123-128.

Desbarats, J. (1986). Ethnic differences in adaptation: Sino-Vietnamese refugees in the United States. *International Migration Review, 20,* 405-427.

Deusen, J. (1982). Health/mental health studies of Indochinese refugees. *Medical Anthropology, 6,* 231-252.

Deutsch, S., & Won, G. (1963). Some factors in the adjustment of foreign nationals in the United States. *Journal of Social Issues, 19*(3), 115-122.

De Verthelyi, R. F. (1995). International students' spouses: Invisible sojourners in the culture shock literature. *International Journal of Intercultural Relations, 19,* 387-411.

De Vos, G. A. (1990a). Conflict, dominance, and exploitation: The sacred and expressive in systems of social segregation. In G. A. De Vos &

M. M. Suárez-Orozco, *Status inequality: The self in culture* (pp. 148-163). Newbury Park, CA: Sage.

De Vos, G. A. (1990b). Internalization and human resonance: From empathy to alienation. In G. A. De Vos & M. M. Suárez-Orozco, *Status inequality: The self in culture* (pp. 75-119). Newbury Park, CA: Sage.

De Vos, G. A. (1990c). Self in society: A multilevel, psychocultural analysis. In G. A. De Vos & M. M. Suárez-Orozco, *Status inequality: The self in culture* (pp. 17-74). Newbury Park, CA: Sage.

De Vos, G. A. (1993). A psychocultural approach to ethnic interaction in contemporary research. In M. Bernal & G. Knight (Eds.), *Ethnic identity: Formation and transmission among Hispanics and other minorities* (pp. 235-270). Albany: State University of New York Press.

De Vos, G. A., & Suárez-Orozco, M. M. (1990a). Ethnic belonging and status mobility. In G. A. De Vos & M. M. Suárez-Orozco, *Status inequality: The self in culture* (pp. 246-264). Newbury Park, CA: Sage.

De Vos, G. A., & Suárez-Orozco, M. M. (1990b). *Status inequality: The self in culture*. Newbury Park, CA: Sage.

Diesing, P. (1991). *How does social science work? Reflections on practice.* Pittsburgh, PA: University of Pittsburgh Press.

Diggs, N., & Murphy, B. (1991). Japanese adjustment to American communities: The case of the Japanese in the Dayton area. *International Journal of Intercultural Relations, 15*, 103-116.

Dimsdale, J. (1976). The coping behavior of Nazi concentration camp survivors. In R. Moos (Ed.), *Human adaptation: Coping with life crises* (pp. 350-360). Lexington, MA: D. C. Heath.

Dinges, N. (1983). Intercultural competence. In D. Landis & R. W. Brislin (Eds.), *Handbook of intercultural training: Vol. 1. Issues in theory and design* (pp. 176-202). New York: Pergamon.

Dinges, N., & Lieberman, D. (1989). Intercultural communication competence: Coping with stressful work situations. *International Journal of Inter-cultural Relations, 13*, 371-386.

DiPrete, T., & Forristal, J. (1994). Multilevel models: Methods and substance. *Annual Review of Sociology, 20*, 331-357.

Dobuzinskis, L. (1987). *The self-organizing polity: An epistemological analysis of political life.* Boulder, CO: Westview.

Dobzhansky, T. (1962). *Mankind evolving: The evolution of the human species.* New Haven, CT: Yale University Press.

Dollard, J., Miller, N. E., Doob, L., Mower, O. H., & Sears, R. R. (1963). *Frustration and aggression.* New Haven, CT: Yale University Press.

Dong, Q., & Tan, A. (1996, May). *Immigrant adolescent socialization via television: A study of adolescent Asian immigrants to the United States.* Paper presented at the annual meeting of the International Communication Association, Chicago.

Dorais, L. (1987). Language use and adaptation. In K. Chan & D. Indra (Eds.), *Uprooting, loss and adaptation: The resettlement of Indochinese refugees in Canada* (pp. 52-64). Ottawa: Canadian Public Health Association.

Dosman, E. (1972). *Indians: The urban dilemma.* Toronto: McClelland & Stewart.

Driedger, L. (1976). Ethnic self-identity: A comparison of ingroup evaluations. *Sociometry, 39,* 131-141.

Dubin, R. (1978). *Theory building* (Rev. ed.). New York: Free Press.

Dublin, T. (1993). *Immigrant voices: New lives in America, 1773-1986.* Urbana: University of Illinois Press.

Dubos, R. (1965). *Man adapting.* New Haven, CT: Yale University Press.

Durgunoglu, A., & Verhoeven, L. (Eds.). (1998). *Literacy development in a multilingual context: A cross-cultural perspective.* Hillsdale, NJ: Lawrence Erlbaum.

Dyal, J., & Dyal, R. (1981). Acculturation, stress and coping. *International Journal of Intercultural Relations, 5,* 301-328.

Eames, E., & Schwab, W. (1964). Urban migration in India and Africa. *Human Organization, 23,* 24-27.

Earlum, N. (1980). The Cherokee nation of Oklahoma: A case study. In U.S. Department of State (Ed.), *Twenty-second executive seminar in national and international affairs.* Washington, DC: Government Printing Office.

Eastman, C. (1985). Establishing social identity through language use. *Journal of Language and Social Psychology, 4,* 1-20.

Easton, D. (1991). The division, integration, and transfer of knowledge. In D. Easton & C. S. Schelling (Eds.), *Divided knowledge: Across disciplines, across cultures* (pp. 7-36). Newbury Park, CA: Sage.

Eaton, W., & Lasry, J. (1978). Mental health and occupational mobility in a group of immigrants. *Science and Medicine, 12,* 53-58.

Eckenrode, J., & Gore, S. (1981). Stressful events and social supports: The significance of context. In B. Gottlieb (Ed.), *Social networks and social support* (pp. 43-68). Beverly Hills, CA: Sage.

Eddy, R. (Ed.). (1996). *Reflections on multiculturalism.* Yarmouth, ME: Intercultural Press.

Edwards, J. (1985). *Language, society and identity.* New York: Basil Blackwell.

Edwards, J. (1994, July). *Parochialism and intercourse: Metaphors for mobility.* Paper presented at the Fifth International Conference on Language and Social Psychology, Brisbane, Queensland.

Ekman, P., & Friesen, W. (1971). Constants across cultures in the face and emotion. *Journal of Personality and Social Psychology, 17,* 124-129.

Elgin, D. (1981). *Voluntary simplicity.* New York: Bantam.

Ellis, C., & Flaherty, M. G. (1992a). An agenda for the interpretation of lived experience. In C. Ellis & M. G. Flaherty (Eds.), *Investigating subjectivity: Research on lived experience* (pp. 1-16). Newbury Park, CA: Sage.

Ellis, C., & Flaherty, M. G. (Eds.). (1992b). *Investigating subjectivity: Research on lived experience.* Newbury Park, CA: Sage.

Enguidanos-Clark, G. (1986). Acculturative stress and its contribution to the development of depression in Hispanic women. *Dissertation Abstracts International, 47*(04), 1719B. (University Microfilms No. AAC86-13539)

Enloe, W., & Lewin, P. (1987). Issues of integration abroad and readjustment to Japan of Japanese returnees. *International Journal of Intercultural Relations, 11,* 223-248.

Epstein, J., Botvin, J., Dusenberry, L., Diaz, T., & Kerner, T. (1996). Validation of an acculturation measure for Hispanic adolescents. *Psychological Reports, 79,* 1075-1079.

Erikson, E. (1959). *Identity and the life cycle.* New York: International Universities Press.

Erikson, E. (1968). *Identity, youth, and crisis.* New York: W. W. Norton.

Erikson, E. (1969). Growth and crises of the healthy personality. In H. Chiang & A. H. Maslow (Eds.), *The healthy personality* (pp. 30-34). New York: Van Nostrand Reinhold.

Eschbach, K., & Gomez, C. (1998). Choosing Hispanic identity: Ethnic identity switching among respondents to high school and beyond. *Social Science Quarterly, 79,* 74-90.

Ethier, K., & Deaux, K. (1994). Negotiating social identity when contexts change: Maintaining identification and responding to threat. *Journal of Personality and Social Psychology, 67,* 243-251.

Fabrega, H., Jr. (1969). Social psychiatric aspects of acculturation and migration: A general statement. *Comprehensive Psychiatry, 10,* 314-326.

Fantini, A. (1985). *Language acquisition of a bilingual child.* Clevedon, England: Multilingual Matters.

Farah, M. (1990). In praise of exile. In J. Glad (Ed.), *Literature in exile* (pp. 64-83). Durham, NC: Duke University Press.

Faust, K., & Wasserman, S. (1992). Centrality and prestige: A review and synthesis. *Journal of Qualitative Anthropology, 4,* 23-78.

Feagin, J. (Ed.). (1984). *Racial and ethnic relations* (2nd ed.). Englewood Cliffs, NJ: Prentice Hall.

Ferguson, C., & Heath, S. (Eds.). (1981). *Language in the USA.* Cambridge, UK: Cambridge University Press.

Fielding, N. G., & Fielding, J. L. (1986). *Linking data.* Beverly Hills, CA: Sage.

Fischer, J. (1961). Art styles as cultural cognitive maps. *American Anthropologist, 63,* 79-93.

Fisher, G. (1988). *Mindsets.* Yarmouth, ME: Intercultural Press.

Fiske, D., & Maddi, S. (Eds.). (1961). *Functions of varied experience.* Homewood, IL: Dorsey.

Florack, A., & Piontkowski, U. (1997). Identification and perceived vitality: The Dutch and the Germans in the European Union. *Journal of Multilingual and Multicultural Development, 18*, 349-363.

Fogel, A. (1993). *Developing through relationships: Origins of communication, self, and culture.* Chicago: University of Chicago Press.

Fogelman, B. (1972). *Adaptive mechanisms of the North American Indian to an urban setting.* Unpublished doctoral dissertation, Southern Methodist University.

Foner, N. (Ed.). (1987). *New immigrants in New York.* New York: Columbia University Press.

Ford, D., & Lerner, R. (1992). *Developmental systems theory: An integrative approach.* Newbury Park, CA: Sage.

Foster, L., & Stockley, S. (1988). *Australian multiculturalism: A documentary history and critique.* Clevedon, England: Multilingual Matters.

Fowler, F. J., Jr., & Mangione, T. W. (1990). *Standardized survey interviewing: Minimizing interviewer-related error.* Newbury Park, CA: Sage.

Francis, E. (1976). *Interethnic relations.* New York: Elsevier.

Frank, L. (1975). Cultural organization. In B. D. Ruben & J. Y. Kim (Eds.), *General systems theory and human communication* (pp. 128-135). Rochelle Park, NJ: Hayden.

French, J., Jr., Rodger, W., & Cobb, S. (1974). Adjustment as person environment fit. In G. Coelho, D. Hamburg, & J. Adams (Eds.), *Coping and adaptation* (pp. 316-333). New York: Basic Books.

Frey, W., & Tilove, J. (1995, August 20). Immigrants in, native whites out. *New York Times Magazine*, pp. 44, 46.

Friedkin, N. (1991). Theoretical foundations for centrality measures. *American Journal of Sociology, 96*, 1478-1504.

Friedlander, J. (Ed.). (1988). *Sojourners and settlers: The Yemeni immigrant experience.* Salt Lake City: University of Utah Press.

Friedrich, O. (1985, July 8). The changing faces of America. *Time*, pp. 26-33.

Furnham, A. (1988). The adjustment of sojourners. In Y. Y. Kim & W. B. Gudykunst (Eds.), *Cross-cultural adaptation: Current approaches* (pp. 42-61). Newbury Park, CA: Sage.

Furnham, A., & Bochner, S. (1982). Social difficulty in a foreign culture: An empirical analysis of culture shock. In S. Bochner (Ed.), *Cultures in contact: Studies in cross-cultural interaction* (pp. 161-198). New York: Pergamon.

Furnham, A., & Bochner, S. (1986). *Culture shock: Psychological reactions to unfamiliar environments.* New York: Routledge.

Gadfields, N., Giles, H., Bourhis, R. Y., & Tajfel, H. (1979). Dynamics of humor in ethnic group relations. *Ethnicity, 6*, 373-382.

Gal, S. (1978). Variation and change in patterns of speaking: Language shift in Austria. In D. Sankoff (Ed.), *Linguistic variation: Models and methods* (pp. 227-238). New York: Academic Press.

Gallagher, W. (1996). *I.D.: How heredity and experience make you who you are.* New York: Random House.

Gallo, P. (1974). *Ethnic alienation: The Italian Americans.* Cranbury, NJ: Fairleigh Dickinson University Press.

Gallois, C., Franklyn-Stokes, A., Giles, H., & Coupland, N. (1988). Communication accommodation in intercultural encounters. In Y. Y. Kim & W. B. Gudykunst (Eds.), *Theories in intercultural communication* (pp. 157-185). Newbury Park, CA: Sage.

Gallois, C., Giles, H., Jones, E., Cargile, A. C., & Ota, H. (1995). Accommodating intercultural encounters: Elaborations and extensions. In R. L. Wiseman (Ed.), *Intercultural communication theory* (pp. 115-147). Thousand Oaks, CA: Sage.

Gans, H. J. (1962). *The urban villagers: Group and class in the life of Italian-Americans.* New York: Free Press.

Gao G., & Gudykunst, W. B. (1990). Uncertainty, anxiety, and adaptation. *International Journal of Intercultural Relations, 14,* 301-317.

Gardner, R. C. (1985). *Social psychology and second language learning: The role of attitudes and motivation.* Baltimore: Edward Arnold.

Gardner, R. C. (1991). Attitudes and motivation in second language learning. In A. Reynolds (Ed.), *Bilingualism, multiculturalism, and second language learning: The McGill Conference in Honour of Wallace E. Lambert* (pp. 43-63). Hillsdale, NJ: Lawrence Erlbaum.

Gardner, R. C., & Clément, R. (1990). Social psychological perspectives on second language acquisition. In H. Giles & W. P. Robinson (Eds.), *Handbook of language and social psychology* (pp. 495-517). Chichester, England: John Wiley.

Gass, S. M., & Varonis, E. M. (1991). Miscommunication in nonnative speaker discourse. In N. Coupland, H. Giles, & J. M. Wiemann (Eds.), *"Miscommunication" and problematic talk* (pp. 121-145). Newbury Park, CA: Sage.

Gebart-Eaglemont, J. (1994, July). *Acculturation and stress in immigrants: A path analysis.* Paper presented at the Fifth International Conference on Language and Social Psychology, Brisbane, Queensland.

Gehl, J. (1984). But I am Danish(?). In AFS International/Intercultural Programs (Ed.), *Occasional papers in intercultural learning, no. 6* (pp. 1, 4-16). New York: AFS International/Intercultural Programs.

Gendlin, E. (1962). *Experiencing and the creation of meaning.* New York: Free Press.

Gendlin, E. (1978). *Focusing.* New York: Everest House.

George, C. (1985). The impact of Western education on intercaste social behavior: A case study of Hindu Indian nationals in the Washington metropolitan area. *Dissertation Abstracts International, 46*(03), 803A. (University Microfilms No. DA85-10248)

Gephart, R. P., Jr. (1988). *Ethnostatistics: Qualitative foundations for quantitative research.* Newbury Park, CA: Sage.

Geyer, R. (1980). *Alienation theories: A general systems approach.* New York: Pergamon.

Gil, A., Vega, W., & Dimas, J. (1994). Acculturative stress and personal adjustment among Hispanic adolescent boys. *Journal of Community Psychology, 22,* 43-54.

Giles, H., Bourhis, R. Y., & Taylor, D. (1977). Towards a theory of language in ethnic group relations. In H. Giles (Ed.), *Language, ethnicity, and intergroup relations* (pp. 307-348). London: Academic Press.

Giles, H., & Byrne, J. (1982). The intergroup theory of second language acquisition. *Journal of Multilingual and Multicultural Development, 3,* 17-40.

Giles, H., Coupland, N., Coupland, J., Williams, A., & Nussbaum, J. F. (1992). Intergenerational talk of communication with older people. *International Journal of Aging and Human Development, 34,* 271-297.

Giles, H., & Johnson, P. (1987). Ethnolinguistic identity theory: A social psychological approach to language maintenance. *International Journal of Social Language, 68,* 69-99.

Giles, H., Mulac, A., Bradac, J. J., & Johnson, P. (1987). Speech accommodation theory: The first decade and beyond. In M. L. McLaughlin (Ed.), *Communication yearbook 10* (pp. 13-48). Newbury Park, CA: Sage.

Giles, H., & Smith, P. (1979). Accommodation theory: Optimal levels of convergence. In H. Giles & R. St. Clair (Eds.), *Language and social psychology* (pp. 45-65). Baltimore: University Park Press.

Giles, H., & Viladot, A. (1994). Ethnolinguistic identity in Catalonia. *Multilingua, 13,* 301-312.

Givón, T. (1989). *Mind, code and context: Essays in pragmatics.* Hillsdale, NJ: Lawrence Erlbaum.

Glad, J. (Ed.). (1990). *Literature in exile.* Durham, NC: Duke University Press.

Glazer, N., & Moynihan, D. P. (1963). *Beyond the melting pot.* Cambridge, PA: MIT Press.

Glazer, N., & Moynihan, D. P. (1975). *Ethnicity: Theory and experience.* Cambridge, MA: Harvard University Press.

Glenn, N. (1977). *Cohort analysis.* Beverly Hills, CA: Sage.

Gmelch, G. (1997). Crossing cultures: Student travel and personal development. *International Journal of Intercultural Relations, 21,* 475-490.

Goffman, E. (1961). *Asylums: Essays on the social situation of mental patients and other inmates.* Garden City, NY: Doubleday.

Goffman, E. (1966). Alienation from interaction. In A. Smith (Ed.), *Communication and culture* (pp. 103-118). New York: Holt, Rinehart & Winston.

Goffman, E. (1979). Facial engagements. In C. Mortensen (Ed.), *Basic readings in communication theory* (2nd ed., pp. 137-163). New York: Harper & Row.

Goldenberg, S., & Haines, V. (1992). Social networks and institutional completeness: From territory to ties. *Canadian Journal of Sociology, 17,* 301-312.

Gordon, M. (1964). *Assimilation in American life: The role of race, religion, and national origins.* New York: Oxford University Press.

Gordon, M. (1973). Assimilation in America: Theory and reality. In P. Rose (Ed.), *The study of society* (pp. 350-365). New York: Random House.

Gordon, M. (1981). Models of pluralism: The new American dilemma. *Annals of the American Academy of Political and Social Science, 454,* 178-188.

Gore, S. (1984). Stress-buffering functions of social supports: An appraisal and clarification of research models. In B. S. Dohrenwend & B. P. Dohrenwend (Eds.), *Stressful life events and their contexts* (pp. 202-233). New Brunswick, NJ: Rutgers University Press.

Gottlieb, B. (1981). Social networks and social support in community mental health. In B. Gottlieb (Ed.), *Social networks and social support* (pp. 11-42). Beverly Hills, CA: Sage.

Goza, F. (1987). Adjustment and adaptation among Southeast Asian refugees in the United States. *Dissertation Abstracts International, 48*(02), 486B. (University Microfilms No. AAC87-08086)

Graafsma, T., Bosma, H., Grotevant, H., & de Levita, D. (1994). Identity and development: An interdisciplinary view. In H. Bosma, T. Graafsma, & D. de Levita (Eds.), *Identity and development: An interdisciplinary approach* (pp. 159-174). Thousand Oaks, CA: Sage.

Granovetter, M. (1973). The strength of weak ties. *American Journal of Sociology, 78,* 1360-1380.

Graves, T. (1967). Acculturation, access, and alcohol in a tri-ethnic community. *American Anthropologist, 69,* 306-321.

Greeley, A. (1974). *Ethnicity in the United States: A preliminary reconnaissance.* New York: John Wiley.

Grotevant, H. (1992). Assigned and chosen identity components: A process perspective on their integration. In G. R. Adams, T. P. Gullotta, & R. Montemayor (Eds.), *Adolescent identity formation* (pp. 73-90). Newbury Park, CA: Sage.

Grotevant, H. (1993). The integrative nature of identity: Bridging the soloists to sing in the choir. In J. Kroger (Ed.), *Discussions on ego identity* (pp. 121-146). Hillsdale, NJ: Lawrence Erlbaum.

Grove, C., & Torbiorn, I. (1985). A new conceptualization of intercultural adjustment and the goals of training. *International Journal of Intercultural Relations, 9,* 205-233.

Gudykunst, W. B. (1983). Similarities and differences in perceptions of initial intracultural and intercultural encounters: An exploratory investigation. *Southern Speech Communication Journal, 49*(1), 49-65.

Gudykunst, W. B. (1995). Anxiety/uncertainty management (AUM) theory: Current status. In R. L. Wiseman (Ed.), *Intercultural communication theory* (pp. 8-58). Thousand Oaks, CA: Sage.

Gudykunst, W. B., & Kim, Y. Y. (1997). *Communicating with strangers: An approach to intercultural communication* (3rd ed.). New York: McGraw-Hill.

Gudykunst, W. B., Wiseman, R. L., & Hammer, M. R. (1977). Determinants of a sojourner's attitudinal satisfaction: A path model. In B. D. Ruben (Ed.), *Communication yearbook 1* (pp. 415-425). Brunswick, NJ: Transaction.

Gullahorn, J., & Gullahorn, J. (1963). An extension of the U-curve hypothesis. *Journal of Social Issues, 19*(3), 33-47.

Gumperz, J. J. (1978). The conversational analysis of interethnic communication. In E. Ross (Ed.), *Interethnic communication* (pp. 13-31). Athens: University of Georgia Press.

Gumperz, J. J., & Cook-Gumperz, J. (1982). Introduction: Language and the communication of social identity. In J. J. Gumperz (Ed.), *Language and social identity* (pp. 1-21). Cambridge, UK: Cambridge University Press.

Gupta, S. (1975). Changes in the food habits of Asian Indians in the U.S. *Sociology and Social Research, 60*(1), 87-99.

Hall, E. T. (1976). *Beyond culture.* Garden City, NY: Anchor.

Hall, E. T. (1979). Adumbration as a feature of intercultural communication. In C. Mortensen (Ed.), *Basic readings in communication theory* (2nd ed., pp. 420-432). New York: Harper & Row.

Hall, E. T. (1983). *The dance of life: The other dimension of time.* Garden City, NY: Anchor.

Hall, P. (1986). The etic-emic distinction: Its observational foundation. In B. Dervin & M. J. Voigt (Eds.), *Progress in communication sciences* (Vol. 7, pp. 123-151). Norwood, NJ: Ablex.

Hamers, J. (1994, July). *How do social networks, attitudes and literacy interact in bilingual development?* Paper presented at the Fifth International Conference on Language and Social Psychology, Brisbane, Queensland.

Hammer, M. R. (1989). Intercultural communication competence. In M. K. Asante & W. B. Gudykunst (Eds.), *Handbook of international and intercultural communication* (pp. 247-260). Newbury Park, CA: Sage.

Hample, D. (1987). Communication and the unconscious. In B. Dervin & M. J. Voigt (Eds.), *Progress in communication sciences* (Vol. 8, pp. 83-121). Norwood, NJ: Ablex.

Hansel, B. (1993). *An investigation of the re-entry adjustment of Indians who studied in the U.S.A.* (Occasional Papers in Intercultural Learning No. 17). New York: AFS Center for the Study of Intercultural Learning.

Harris, L. (1979, May). *Communication competence: An argument for a systemic view.* Paper presented at the annual meeting of the International Communication Association, Philadelphia.

Harrison, J., Chadwick, M., & Scales, M. (1996). The relationship between cross-cultural adjustment and the personality variables of self-efficacy and self-monitoring. *International Journal of Intercultural Relations, 20,* 167-188.

Harwood, J., Giles, H., & Bourhis, R. Y. (1994). The genesis of vitality theory: Historical patterns and discoursal dimensions. *International Journal of the Sociology of Language, 108,* 167-206.

Haslett, B., & Alexander, A. (1988). Developing communication skills. In R. Hawkins, J. M. Wiemann, & S. Pingree (Eds.), *Advancing communication science: Merging mass and interpersonal processes* (pp. 224-252). Newbury Park, CA: Sage.

Havel, V. (1995, January-February). A time for transcendence. *Utne Reader, 53,* 112-113.

Hawes, F., & Kealey, D. (1981). An empirical study of Canadian technical assistance. *International Journal of Intercultural Relations, 5,* 239-258.

Hays, R. (1989). The day-to-day functioning of close versus casual friendships. *Journal of Social and Personal Relationships, 6,* 21-37.

Headland, T., Pike, K., & Harris, M. (1990). *Emics and etics: The insider/outsider debate.* Newbury Park, CA: Sage.

Healy, J., Jr., & Stewart, A. (1984). Adaptation to life changes in adolescence. In P. Karoly & J. Steffen (Eds.), *Adolescent behavior disorders: Foundations and contemporary concerns* (pp. 61-96). Lexington, MA: D. C. Heath.

Heath, D. (1965). *Explorations of maturity: Studies of mature and immature college men.* New York: Appleton-Century-Crofts.

Heath, D. (1977). *Maturity and competence: A transcultural view.* New York: Gardner.

Heckathorn, D. (1990). Collective sanctions and compliance norms: A formal theory of group-mediated social control. *American Sociological Review, 55,* 366-384.

Hegde, R. S. (1998). Swinging the trapeze: The negotiation of identity among Asian Indian immigrant women in the United States. In D. V. Tanno & A. González (Eds.), *Communication and identity across cultures* (pp. 34-55). Thousand Oaks, CA: Sage.

Herberg, E. (1989). *Ethnic groups in Canada: Adaptations and transitions.* Scarborough, ON: Nelson Canada.

Herman, S., & Schield, E. (1960). The stranger group in a cross-cultural situation. *Sociometry, 4,* 165-176.

Herskovits, M. (1958). *Acculturation: The study of culture contact.* Gloucester, MA: Peter Smith.

Herskovits, M. (1966). *Cultural dynamics.* New York: Alfred A. Knopf. (Original work published 1947)

Hettema, P. (1979). *Personality and adaptation.* New York: North-Holland.

Hevesi, D. (1991, December 28). Future cabbies may face tougher language exam. *New York Times,* p. B28.

Hirsch, B. (1981). Social networks and the coping process: Creating personal communities. In B. Gottlieb (Ed.), *Social networks and social support* (pp. 149-170). Beverly Hills, CA: Sage.

Ho, T., & Sung, K. (1990). Role of infrastructure networks in supporting social values to sustain economic success in newly-industrialized nations. *International Journal of Psychology, 25,* 887-900.

Hogg, M. A. (1996). Identity, cognition, and language in intergroup context. *Journal of Language and Social Psychology, 15,* 372-384.

Hogg, M. A., & Rigoli, N. (1996). Effects of ethnolinguistic vitality, ethnic identification, and linguistic contacts on minority language use. *Journal of Language and Social Psychology, 15,* 76-89.

Hoijer, H. (1985). The Sapir-Whorf hypothesis. In L. A. Samovar & R. E. Porter (Eds.), *Intercultural communication: A reader* (4th ed., pp. 210-217). Belmont, CA: Wadsworth.

Holmes, T., & Rahe, R. (1967). The social readjustment rating scale. *Journal of Psychometric Research, 11,* 213-218.

Holmgren, C., Fitzgerald, B., & Carman, R. (1983). Alienation and alcohol use by American Indian and Caucasian high school students. *Journal of Social Psychology, 120,* 139-140.

Holmsten, V. (1978, May 27). My two years in the Peace Corps. *Chicago Tribune,* sec. 1, p. 10.

Hong, L. (1976). Recent immigrants in the Chinese-American community: Issues of adaptations and impacts. *International Migration Review, 10,* 509-514.

Horowitz, M. J. (1991). Person schemas. In M. J. Horowitz (Ed.), *Person schemas and maladaptive interpersonal patterns* (pp. 13-31). Chicago: University of Chicago Press.

Horton, D., & Wohl, R. (1979). Mass communication and para-social interaction: Observations on intimacy at a distance. In G. Gumpert & R. Cathcart (Eds.), *Inter/media: Interpersonal communication in a media world* (pp. 32-55). New York: Oxford University Press.

Houston, J. W. (1981, May 14). *Beyond Manzanar: A personal view on Asian-American womanhood.* Guest lecture delivered at Governors State University, University Park, IL.

Hsu, F. (1981). *The challenge of the American dream: The Chinese in the United States.* Belmont, CA: Wadsworth.

Hsu, T., Grant, A., & Huang, W. (1993). The influence of social networks on the acculturation behavior of foreign students. *Connections, 16*(1-2), 23-30.

Hunter, E. (1960). *In many voices: Our fabulous foreign-language press.* Norman Park, CA: Norman College.

Hurh, W., & Kim, K. C. (1990). Adaptation stages and mental health of Korean male immigrants in the United States. *International Migration Review, 24,* 456-479.

Hurst, J. (1977, October 30). Ja, Chicago still has lots of German soul. *Chicago Tribune Magazine,* pp. 22-26, 48-50.

Hutnik, N. (1986). Patterns of ethnic minority identification and modes of social adaptation. *Ethnic and Racial Studies, 9,* 150-167.

Hutnik, N., & Bhola, P. (1994, July). *Self-categorization and response to threat.* Paper presented at the Fifth International Conference on Language and Social Psychology, Brisbane, Queensland.

Hymes, D. (1979). On communicative competence. In J. Pride & J. Holmes (Eds.), *Sociolinguistics* (pp. 269-293). New York: Penguin.

Igoa, C. (1995). *The inner world of the immigrant child.* Hillsdale, NJ: Lawrence Erlbaum.

Imahori, T., & Lanigan, M. (1989). Relational model of intercultural communication competence. *International Journal of Intercultural Relations, 13,* 269-286.

Inglis, M., & Gudykunst, W. B. (1982). Institutional completeness and communication acculturation: A comparison of Korean immigrants in Chicago and Hartford. *International Journal of Intercultural Relations, 6,* 251-272.

Ireland, P. (1994). *The policy challenge of ethnic diversity: Immigrant politics in France and Switzerland.* Cambridge, MA: Harvard University Press.

Jaeger, S., & Sandu, H. (1985). *Southeast Asian refugees: English language development and acculturation.* Rosslyn, VA: National Clearinghouse for Bilingual Education.

Jahoda, M. (1958). *Current concepts of positive mental health.* New York: Basic Books.

Janofsky, M. (1997, July 6). Amish life is changing, but slowly. *New York Times,* p. A7.

Jantsch, E. (1980). *The self-organizing universe: Scientific and human implications of the emerging paradigm of evolution.* New York: Pergamon.

Jaret, C. (1979). The Greek, Italian, and Jewish American ethnic press: A comparative analysis. *Journal of Ethnic Studies, 7*(2), 47-70.

Jaspars, J., & Hewstone, M. (1982). Cross-cultural interaction, social attribution and inter-group relations. In S. Bochner (Ed.), *Cultures in contact: Studies in cross-cultural interaction* (pp. 127-156). New York: Pergamon.

Jeffres, L., & Hur, K. (1981). Communication channels within ethnic groups. *International Journal of Intercultural Relations, 5,* 115-132.

Joas, H. (1993). *Pragmatism and social theory.* Chicago: University of Chicago Press.

Jones, F. (1987). Age at immigration and education: Further explorations. *International Migration Review, 21,* 70-85.

Jones, S. (1979). Integrating etic and emic approaches in the study of intercultural communication. In M. K. Asante, E. Newmark, & C. Blake (Eds.), *Handbook of intercultural communication* (pp. 57-74). Beverly Hills, CA: Sage.

Jou, Y., & Fukada, H. (1995). Effects of social support on adjustment of Chinese students in Japan. *Journal of Social Psychology, 135,* 39-47.

Jourard, S. (1974). Growing awareness and the awareness of growth. In B. Patton & K. Griffin (Eds.), *Interpersonal communication* (pp. 456-465). New York: Harper & Row.

Jung, C. G. (1959). *The archetypes and the collective unconscious.* Princeton, NJ: Bollingen Series.

Jung, C. G., with von Franz, M.-L., Henderson, J. L., Jacobi, J., & Jaffé, A. (1964). *Man and his symbols.* Garden City, NY: Doubleday.

Kagan, J. (1984). *The nature of the child.* New York: Basic Books.

Kahane, R. (1986). Informal agencies of socialization and the integration of immigrant youth into society: An example from Israel. *International Migration Review, 20,* 21-39.

Kalbach, W., & Richard, M. (1990). *Ethnic connectedness and the gender gap.* Paper presented at the annual meeting of the Canadian Sociological and Anthropological Association, Victoria, BC.

Kamali, A. (1987). The process of adjustment: An analysis of some correlates affecting the adjustment process of individuals in a new environment. *Dissertation Abstracts International, 47*(09), 3566A. (University Microfilms No. AAC87-00485)

Kameda, T., Ohtsubo, Y., & Takezawa, M. (1997). Centrality in sociocognitive networks and social influence: An illustration in a group decision-making context. *Journal of Personality and Social Psychology, 73,* 296-310.

Kantima, K. (1982). *Communication patterns of Thai students in the process of acculturation.* Unpublished doctoral dissertation, University of Oklahoma, Norman.

Kao, C. (1975). *Search for maturity.* Philadelphia: Westminster.

Kapoor, S., & Williams, W., Jr. (1979, May). *Acculturation of foreign students by television: A Q methodology approach.* Paper presented at the annual meeting of the International Communication Association, Philadelphia.

Karl, R. (1984). A-doka. In AFS International/Intercultural Programs (Ed.), *Occasional papers in intercultural learning, no. 6* (pp. 3, 17-24). New York: AFS International/Intercultural Programs.

Kauffman, S. (1995). *At home in the universe: The search for the laws of self-organization and complexity.* New York: Oxford University Press.

Kauffmann, N., Martin, J., & Weaver, H., with Weaver, J. (1992). *Students abroad: Strangers at home.* Yarmouth, ME: Intercultural Press.

Kealey, D. (1989). A study of cross-cultural effectiveness: Theoretical issues, practical applications. *International Journal of Intercultural Relations, 13,* 387-428.

Kealey, D., & Ruben, B. D. (1983). Cross-cultural personnel selection criteria, issues and methods. In D. Landis & R. W. Brislin (Eds.), *Handbook of intercultural training: Vol. 1. Issues in theory and design* (pp. 155-175). New York: Pergamon.

Keenan, B. (1992). *An evil cradling: The five-year ordeal of a hostage.* New York: Viking.

Keene, D. (1994). *On familiar terms: A journey across cultures.* New York: Kodansha International.

Kelly, G. (1955). *The psychology of personal constructs.* New York: W. W. Norton.

Kelly, J. (1985, July 8). To the land of free speech. *Time,* pp. 95-97.

Kemnitzer, L. (1973). Adjustment and value conflict in urbanizing Dakota Indians measured by Q sort techniques. *American Anthropologist, 75,* 687-707.

Kennedy, G. (1991a). Foreword. In G. Kennedy (Ed.), *From the center of the earth: Stories out of the Peace Corps* (pp. 9-12). Santa Monica, CA: Clover Park.

Kennedy, G. (Ed.). (1991b). *From the center of the earth: Stories out of the Peace Corps.* Santa Monica, CA: Clover Park.

Kim, H. K. (1991). Influence of language and similarity on initial intercultural attraction. In S. Ting-Toomey & F. Korzenny (Eds.), *Cross-cultural interpersonal communication* (pp. 213-229). Newbury Park, CA: Sage.

Kim, H. S. (1991). Coorientation and communication. In B. Dervin & M. J. Voigt (Eds.), *Progress in communication sciences* (Vol. 7, pp. 31-54). Norwood, NJ: Ablex.

Kim, J. (1980). Explaining acculturation in a communication framework: An empirical test. *Communication Monographs, 47,* 155-179.

Kim, J., Lee, B., & Jeong, W. (1982, July). *Uses of mass media in acculturation: Dependency, information preference, and gratifications.* Paper presented at the annual meeting of the Association for Education in Journalism, Athens, OH.

Kim, Y. Y. (1976). *Communication patterns of foreign immigrants in the process of acculturation: A survey among the Korean population in Chicago.* Unpublished doctoral dissertation, Northwestern University.

Kim, Y. Y. (1977). Communication patterns of foreign immigrants in the process of acculturation. *Human Communication Research, 4,* 66-77.

Kim, Y. Y. (1978a, November). *Acculturation and patterns of interpersonal communication relationships: A study of Japanese, Mexican, and Korean communities in the Chicago area.* Paper presented at the annual meeting of the Speech Communication Association, Minneapolis.

Kim, Y. Y. (1978b). A communication approach to acculturation processes: Korean immigrants in Chicago. *International Journal of Intercultural Relations, 2,* 197-224.

Kim, Y. Y. (1978c). Interethnic and intraethnic communication: A study of Korean immigrants in Chicago. In N. Jain (Ed.), *International and intercultural communication annual* (Vol. 4, pp. 53-68). Falls Church, VA: Speech Communication Association.

Kim, Y. Y. (1979a, November). *Dynamics of intrapersonal and interpersonal communication: A study of Indochinese refugees in the initial phase of acculturation.* Paper presented at the annual meeting of the Speech Communication Association, San Antonio, TX.

Kim, Y. Y. (1979b, May). *Mass media and acculturation: Toward development of an interactive theory.* Paper presented at the annual meeting of the Eastern Communication Association, Philadelphia.

Kim, Y. Y. (1979c). Toward an interactive theory of communication-acculturation. In D. Nimmo (Ed.), *Communication yearbook 3* (pp. 435-453). New Brunswick, NJ: Transaction.

Kim, Y. Y. (1980). *Indochinese refugees in Illinois* (5 vols.) (Research report submitted to the Department of Health, Education and Welfare Region V, Grant P: 95-549). Chicago: Travelers Aid Society.

Kim, Y. Y. (1986). Understanding the social context of intergroup communication: A personal network approach. In W. B. Gudykunst (Ed.), *Intergroup communication* (pp. 86-95). London: Edward Arnold.

Kim, Y. Y. (1987). Facilitating immigrant adaptation: The role of communication and interpersonal ties. In T. L. Albrecht & M. B. Adelman (Eds.), *Communicating social support: Process in context* (pp. 192-211). Newbury Park, CA: Sage.

Kim, Y. Y. (1988). *Communication and cross-cultural adaptation: An integrative theory.* Clevedon, England: Multilingual Matters.

Kim, Y. Y. (1989). Personal, social, and economic adaptation: The case of 1975-1979 arrivals in Illinois. In D. Haines (Ed.), *Refugees as immigrants: Survey research on Cambodians, Laotians, and Vietnamese in America* (pp. 86-104). Totowa, NJ: Rowman & Littlefield.

Kim, Y. Y. (1990). Communication and adaptation of Asian Pacific refugees in the United States. *Journal of Pacific Rim Communication, 1,* 191-207.

Kim, Y. Y. (1991). Intercultural communication competence: A systems-theoretic view. In S. Ting-Toomey & F. Korzenny (Eds.), *Cross-cultural interpersonal communication* (pp. 259-275). Newbury Park, CA: Sage.

Kim, Y. Y. (1993, May). *Synchrony and intercultural communication competence: A theoretical exploration.* Paper presented at the annual meeting of the International Communication Association, Washington, DC.

Kim, Y. Y. (1994). Interethnic communication: The context and the behavior. In S. A. Deetz (Ed.), *Communication yearbook 17* (pp. 511-538). Thousand Oaks, CA: Sage.

Kim, Y. Y. (1995a). Cross-cultural adaptation: An integrative theory. In R. L. Wiseman (Ed.), *Intercultural communication theory* (pp. 170-193). Thousand Oaks, CA: Sage.

Kim, Y. Y. (1995b). Identity development: From cultural to intercultural. In H. B. Mokros (Ed.), *Interaction and identity* (pp. 347-369). New Brunswick, NJ: Transaction.

Kim, Y. Y. (1997a). The behavior-context interface in interethnic communication. In J. Owen (Ed.), *Context and communication behavior* (pp. 261-291). Reno, NV: Context.

Kim, Y. Y. (1997b). Intercultural personhood: An integration of Eastern and Western perspectives. In L. A. Samovar & R. E. Porter (Eds.), *Intercultural communication: A reader* (8th ed., pp. 434-447). Belmont, CA: Wadsworth.

Kim, Y. Y. (1999). Unum and pluribus: Ideological underpinnings of interethnic communication in the United States. *International Journal of Intercultural Relations, 34,* 591-611.

Kim, Y. Y., Lujan, P., & Dixon, L. (1998a). "I can walk both ways": Identity integration of American Indians in Oklahoma. *Human Communication Research, 25,* 252-274.

Kim, Y. Y., Lujan, P., & Dixon, L. (1998b). Patterns of communication and interethnic integration: A study of American Indians in Oklahoma. *Canadian Journal of Native Education, 22*(1), 120-137.

Kim, Y. Y., & Paulk, S. (1994a). Intercultural challenges and personal adjustments: A qualitative analysis of the communication experiences of American and Japanese coworkers. In R. L. Wiseman & R. Shutter (Eds.), *Communicating in multinational organizations* (pp. 117-140). Thousand Oaks, CA: Sage.

Kim, Y. Y., & Paulk, S. (1994b, November). *Intercultural communication in a multinational organization: A replication study.* Paper presented at the annual meeting of the Speech Communication Association, New Orleans, LA.

Kim, Y. Y., & Ruben, B. D. (1988). Intercultural transformation: A systems theory. In Y. Y. Kim & W. B. Gudykunst (Eds.), *Theories in intercultural communication* (pp. 299-321). Newbury Park, CA: Sage.

Kincaid, D. (1988). The convergence theory and intercultural communication. In Y. Y. Kim & W. B. Gudykunst (Eds.), *Theories in intercultural communication* (pp. 280-298). Newbury Park, CA: Sage.

Kincaid, D., Yum, J., Woelfel, J., & Barnett, G. (1983). The cultural convergence of Korean immigrants in Hawaii: An empirical test of a mathematical theory. *Quality and Quantity, 18,* 59-78.

King, S. (1984, June). *Natural helping networks among ethnic groups in Hawaii: Yearbook II. Help seeking behavior survey.* Washington, DC: National Institute of Mental Health.

Kino, F. (1973). Aliens' paranoid reaction. In C. Zwingmann & M. Pfister-Ammende (Eds.), *Uprooting and after . . .* (pp. 60-66). New York: Springer-Verlag.

Kinzie, J., Tran, K., Breckenridge, A., & Bloom, J. (1980). An Indochinese refugee psychiatric clinic: Culturally accepted treatment approaches. *American Journal of Psychiatry, 137,* 1429-1432.

Kirby, J. (1989). Overseas Chinese: An accent on harmony. *Free China Review, 39*(7), 4-9.

Kirkland, S., Greenberg, J., & Pysczynski, T. (1987). Further evidence of the deleterious effects of overheard DELs: Derogation beyond the target. *Personality and Social Psychological Bulletin, 13,* 126-227.

Kirschner, G. (1994). Equilibrium processes: Creativity and depression. *Mind and Human Interaction, 5*(4), 165-171.

Kleiner, R., & Parker, S. (1969). Social-psychological aspects of migration and mental disorder in a Negro population. In E. Brody (Ed.), *Behavior in new environments: Adaptation of migrant populations* (pp. 353-374). Beverly Hills, CA: Sage.

Klineberg, O., & Hull, W., IV. (1979). *At a foreign university: An international study of adaptation and coping.* New York: Praeger.

Knoke, D., & Kuklinski, J. (1982). *Network analysis.* Beverly Hills, CA: Sage.

Koenig, H. (1990, February). *Tie strength: A new wrinkle on an old friend.* Paper presented at the International Sunbelt Social Network Conference, San Diego, CA.

Koester, J., & Olebe, M. (1988). The behavioral assessment scale for intercultural communication effectiveness. *International Journal of Intercultural Relations, 12,* 233-246.

Koestler, A. (1967). *The ghost in the machine.* New York: Macmillan.

Kogon, E. (1958). *The theory and practice of hell.* New York: Berkeley Medallion.

Korzybski, A. (1958). *Science and sanity* (4th ed.). Lakeville, CT: International Non-Aristolelian Library.

Kramarae, C., Schulz, M., & O'Barr, W. M. (1984). Introduction: Toward an understanding of language and power. In C. Kramarae, M. Schulz, & W. M. O'Barr (Eds.), *Language and power* (pp. 9-22). Beverly Hills, CA: Sage.

Krashen, S. (1981). *Second language acquisition and second language learning.* New York: Pergamon.

Krau, E. (1991). *The contradictory immigrant problem: A sociopsychological analysis.* New York: Peter Lang.

Krause, C. (1978). Urbanization without breakdown: Italian, Jewish and Slavic immigrant women in Pittsburgh, 1900-1945. *Journal of Urban History, 4,* 291-306.

Kraybill, D. (1995). *Amish enterprise: From ploughs to profits.* Baltimore: Johns Hopkins University Press.

Kroger, J. (1993). On the nature of structural transition in the identity formation process. In J. Kroger (Ed.), *Discussions on ego identity* (pp. 205-234). Hillsdale, NJ: Lawrence Erlbaum.

Krueger, R. A. (1988). *Focus groups: A practical guide for applied research.* Newbury Park, CA: Sage.

Krull, R., & Paulson, A. (1977). Time series analysis in communication research. In P. Hirsch, P. Miller, & F. G. Kline (Eds.), *Strategies for communication research* (pp. 231-256). Beverly Hills, CA: Sage.

Kuhn, A. (1975). Social organization. In B. D. Ruben & J. Y. Kim (Eds.), *General systems theory and human communication* (pp. 114-127). Rochelle Park, NJ: Hayden.

Kurth, S. (1970). Friendships and friendly relations. In G. McNall (Ed.), *Social relationships* (pp. 136-170). Chicago: Aldine.

Lam, L. (1980). The role of ethnic media for immigrants: A case study of Chinese immigrants and their media in Toronto. *Canadian Ethnic Studies, 12*(1), 74-92.

Lambert, W. (1979). Language as a factor in inter-group relations. In H. Giles & R. St. Clair (Eds.), *Language and social psychology* (pp. 186-192). Baltimore: University Park Press.

Lamphere, L. (Ed.). (1992). *Structuring diversity: Ethnographic perspectives on the new immigration.* Chicago: University of Chicago Press.

Lanca, M., Alksnis, C., Roese, N. J., & Gardner, R. C. (1994). Effects of language choice on acculturation: A study of Portuguese immigrants in a multicultural setting. *Journal of Language and Social Psychology, 13,* 315-330.

Landis, D., & Bhagat, R. S. (Eds.). (1996). *Handbook of intercultural training* (2nd ed.). Thousand Oaks, CA: Sage.

Landry, R., & Bourhis, R. Y. (1997). Linguistic landscape and ethnolinguistic vitality: An empirical study. *Journal of Language and Social Psychology, 16,* 23-49.

Langsdorf, L., & Smith, A. (Ed.). (1995). *Recovering pragmatism's voice: The classical tradition, Rorty, and the philosophy of communication.* Albany: State University of New York Press.

Lanigan, R. (1988). *Phenomenology of communication: Merleau-Ponty's thematics in communicology and semiology.* Pittsburgh, PA: Duquesne University Press.

Lapierre, D. (1985). *The city of joy.* New York: Warner/Doubleday.

LaRose, C., & Gebart-Eaglemont, J. (1994, July). *The effects of problem-solving ability and linguistic aspects of acculturation and life satisfaction in two immigrant population.* Paper presented at the Fifth International Conference on Language and Social Psychology, Brisbane, Queensland.

Lasswell, H. (1964). The structure and function of communication in society. In L. Bryson (Ed.), *The communication of ideas* (pp. 37-51). New York: Cooper Systems. (Original work published 1948)

Laszlo, E. (1972). *The systems view of the world.* New York: George Braziller.

Laumann, E. (1973). *Bonds of pluralism: The form and substance of urban social networks.* New York: John Wiley.

Lauver, P., & Schram, J. (1988). Alienation in international students. *Journal of College Student Development, 29,* 146-150.

Lazarus, R. (1966). *Psychological stress and the coping process.* St. Louis, MO: McGraw-Hill.

Lazarus, R., Cohen, J., Folkman, S., Kanner, A., & Schnefer, C. (1980). Psychological stress and adaptation: Some unresolved issues. In H. Selye (Ed.), *Selye's guide to stress research* (Vol. 1, pp. 90-117). New York: Van Nostrand Reinhold.

Lee, W. (1994). Communication about humor as procedural competence in intercultural encounters. In L. A. Samovar & R. E. Porter (Eds.), *Intercultural communication: A reader* (7th ed., pp. 373-382). Belmont, CA: Wadsworth.

Leenders, R. (1996). Evolution of friendship and best friendship choices. *Journal of Mathematical Sociology, 21*(1-2), 133-148.

Leets, L., & Giles, H. (1995). Intergroup cognition and communication climates: New dimensions of minority language maintenance. In W. Fase, K. Jaspaert, & S. Kroon (Eds.), *The state of minority languages: International perspectives on survival and decline* (pp. 37-74). Lisse, Netherlands: Swets & Zeitlinger.

Lefcourt, H. (1984). Locus of control and stressful life events. In B. Dohrenwend & B. Dohrenwend (Eds.), *Stressful life events and their contexts* (pp. 157-166). New Brunswick, NJ: Rutgers University Press.

Lehnen, R., & Koch, G. (1974). Analyzing panel data with uncontrolled attrition. *Public Opinion Quarterly, 38,* 40-56.

Lepkowski, J. (1989). Treatment of wave nonresponse in panel surveys. In D. Kasprzyk, G. Duncan, G. Kalton, & M. Singh (Eds.), *Panel surveys* (pp. 348-374). New York: John Wiley.

Leslie, L. (1992). The role of informal support networks in the adjustment of Central American immigrant families. *Journal of Community Psychology, 20,* 243-256.

Leuthold, S. (1991, November). *Aesthetics and cultural identification in environments of cultural contact and change.* Paper presented at the annual meeting of the Speech Communication Association, Atlanta.

Levine, D. (1992). The sociology of the stranger. In W. B. Gudykunst & Y. Y. Kim (Eds.), *Readings on intercultural communication* (pp. 33-46). New York: McGraw-Hill. (Original work published 1979)

Levine, R., & Campbell, D. (1972). *Ethnocentrism: Theories of conflict, ethnic attitudes and group behavior.* New York: John Wiley.

Lewin, K. (1951). *Field theory in social science.* New York: Harper & Row.

Lewin, P. (1992, January 8). Study points to increase in tolerance of ethnicity. *New York Times,* p. A12.

Lewis, M. (1948). *Language and society.* New York: Social Science.

Lewis, T., & Jungman, R. (Eds.). (1986). *On being foreign: Culture shock in short fiction.* Yarmouth, ME: Intercultural Press.

Lifton, R. J. (1993). *The Protean self: Human resilience in an age of fragmentation.* New York: Basic Books.

Limonov, E. (1990). Thirteen studies on exile. In J. Glad (Ed.), *Literature in exile* (pp. 49-58). Durham, NC: Duke University Press.

Lincoln, Y. S., & Guba, E. G. (1985). *Naturalistic inquiry.* Beverly Hills, CA: Sage.

Lind, M. (1995). *The next American nation: The new nationalism and the fourth American revolution.* New York: Free Press.

Lindgren, H., & Yu, R. (1975). Cross-cultural insight and empathy among Chinese immigrants to the U.S. *Journal of Social Psychology, 96,* 305-306.

Little, R., & Su, H. (1989). Item nonresponse in panel surveys. In D. Kasprzyk, G. Duncan, G. Kalton, & M. Singh (Eds.), *Panel surveys* (pp. 400-425). New York: John Wiley.

Liu Z. (1984). *Two years in the melting pot.* San Francisco: China.

Lukens, J. (1979). Interethnic conflict and communicative distance. In H. Giles & B. Saint-Jacques (Eds.), *Language and ethnic relations* (pp. 143-158). New York: Pergamon.

Lum, M. (1991). Communication and cultural insularity: The Chinese immigrant experience. *Critical Studies in Mass Communication, 8,* 91-101.

Lutzker, D. (1960). Internationalism as a predictor of cooperative behavior. *Journal of Conflict Resolution, 4,* 426-430.

Lvovich, N. (1997). *The multilingual self: An inquiry into language learning.* Mahwah, NJ: Lawrence Erlbaum.

Mackey, W. (1979). Language policy and language planning. *Journal of Communication, 29*(2), 48-53.

MacKinnon, D. W. (1978). *In search of human effectiveness: Identifying and developing creativity.* Buffalo, NY: Creative Education Foundation.

Mansell, M. (1981). Transcultural experience and expressive response. *Communication Education, 30,* 93-108.

Maquet, J. (1979). *Introduction to aesthetic anthropology.* Malibu, CA: Undena.

Marcia, J. (1993). The relational roots of identity. In J. Kroger (Ed.), *Discussions on ego identity* (pp. 101-120). Hillsdale, NJ: Lawrence Erlbaum.

Marden, C., & Meyer, G. (1968). *Minorities in America* (3rd ed.). New York: Van Nostrand Reinhold.

Marmot, M., & Syme, S. (1976). Acculturation and coronary heart disease in Japanese-Americans. *American Journal of Epidemiology, 104,* 225-247.

Marrett, C. B., & Leggon, C. (Eds.). (1982). *Research in race and ethnic relations* (Vol. 3). Greenwich, CT: JAI.

Marsden, P. (1993). The reliability of network density and composition measures. *Social Networks, 15,* 399-421.

Marsden, P., & Campbell, K. (1983, September). *Measuring tie strength.* Paper presented at the annual meeting of the American Sociological Association, Detroit, MI.

Marshall, C., & Rossman, G. B. (1989). *Designing qualitative research.* Newbury Park, CA: Sage.

Martin, J. (1984). The intercultural reentry: Conceptualization and directions for future research. *International Journal of Intercultural Relations, 8,* 115-134.

Martin, J., Bradford, L., & Rohrlich, B. (1995). Comparing pre-departure expectations and post-sojourn reports: A longitudinal study of U.S. students abroad. *International Journal of Intercultural Relations, 19,* 87-110.

Maruyama, M. (1998). *Cross-cultural adaptation and host environment: A study of international students in Japan.* Unpublished doctoral dissertation, University of Oklahoma, Norman.

Maruyama, M., & Kim, Y. Y. (1997, May). *Cross-cultural adaptation of international students in Japan: An exploratory survey.* Paper presented at the annual meeting of the International Communication Association, Montreal.

Marzolf, M. (1973, August). *America's enduring ethnic press.* Paper presented at the annual meeting of the Association for Education in Journalism, Ft. Collins, CO.

Marzolf, M. (1979). *The Danish-language press in America.* New York: Arno.

Maslow, A. H. (1969). A theory of metamotivation: The biological rooting of the value-life. In H. Chiang & A. H. Maslow (Eds.), *The healthy personality* (pp. 35-56). New York: Van Nostrand Reinhold.

Maslow, A. H. (1970). *Motivation and personality* (2nd ed.). New York: Harper & Row.

Massey, D. (1987). Understanding Mexican migration to the United States. *American Journal of Sociology, 92,* 1372-1403.

Masterpasqua, F., & Perna, P. (1997). *The psychological meaning of chaos: Translating theory into practice.* Washington, DC: American Psychological Association.

Masuda, M., Matsumoto, G., & Meredith, G. (1970). Ethnic identity in three generations of Japanese Americans. *Journal of Social Psychology, 81,* 199-207.

McAllister, I. (1986). Speaking the language: Maintenance and English proficiency among immigrant youth in Australia. *Ethnic and Racial Studies, 9,* 24-42.

McCauley, T. (1991, June). *Social change in a bi-cultural community: A case study of Penetanguishene.* Paper presented at the annual meeting of the Canadian Society for Sociology and Anthropology, Kingston, ON.

McConahay, J., & Hough, J. (1976). Symbolic racism. *Journal of Social Issues, 32*(1), 23-45.

McCracken, G. (1988). *The long interview.* Newbury Park, CA: Sage.

McCrae, R. R., & Costa, P. T., Jr. (1985). Openness to experience. In R. Hogan & W. Jones (Eds.), *Perspectives in personality* (Vol. 1, pp. 145-172). Greenwich, CT: JAI.

McCroskey, J. C., & Richmond, V. P. (1991). Willingness to communicate: A cognitive view. In M. Booth-Butterfield (Ed.), *Communication, cognition, and anxiety* (pp. 19-37). Newbury Park, CA: Sage.

McDermott, V. (1980). Interpersonal communication networks: An approach through the understanding of self-concept, significant others, and the social influence process. *Communication Quarterly, 28,* 13-25.

McEvoy-Jamil, P. (1996). Acculturation, second language acquisition, and academic environment: A neo-ethnographic case study of an international student's coping strategies and academic achievement (Doctoral dissertation, University of San Francisco University, 1996) [Abstract]. *Connections, 20*(1), 64.

McGrath, J. E. (1982). Dilemmatics: The study of research choices and dilemmas. In J. E. McGrath, J. Martin, & R. A. Kulka (Eds.), *Judgment calls in research* (pp. 69-128). Beverly Hills, CA: Sage.

McKay, J. (1989). *Phoenician farewell: Three generations of Lebanese Christians in Australia.* Melbourne: Ashwood House.

McKeown, B., & Thomas, D. (1988). *Q methodology.* Newbury Park, CA: Sage.

McLuhan, M. (1962). *The Gutenberg galaxy.* New York: New American Library.

McPherson, J. (1991, February). *Opportunities for contact and network diversity: Further explorations of homophily in voluntary organizations.* Paper presented at the International Sunbelt Social Network Conference, Tampa, FL.

Mead, M. (1964). *Continuities in cultural evolution.* New Haven, CT: Yale University Press.

Mechanic, D. (1974). Social structure and personal adaptation: Some neglected dimensions. In G. Coelho, D. Hamburg, & J. Adams (Eds.), *Coping and adaptation* (pp. 32-44). New York: Basic Books.

Melchior, L. A., & Cheek, J. M. (1991). Shyness and anxious self-preoccupation during a social interaction. In M. Booth-Butterfield (Ed.), *Communication, cognition, and anxiety* (pp. 117-130). Newbury Park, CA: Sage.

Menard, S. (1991). *Longitudinal research.* Newbury Park, CA: Sage.

Mendenhall, M., & Oddou, G. (1985). The dimensions of expatriate acculturation. *Academy of Management Review, 10*(1), 39-47.

Mercer, N., Mead, E., & Mears, R. (1979). Linguistic and cultural affiliation among young Asian people in Leicester. In H. Giles & B. St. Jacques (Eds.), *Language and ethnic relations* (pp. 15-26). Oxford: Pergamon.

Mezirow, J. (1984). A critical theory of adult learning and education. In S. Merriam (Ed.), *Selected writings on philosophy and adult education* (pp. 123-139). Malabar, FL: Robert E. Krieger.

Mezirow, J. (1991). *Transformative dimensions of adult learning.* San Francisco: Jossey-Bass.

Meznaric, S. (1984). Sociology of migration in Yugoslavia. *Current Sociology, 32,* 41-59.

Mifflin, L. (1996, February 11). ABC sends a young point of view into the field: Up and coming Anderson Cooper. *New York Times,* p. H32.

Miles, M. B., & Huberman, A. M. (1994). *Qualitative data analysis: An expanded sourcebook* (2nd ed.). Thousand Oaks, CA: Sage.

Miller, L. (1991). Verbal listening behavior in conversation between Japanese and Americans. In J. Blommaert & J. Verschueren (Eds.), *The pragmatics of international and intercultural communication* (pp. 111-130). Amsterdam: John Benjamins.

Miller, M. (1988). *Reflections on reentry after teaching in China* (Occasional Papers in Intercultural Learning No. 14). New York: AFS Center for the Study of Intercultural Learning.

Miller, S. M. (1987). *The ethnic press in the United States: A historical analysis and handbook.* Westport, CT: Greenwood.

Milroy, L. (1980). *Language and social networks.* Baltimore: University Park Press.

Milroy, L. (1982). Social network and linguistic focusing. In S. Romaine (Ed.), *Sociolinguistic variation in speech communities* (pp. 141-152). London: Edward Arnold.

Milroy, L. (1987). *Language and social networks* (2nd ed.). Oxford, UK: Basil Blackwell.

Minatoya, L. (1992). *Talking to high monks in the snow: An Asian American odyssey.* New York: HarperCollins.

Miranda, M., & Castro, F. (1977). Culture distance and success in psychotherapy with Spanish speaking clients. In J. Martinez, Jr. (Ed.), *Chicano psychology* (pp. 249-262). New York: Academic Press.

Mirowsky, J., & Ross, C. E. (1983, September). *Language networks and social status among Mexican Americans.* Paper presented at the annual meeting of the American Sociological Association, Detroit, MI.

Mishra, R. C., Sinha, D., & Berry, J. W. (1996). *Ecology, acculturation, and psychological adaptation: A study of Adivasis in Bihar.* Thousand Oaks, CA: Sage.

Mitchell, C. (1994). Situational analysis and network analysis. *Connections, 17*(1), 16-22.

Monge, P. R. (1973). Theory construction in the study of communication: The system paradigm. *Journal of Communication, 23*(1), 5-16.

Monge, P. R. (1977). The systems perspective as a theoretical basis for the study of human communication. *Communication Quarterly, 25,* 19-29.

Monge, P. R. (1990). Theoretical and analytical issues in studying organizational processes. *Organization Science, 1,* 406-430.

Monge, P. R., & Contractor, N. S. (1988). Communication networks: Measurement techniques. In C. H. Tardy (Ed.), *A handbook for the study of human communication: Methods and instruments for observing, measuring, and assessing communication processes* (pp. 107-138). Norwood, NJ: Ablex.

Montalvo, F. (1991). Phenotyping, acculturation, and biracial assimilation of Mexican Americans. In M. Sotomayor (Ed.), *Empowering Hispanic families:*

A critical issue for the '90s (pp. 97-119). Milwaukee, WI: Family Service America.

Moos, R. (1974). Psychological techniques in the assessment of adaptive behavior. In G. Coelho, D. Hamburg, & J. Adams (Eds.), *Coping and adaptation* (pp. 334-399). New York: Basic Books.

Moos, R. (Ed.). (1976). *Human adaptation: Coping with life crises.* Lexington, MA: D. C. Heath.

Moos, R. (Ed.). (1986). *Coping with life crises.* New York: Plenum.

Moos, R., & Mitchell, R. (1982). Social network resources and adaptation: A conceptual framework. In T. Wills (Ed.), *Basic processes in helping relationships* (pp. 213-232). New York: Academic Press.

Moos, R., & Tsu, V. (1976). Human competence and coping. In R. Moos (Ed.), *Human adaptation: Coping with life crises* (pp. 3-16). Lexington, MA: D. C. Heath.

Morgan, D. L. (1988). *Focus groups as qualitative research.* Newbury Park, CA: Sage.

Morgan, D. L., Neal, M. B., & Carder, P. (1997). The stability of core and peripheral networks over time. *Social Networks, 19,* 9-25.

Morgan, N. (1987). *Language maintenance and shift among Haitians in the Dominican Republic.* Unpublished doctoral dissertation, University of New Mexico, Albuquerque.

Morris, R. (1960). *The two-way mirror.* Minneapolis: University of Minnesota Press.

Mortland, C., & Ledgerwood, J. (1988). Refugee resource acquisition: The invisible communication system. In Y. Y. Kim & W. B. Gudykunst (Eds.), *Cross-cultural adaptation: Current approaches* (pp. 286-306). Newbury Park, CA: Sage.

Moustakas, C. (1977). *Creative life.* New York: Van Nostrand Reinhold.

Mullen, W. (1984, July 1). Starting over. *Sunday: The Chicago Tribune Magazine,* pp. 8, 13-15, 19.

Mura, D. (1991). *Turning Japanese: Memoirs of a sansei.* New York: Atlantic Monthly Press.

Murphy-Shigematsu, S. (1987). The voices of Amerasians: Ethnicity, identity, and empowerment in interracial Japanese Americans (Doctoral dissertation, Harvard University, 1987). *Dissertation Abstracts International, 48,* 1143B.

Murray, A., & Sondhi, R. (1987). Socio-political influences on cross-cultural encounters: Notes towards a framework for the analysis of context. In K. Knapp, W. Enninger, & A. Knapp-Potthoff (Eds.), *Analyzing intercultural communication* (pp. 17-33). New York: Mouton de Gruyter.

Nagata, G. (1969). *A statistical approach to the study of acculturation of an ethnic group based on communication oriented variables: The case of Japanese Americans in*

Chicago. Unpublished doctoral dissertation, University of Illinois, Urbana-Champaign.

Namazi, K. (1984). Assimilation and need assessment among Mexican, Cuban, and Middle Eastern immigrants: A multivariate analysis. *Dissertation Abstracts International, 45*(03), 949A. (University Microfilms No. DA84-14649)

Nash, M. (1989). *The cauldron of ethnicity in the modern world*. Chicago: University of Chicago Press.

Neidert, L., & Farley, R. (1985). Assimilation in the United States: An analysis of ethnic and generation differences in status and achievement. *American Sociological Review, 50*, 840-850.

Neumann, M. (1992). The trail through experience: Finding self in the recollection of travel. In C. Ellis & M. G. Flaherty (Eds.), *Investigating subjectivity: Research on lived experience* (pp. 176-201). Newbury Park, CA: Sage.

Nishida, H. (1985). Japanese intercultural communication competence and cross-cultural adjustment. *International Journal of Intercultural Relations, 9*, 247-269.

Noels, K., Pon, G., & Clément, R. (1996). Language, identity, and adjustment: The role of linguistic self-confidence in the acculturation process. *Journal of Language and Social Psychology, 15*, 246-264.

Norrick, N. (1991). On the organization of corrective exchange in conversation. *Journal of Pragmatics, 16*, 59-83.

Novak, M. (1971). *The rise of the unmeltable ethnics*. New York: Macmillan.

Novak, M. (1973, May-June). The new ethnicity. *Humanist*, pp. 18-21.

Oberg, K. (1960). Cultural shock: Adjustment to new cultural environments. *Practical Anthropology, 7*, 170-179.

Oberg, K. (1979). Culture shock and the problem of adjustment in new cultural environments. In E. C. Smith & L. F. Luce (Eds.), *Toward internationalism: Readings in cross-cultural communication* (pp. 43-45). Rowley, MA: Newbury.

Oddou, G., & Mendenhall, M. (1984). Person perception in cross-cultural settings. *International Journal of Intercultural Relations, 8*, 77-96.

Oehlkers, P. (1991, November). *Networks of social support and the adjustment of Japanese sojourners in the United States*. Paper presented at the annual meeting of the Speech Communication Association, Atlanta, GA.

Office of Refugee Resettlement. (1984). *A study of English language training for refugees in the United States*. Washington, DC: U.S. Department of Health and Human Services.

O'Halloran, M. (1994). *Pure heart, enlightened mind*. Boston: Charles E. Tuttle.

Okazaki-Luff, K. (1991). On the adjustment of Japanese sojourners: Beliefs, contentions, and empirical findings. *International Journal of Intercultural Relations, 15*, 85-102.

Olebe, M., & Koester, J. (1989). Exploring the cross-cultural equivalence of the Behavioral Assessment Scale for intercultural communication. *International Journal of Intercultural Relations, 12,* 233-246.

Opotow, S. (1990). Moral exclusion and inclusion. *Journal of Social Issues, 46*(1), 1-20.

Orbach, M., & Beckwith, J. (1982). Indochinese adaptation and local government policy: An example from Monterey. *Anthropological Quarterly, 55*(3), 135-145.

Ostrom, C., Jr. (1978). *Time series analysis: Regression techniques.* Beverly Hills, CA: Sage.

Ostwald, P., & Bittner, E. (1976). Life adjustment after severe persecution. In R. Moos (Ed.), *Human adaptation: Coping with life crises* (pp. 361-371). Lexington, MA: D. C. Heath.

Ota, H., & Gudykunst, W. B. (1994, May). *Sojourners' social support networks in the United States.* Paper presented at the annual meeting of the International Communication Association, Sydney.

Owusu, T. (1996). The adaptation of black African immigrants in Canada: A case study of residential behavior and ethnic community formation among Ghanaians in Toronto (Ontario) (Doctoral dissertation, University of Toronto, 1996) [Abstract]. *Connections, 20*(1), 68.

Padilla, A. (1980a). Introduction. In A. Padilla (Ed.), *Acculturation: Theory, models and some new findings* (pp. 1-8). Boulder, CO: Westview.

Padilla, A. (1980b). The role of cultural awareness and ethnic loyalty in acculturation. In A. Padilla (Ed.), *Acculturation: Theory, models and some new findings* (pp. 47-84). Boulder, CO: Westview.

Padilla, A., Wagatsuma, Y., & Lindholm, K. (1985). Acculturation and personality as predictors of stress in Japanese and Japanese-Americans. *Journal of Social Psychology, 125,* 295-305.

Page, J. (1994, January-February). Japanese Brazilian style. *Américas,* pp. 34-41.

Palisi, B., & Ransford, H. (1987). Friendship as a voluntary relationship: Evidence from national surveys. *Journal of Social and Personal Relationships, 4,* 243-259.

Parenti, M. (1967). Ethnic politics and the persistence of ethnic voting identification. *American Political Science Review, 67,* 717-726.

Park, R. (1922). *The immigrant press and its controls.* New York: Harper.

Park, R. (1928). Human migration and the marginal man. *American Journal of Sociology, 33,* 881-893.

Park, R. (1939). Reflections on communication and culture. *American Journal of Sociology, 44,* 191-205.

Parks, T. (1992). *Italian neighbors: An Englishman in Verona.* London: Heineman.

Parrillo, V. (1966). *Strangers to these shores: Race and ethnic relations in the United States.* Boston: Houghton Mifflin.

Pearce, W. B. (1989). *Communication and the human condition.* Carbondale: Southern Illinois University Press.

Pearce, W. B., & Stamm, K. (1973). Communication behavior and coorientation relations. In P. Clarke (Ed.), *New models for mass communication research* (pp. 177-203). Beverly Hills, CA: Sage.

Peck, J. (1972). Urban station-migration of the Lumbee Indians (Doctoral dissertation, University of North Carolina, Chapel Hill, 1972). *Dissertation Abstracts International, 33,* 1362B.

Pedone, R. (1980). *The retention of minority language in the United States.* Washington, DC: National Center for Education Statistics.

Penalosa, F. (1972). Pre-migration background and assimilation of Latin-American immigrants in Israel. *Jewish Social Studies, 34*(2), 122-139.

Peng, F. (1974). Communicative distance. *Language Sciences, 31,* 32-38.

Penninx, R. (1986). International migration in West Europe since 1973: Developments, mechanisms and controls. *International Migration Review, 20,* 951-971.

Perreault, S., & Bourhis, R. Y. (1998). Social identification, interdependence and discrimination. *Group Processes and Intergroup Relations, 1*(1), 49-66.

Pescosolido, B. (1992). Beyond rational choice: The social dynamics of how people seek help. *American Journal of Sociology, 97,* 1096-1138.

Peterson, T., Jensen, J., & Rivers, W. (1965). *The mass media and modern society.* New York: Holt, Rinehart & Winston.

Pettigrew, T. F. (1979). The ultimate attribution error: Extending Allport's cognitive analysis of prejudice. *Personality and Social Psychology Bulletin, 5,* 461-476.

Pettigrew, T. F. (1982). Cognitive styles and social behavior. In L. Wheeler (Ed.), *Review of personality and social psychology* (Vol. 3). Beverly Hills, CA: Sage.

Pettigrew, T. F. (1988). Integration and pluralism. In P. Katz & D. Taylor (Eds.), *Eliminating racism* (pp. 13-30). New York: Plenum.

Philip, L. (1989). *The road through Miyama.* New York: Random House.

Phinney, J. (1993). Multiple group identities: Differentiation, conflict, and integration. In J. Kroger (Ed.), *Discussions on ego identity* (pp. 47-73). Hillsdale, NJ: Lawrence Erlbaum.

Phinney, J., & Rosenthal, D. (1992). Ethnic identity in adolescence: Process, context, and outcome. In G. R. Adams, T. P. Gullotta, & R. Montemayor (Eds.), *Adolescent identity formation* (pp. 145-172). Newbury Park, CA: Sage.

Phinney, J., & Rotheram, M. (Eds.). (1987). *Children's ethnic socialization: Pluralism and development.* Newbury Park, CA: Sage.

Phizacklea, A. (1984). A sociology of migration or "race relations"? A view from Britain. *Current Sociology, 32,* 199-209.

Piaget, J. (1963). *The origins of intelligence in children.* New York: W. W. Norton.

Plummer, K. (1983). *Documents of life.* London: Allen & Unwin.

Pogrebin, L. C. (1987). *Among friends: Who we like, why we like them, and what we do with them.* New York: McGraw-Hill.

Postiglione, G. (1983). *Ethnicity and American social theory: Toward critical pluralism.* Lanham, MD: University Press of America.

Price, J. (1968). The migration and adaptation of American Indians to Los Angeles. *Human Organization, 27,* 168-175.

Puente, M. (1995, July 5). Immigrants favor ID cards. *USA Today,* pp. 1A, 5A.

Punetha, D., Giles, H., & Young, L. (1988). Interethnic perceptions and relative deprivation: British data. In Y. Y. Kim & W. B. Gudykunst (Eds.), *Cross-cultural adaptation: Current approaches* (pp. 252-266). Newbury Park, CA: Sage.

Quisumbing, M. (1982). *Life events, social support and personality: Their impact upon Filipino and psychological adjustment.* Unpublished doctoral dissertation, University of Chicago.

Rankin, D. (1981). *Country school legacy: Humanities on the frontier.* Silt, CO: Country School Legacy Project. (ERIC Document Reproduction Service No. ED 211 243)

Rapoport, A. (1986). *General system theory: Essential concepts and applications.* Cambridge, MA: Abacus.

Rappaport, R. (1971). Ritual, sanctity, and cybernetics. *American Anthropologist, 73,* 53-76.

Redfield, R., Linton, R., & Herskovits, M. (1936). Outline for the study of acculturation. *American Anthropologist, 38,* 149-152.

Redmond, M. V., & Bunyi, J. M. (1993). The relationship of intercultural communication competence with stress and the handling of stress as reported by international students. *International Journal of Intercultural Relations, 17,* 235-354.

Reece, D., & Palmgreen, P. (1996, May). *Coming to America: The influence of cultural variables on media use among Indian sojourners in the US.* Paper presented at the annual meeting of the International Communication Association, Chicago.

Reid, S., & Ng, S. H. (1999). Language, power, and intergroup relations. *Journal of Social Issues, 55*(1), 119-139.

Rei Doval, G. (1994, July). *Towards an integrated typology of linguistic competence in Spain's languages: The Gallician case.* Paper presented at the Fifth International Conference on Language and Social Psychology, Brisbane, Queensland.

Rex, J., Joly, D., & Wilpert, C. (1987). *Immigrant associations in Europe.* Brookfield, VT: Gower.

Richler, M. (1992). *Oh Canada! Oh Quebec!* New York: Alfred A. Knopf.

Richmond, A. (1967). *Post-war immigration in Canada.* Toronto: University of Toronto Press.

Ricoeur, P. (1992). *Oneself as another* (K. Blamey, Trans.). Chicago: University of Chicago Press.

Rimer, S. (1991, December 27). Listen, New York, this man just wants to learn English. *New York Times,* pp. B1, B4.

Rivera-Sinclair, E. (1997). Acculturation/biculturalism and its relationship to adjustment in Cuban-Americans. *International Journal of Intercultural Relations, 21,* 379-391.

Roberts, S. (1993). *Who we are: A portrait of America.* New York: Random House.

Robinson, J., & Preston, J. (1976). Equal status contact and modification of racial prejudice: A reexamination of the contact hypothesis. *Social Forces, 54,* 911-924.

Robinson, P. (1985). Language retention among Canadian Indians: A simultaneous equations model with dichotomous endogenous variables. *American Sociological Review, 50,* 515-529.

Robinson, V. (1986). *Transients, settlers, and refugees.* Oxford: Clarendon.

Rodriguez, R. (1981). *Hunger of memory: The education of Richard Rodriguez.* Boston: D. R. Godine.

Rogers, E. (1979). Mass media and interpersonal communication. In G. Gumpert & R. Cathcart (Eds.), *Inter/media: Interpersonal communication in a media world* (pp. 192-213). New York: Oxford University Press.

Rogers, E. (1999). Georg Simmel's concept of the stranger and intercultural communication research. *Communication Theory, 9,* 58-74.

Rogers, E., & Kincaid, D. (1981). *Communication networks: A new paradigm for research.* New York: Free Press.

Roosens, E. (1989). *Creating ethnicity: The process of ethnogenesis.* Newbury Park, CA: Sage.

Rosenthal, D., & Hrynevich, C. (1985). Ethnicity and ethnic identity: A comparative study of Greek-, Italian-, and Anglo-Australian working-class adolescents. *Journal of Youth and Adolescence, 12,* 117-135.

Rosenthal, R., & Rosnow, R. (1991). *Essentials of behavioral research: Methods and data analysis* (2nd ed.). New York: McGraw-Hill.

Rotter, J. (1990, April). Internal versus external control of reinforcement: A case history of a variable. *American Psychologist,* pp. 489-493.

Roy, S. (1987). Sociodemographic factors and their effect on the type and degree of acculturation. *Dissertation Abstracts International, 48*(03), 919B. (University Microfilms No. AAC87-13207)

Ruben, B. D. (1972). General systems theory: An approach to human communication. In R. Budd & B. D. Ruben (Eds.), *Approaches to human communication* (pp. 120-144). Rochelle Park, NJ: Hayden.

Ruben, B. D. (1975). Intrapersonal, interpersonal, and mass communication processes in individual and multi-person systems. In B. D. Ruben &

J. Y. Kim (Eds.), *General systems theory and human communication* (pp. 164-190). Rochelle Park, NJ: Hayden.

Ruben, B. D. (1976). Assessing communication competency for intercultural adaptation. *Group & Organization Studies, 1,* 334-354.

Ruben, B. D. (1980, March). *Culture shock: The skull and the lady—Reflections on cultural adjustment and stress.* Paper presented at the annual meeting of the Society for Intercultural Education, Training and Research, Mt. Pocono, PA.

Ruben, B. D. (1983). A system-theoretic view. In W. B. Gudykunst (Ed.), *International and intercultural communication annual: Vol. 12. Intercultural communication theory* (pp. 131-145). Beverly Hills, CA: Sage.

Ruben, B. D. (1988). *Communication and human behavior* (2nd ed.). New York: Macmillan.

Ruben, B. D. (1989). The study of cross-cultural competence: Traditions and contemporary issues. *International Journal of Intercultural Relations, 13,* 229-240.

Ruben, B. D., & Kealey, D. (1979). Behavioral assessment of communication competency and the prediction of cross-cultural adaptation. *International Journal of Intercultural Relations, 3,* 15-27.

Rubin, H. J., & Rubin, I. S. (1995). *Qualitative interviewing: The art of hearing data.* Thousand Oaks, CA: Sage.

Ruesch, J. (1972). *Disturbed communication.* New York: W. W. Norton. (Original work published 1957)

Ruesch, J., & Bateson, G. (1968). *Communication: The social matrix of psychiatry.* New York: W. W. Norton. (Original work published 1951)

Ruggiero, K., Taylor, D., & Lambert, W. (1996). A model of heritage culture maintenance: The role of discrimination. *International Journal of Intercultural Relations, 20,* 47-67.

Ruidl, R. (1982). Idiomatic communication behaviors as indicators of acculturation. *Dissertation Abstracts International, 43*(06), 1738A. (University Microfilms No. DA82-26594)

Runyan, W. (1982). *Life histories and psychobiography.* New York: Oxford University Press.

Rushdie, S. (1992). *Imaginary homelands: Essays and criticism 1981-1991.* New York: Penguin.

Rushdie, S. (1994). *East, West: Stories.* New York: Pantheon.

Ryan, C. (1987). Indochinese refugees in the U.S.: Background characteristics, initial adjustment patterns, and the role of policy. *Dissertation Abstracts International, 48*(04), 1025B. (University Microfilms No. AAC87-15554)

Ryu, J. (1978, May). *Mass media's role in the assimilation process: A study of Korean immigrants in the Los Angeles area.* Paper presented at the annual meeting of the International Communication Association, Chicago.

Sachdev, I., & Wright, A. (1996). Social influence and language learning: An experimental study. *Journal of Language and Social Psychology, 15,* 230-245.

Sahlins, M. (1964). Culture and environment: The study of cultural ecology. In S. Tax (Ed.), *Horizons of anthropology* (pp. 132-147). Chicago: Aldine.

Saldaña, D. (1994). Acculturative stress: Minority status and distress. *Hispanic Journal of Behavioral Sciences, 16,* 116-128.

Salzman, M. (1986). *Iron and silk.* New York: Random House.

Samter, W., Burleson, B. R., & Basden-Murphy, L. (1989). Behavioral complexity is in the eye of the beholder: Effects of cognitive complexity and message complexity on impressions of the source of comforting messages. *Human Communication Research, 15,* 612-629.

Sapir, E. (1937). Communication. In E. Seligman & A. Johnson (Eds.), *Encyclopedia of the social sciences* (Vol. 4, pp. 78-80). New York: Macmillan.

Sarason, I. G., Sarason, B. R., & Pierce, G. R. (1991). Anxiety, cognitive interference, and performance. In M. Booth-Butterfield (Ed.), *Communication, cognition, and anxiety* (pp. 1-18). Newbury Park, CA: Sage.

Sarbaugh, L. (1988). *Intercultural communication* (2nd ed.). New Brunswick, NJ: Transaction.

Sarter, B. (1988). *The stream of becoming: A study of Martha Rogers's theory.* New York: National League for Nursing.

Sauna, V. (1969). Immigration, migration and mental illness: A review of the literature with special emphasis on schizophrenia. In E. Brody (Ed.), *Behavior in new environments: Adaptation of migrant populations* (pp. 291-352). Beverly Hills, CA: Sage.

Schramm, W. (1979). Channels and audiences. In G. Gumpert & R. Cathcart (Eds.), *Inter/media: Interpersonal communication in a media world* (pp. 160-174). New York: Oxford University Press.

Schroder, H., Driver, M., & Streufert, S. (1967). *Human information processing: Individuals and groups functioning in complex social situations.* New York: Holt, Rinehart & Winston.

Schroder, H., Driver, M., & Streufert, S. (1975). Intrapersonal organization. In B. D. Ruben & J. Y. Kim (Eds.), *General systems theory and human communication* (pp. 96-113). Rochelle Park, NJ: Hayden.

Schuetz, A. (1963). The stranger: An essay in social psychology. In M. R. Stein & A. J. Vidich (Eds.), *Identity and anxiety survival of the person in mass society* (pp. 98-109). Glencoe, IL: Free Press. (Original work published 1944)

Schuetz, A. (1964). Making music together. In A. Schuetz, *Collected papers II* (pp. 159-178). The Hague: Nijhoff.

Schuetz, A. (1970). *On phenomenology and social relations.* Chicago: University of Chicago Press.

Scott, J. (1991). *Social network analysis: A handbook.* Newbury Park, CA: Sage.

Searle, W., & Ward, C. (1990). The prediction of psychological and sociocultural adjustment during cross-cultural transitions. *International Journal of Intercultural Relations, 14*, 449-464.

Sechrest, L., Fay, T., & Zaidi, S. (1982). Problems of translation in cross-cultural communication. In L. A. Samovar & R. E. Potter (Eds.), *Intercultural communication: A reader* (3rd ed., pp. 223-233). Belmont, CA: Wadsworth.

Seelye, H., & Wasilewski, J. (1981, March). *Social competency development in multicultural children, aged 6-13* (Final report of exploratory research on Hispanic-background children submitted to National Institute of Education, Contract No. 400-80-0003). LaGrange, IL: International Resource Development.

Seelye, H., & Wasilewski, J. (1996). *Between cultures: Developing self-identity in a world of diversity.* Lincolnwood, IL: NTC Business Books.

Seeman, J. (1983). *Personality integration: Studies and reflections.* New York: Human Sciences.

Seligman, M. E. P., & Weiss, J. (1980). Coping behavior: Learned helplessness, physiological change and learned inactivity. *Behavior Research and Therapy, 18*, 159-512.

Selltiz, C., Christ, J. R., Havel, J., & Cook, S. W. (1963). *Attitudes and social relations of foreign students in the United States.* Minneapolis: University of Minnesota Press.

Selltiz, C., & Cook, S. W. (1962). Factors influencing attitudes of foreign students toward the host country. *Journal of Social Issues, 18*(1), 7-23.

Sewell, W., & Davidsen, O. (1961). *Scandinavian students on an American campus.* Minneapolis: University of Minnesota Press.

Shah, H. (1991). Communication and cross-cultural adaptation patterns among Asian Indians. *International Journal of Intercultural Relations, 15*, 311-321.

Sheehy, G. (1987). *Spirit of survival.* New York: Bantam.

Sherman, S. (1988, October). The Hmong in America. *National Geographic,* pp. 586-610.

Shibutani, T., & Kwan, K. M. (1965). *Ethnic stratification: A comparative approach.* New York: Macmillan.

Shim, J. (1994, May). *Community orientations and newspaper use: Within and between Korean American communities in Southern California.* Paper presented at the annual meeting of the International Communication Association, Sydney.

Shoemaker, P. J. (1991). *Gatekeeping.* Newbury Park, CA: Sage.

Shook, D., & Finet, D. (1987, February). *A dimensional analysis of network centrality and interpersonal trust and influence in organizations.* Paper presented at the International Sunbelt Social Network Conference, Clearwater, FL.

Shuval, J. (1963). *Immigrants on the threshold.* New York: Atherton.

Silverman, M. (1979, October). *Vietnamese in Denver: Cultural conflicts in health care*. Paper presented at the Conference on Indochinese Refugees, Fairfax, VA.

Silvers, R. (1965). Structure and values in the explanation of acculturation rates. *British Journal of Sociology, 16*(1), 68-79.

Simard, L. (1981). Cross-cultural interaction: Potential invisible barriers. *Journal of Social Psychology, 113,* 171-192.

Simmel, G. (1921). The social significance of the "stranger." In R. E. Park & E. W. Burgess (Eds.), *Introduction to the science of sociology* (pp. 322-327). Chicago: University of Chicago Press.

Simmel, G. (1950). The stranger. In G. Simmel, *The sociology of Georg Simmel* (K. H. Wolff, Ed. & Trans.). Glencoe, IL: Free Press. (Original work published 1908)

Simmel, G. (1955). *Conflict and the web of group affiliation* (L. Bendix, Trans.). Glencoe, IL: Free Press.

Singelis, T. M. (1996). The context of intergroup communication. *Journal of Language and Social Psychology, 15,* 360-371.

Slavin, M., & Kriegman, D. (1992). *The adaptive design of the human psyche.* New York: Guilford.

Smith, A. (1981). *The ethnic revival in the modern world.* Cambridge, UK: Cambridge University Press.

Smith, M. (1976). Networks and migration resettlement: Cherchez la femme. *Anthropological Quarterly, 49*(1), 20-27.

Smith, S., Scholnick, N., Crutcher, A., & Simeone, M. (1991). Foreigner talk revisited: Limits on accommodation to nonfluent speakers. In J. Blommaert & J. Verschueren (Eds.), *The pragmatics of international and intercultural communication* (pp. 173-185). Philadelphia: John Benjamins.

Snyder, P. (1976). Neighborhood gatekeepers in the process of urban adaptation: Cross-ethnic commonalities. *Urban Anthropology, 5*(1), 35-52.

Social Science Research Council. (1954). Acculturation: An exploratory formulation. *American Anthropologist, 56,* 973-1002.

Southall, A. (1961). Kinship, friendship and the network of relations in Kisengi, Kampala. In A. Southall (Ed.), *Social change in modern Africa* (pp. 217-229). London: Oxford University Press.

Spicer, E. (1968). Acculturation. In D. Sills (Ed.), *International encyclopedia of the social sciences* (pp. 21-27). New York: Macmillan.

Spindler, G. (1955). *Sociocultural and psychological processes in Menomini acculturation.* Berkeley: University of California Press.

Spindler, G., & Goldschmidt, W. (1952). Experimental design in the study of culture change. *Southwestern Journal of Anthropology, 8,* 68-83.

Spiro, M. (1955). The acculturation of American ethnic groups. *American Anthropologist, 57,* 1240-1252.

Spiro, M. (1987). *Culture and human nature: Theoretical papers of Melford E. Spiro* (B. Kilborne & L. Langness, Eds.). Chicago: University of Chicago Press.

Spitzberg, B. H. (1988). Communication competence: Measures of perceived effectiveness. In C. H. Tardy (Ed.), *A handbook for the study of human communication: Methods and instruments for observing, measuring, and assessing communication processes* (pp. 67-105). Norwood, NJ: Ablex.

Spitzberg, B. H. (1989). Issues in the development of a theory of inter-personal competence in the intercultural context. *International Journal of Intercultural Relations, 13,* 241-268.

Spitzberg, B. H., & Cupach, W. R. (1984). *Interpersonal communication competence.* Beverly Hills, CA: Sage.

Sreenivasan, S. (1996, July 22). As mainstream papers struggle, the ethnic press is thriving. *New York Times,* p. C7.

Stake, R. E. (1995). *The art of case study research.* Thousand Oaks, CA: Sage.

Steen, S. (1998, April). *"I've become a bicultural entity": The cultural adaptation processes of USM students abroad.* Paper presented at the annual meeting of Southern States Communication Association, San Antonio, TX.

Steiner, J. (1967). *Treblinka* (H. Weaver, Trans.). New York: Simon & Schuster.

Stephan, W., & Stephan, C. (1985). Intergroup anxiety. *Journal of Social Issues, 41*(3), 157-175.

Stephan, W., & Stephan, C. (1989). Antecedents of intergroup anxiety in Asian Americans and Hispanic Americans. *International Journal of Intercultural Relations, 13,* 203-219.

Stephan, W., & Stephan, C. (1992). Reducing intercultural anxiety through intercultural contact. *International Journal of Intercultural Relations, 16,* 89-106.

Stephenson, W. (1953). *The study of behavior.* Chicago: University of Chicago Press.

Stewart, A., & Healy, J., Jr. (1984). Processing affective responses to life experiences: The development of the adult self. In C. Malatesta & C. Izard (Eds.), *Emotion in adult development* (pp. 277-295). Beverly Hills, CA: Sage.

Stewart, A., & Healy, J., Jr. (1985). Personality and adaptation to change. In R. Hogan & W. Jones (Eds.), *Perspectives in personality* (Vol. 1, pp. 117-144). Greenwich, CT: JAI.

Stewart, D. W., & Shamdasani, P. N. (1990). *Focus groups: Theory and practice.* Newbury Park, CA: Sage.

Stilling, E. (1997). The electronic melting pot hypothesis: The cultivation of acculturation among Hispanics through television viewing. *Howard Journal of Communication, 8,* 77-100.

Stonequist, E. (1935). The problem of the marginal man. *American Journal of Sociology, 41,* 1-12.

Stonequist, E. (1937). *The marginal man.* New York: Scribner's.

Stonequist, E. (1964). The marginal man: A study in personality and culture conflict. In E. W. Burgess & D. Bogue (Eds.), *Contributions to urban sociology* (pp. 327-345). Chicago: University of Chicago Press.

Stopes-Roe, M., & Cochrane, R. (1990). Support networks of Asian and British families: Comparisons between ethnicities and between generations. *Social Behavior, 5,* 71-85.

Strauss, A. L., & Corbin, J. (1990). *Basics of qualitative research: Grounded theory procedures and techniques.* Newbury Park, CA: Sage.

Suárez-Orozco, M. M. (1990). Migration and education: United States-Europe comparisons. In G. A. De Vos & M. M. Suárez-Orozco, *Status inequality: The self in culture* (pp. 265-287). Newbury Park, CA: Sage.

Subervi-Velez, F. (1986). The mass media and ethnic assimilation and pluralism: A review and research proposal with special focus on Hispanics. *Communication Research, 13,* 71-96.

Suro, R. (1998). *Strangers among us: How Latino immigration is transforming America.* New York: Alfred A. Knopf.

Suzuki, D. (1968). *The essence of Buddhism.* Kyoto, Japan: Hozokan.

Szalay, L., & Inn, A. (1988). Cross-cultural adaptation and diversity: Hispanic Americans. In Y. Y. Kim & W. B. Gudykunst (Eds.), *Cross-cultural adaptation: Current approaches* (pp. 212-232). Newbury Park, CA: Sage.

Szapocznik, J., & Kurtines, W. (1980). Acculturation, biculturalism and adjustment of Cuban Americans. In A. Padilla (Ed.), *Acculturation: Theory, models and some new findings* (pp. 139-159). Boulder, CO: Westview.

Szapocznik, J., Scopetta, M., Kurtines, W., & Aranalde, M. (1978). Theory and measurement of acculturation. *International Journal of Psychology, 12,* 113-130.

Taft, R. (1957). A psychological model for the study of social assimilation. *Human Relations, 10,* 141-156.

Taft, R. (1966). *From stranger to citizen.* London: Tavistock.

Taft, R. (1977). Coping with unfamiliar cultures. In N. Warren (Ed.), *Studies in cross-cultural psychology* (Vol. 1, pp. 121-153). London: Academic Press.

Taft, R. (1986). Methodological considerations in the study of immigrant adaptation in Australia. *Australian Journal of Psychology, 38,* 339-346.

Taft, R. (1988). The psychological adaptation of Soviet immigrants in Australia. In Y. Y. Kim & W. B. Gudykunst (Eds.), *Cross-cultural adaptation: Current approaches* (pp. 150-167). Newbury Park, CA: Sage.

Tagore, R. (1961). *Towards universal man.* New York: Asia.

Tajfel, H. (1970). Experiments in intergroup discrimination. *Scientific American, 223*(2), 96-102.

Tajfel, H., & Turner, J. C. (1979). An integrative theory of intergroup conflict. In W. G. Austin & S. Worchel (Eds.), *The social psychology of intergroup relations* (pp. 33-47). Monterey, CA: Brooks/Cole.

Tajfel, H., & Turner, J. C. (1986). The social identity theory of intergroup behavior. In S. Worchel & W. G. Austin (Eds.), *Psychology of intergroup relations* (2nd ed., pp. 7-24). Chicago: Nelson-Hall.

Takai, J. (1991). Host contact and cross-cultural adjustment in international students in Japan: Assessment instruments and some descriptive statistics. *Research in Higher Education-Daigaku Ronshu, 20,* 195-228.

Tamam, E. (1993). *The influence of ambiguity tolerance, open-mindedness, and empathy on sojourners' psychological adaptation and perceived intercultural communication effectiveness.* Unpublished doctoral dissertation, University of Oklahoma, Norman.

Tanaka, T., Takai, J., Kohyama, T., Fujihara, T., & Minami, H. (1994). Social networks of international students in Japan: Perceived social support and relationship satisfaction. *Japanese Journal of Experimental Social Psychology, 33,* 213-223.

Taylor, D., & Simard, L. (1975). Social interaction in a bilingual setting. *Canadian Psychological Review, 16,* 240-254.

Taylor, S. E. (1991). *Positive illusions: Creative self-deception and the healthy mind.* New York: Basic Books.

Terkel, S. (1987). *Studs Terkel with Ursula Bender* [Audiocassette of radio interview]. Chicago: Window to the World Communications, WFMT-FM.

Terry, D., Rawle, R., & Callan, V. (1995). The effects of social support on adjustment to stress: The mediating role of coping. *Personal Relationships, 2,* 97-124.

Teske, R., & Nelson, B. (1974). Acculturation and assimilation: A clarification. *American Anthropologist, 76,* 351-367.

Thayer, L. (1975). Knowledge, order, and communication. In B. D. Ruben & J. Y. Kim (Eds.), *General systems theory and human communication* (pp. 237-245). Rochelle Park, NJ: Hayden.

Thomas, J. (1991). Indochinese adjustment and assimilation in an Alabama coastal fishing community. *Comparative Civilizations Review, 24,* 1-12.

Thornton, M. (1996). Hidden agendas, identity theories, and multiracial people. In M. P. P. Root (Ed.), *The multiracial experience: Racial borders as the new frontier* (pp. 101-120). Thousand Oaks, CA: Sage.

Ting-Toomey, S. (1981). Ethnic identity and close friendship in Chinese-American college students. *Journal of Intercultural Relations, 5,* 383-406.

Ting-Toomey, S. (1993). Communicative resourcefulness: An identity negotiation perspective. In R. L. Wiseman & J. Koester (Eds.), *Intercultural communication competence* (pp. 72-111). Newbury Park, CA: Sage.

Tinker, J. (1973). Intermarriage and ethnic boundaries: The Japanese American case. *Journal of Social Issues, 29*(2), 49-66.

Toffler, A. (1980). *The third wave.* New York: Bantam.

Torbiorn, I. (1982). *Living abroad: Personal adjustment and personnel policy in the overseas setting.* New York: John Wiley.

Torbiorn, I. (1988). Culture barriers as a social psychological construct: An empirical validation. In Y. Y. Kim & W. B. Gudykunst (Eds.), *Cross-cultural adaptation: Current approaches* (pp. 168-190). Newbury Park, CA: Sage.

Tran, T. (1987). Ethnic community supports and psychological well-being of Vietnamese refugees. *International Migration Review, 21,* 833-844.

Triandis, H., Kashima, Y., Shimada, E., & Villareal, M. (1986). Acculturation indices as a means of confirming cultural differences. *International Journal of Psychology, 21,* 43-70.

Trifonovitch, G. (1977). Culture learning/culture teaching. *Educational Perspectives, 16*(4), 18-22.

Turner, J. C. (1978). Social categorization and social discrimination in a minimal group paradigm. In H. Tajfel (Ed.), *Differentiation between social groups* (pp. 213-235). Beverly Hills, CA: Sage.

Turner, J. C. (1987). *Rediscovering the social group.* Oxford: Blackwell.

Turner, J. C., & Giles, H. (1981). *Intergroup behavior.* Chicago: University of Chicago Press.

Tyler, A., & Davies, C. (1990). Cross-linguistic communication missteps. *Text, 10,* 385-411.

Uehara, A. (1986). The nature of American student reentry adjustment and perceptions of the sojourn experience. *International Journal of Intercultural Relations, 10,* 415-438.

Useem, J. (1963). The community of man: A study of the third culture. *Centennial Review, 7,* 481-498.

Valdéz, A. (1979). *The social and occupational integration among Mexican and Puerto Rican ethnics in an urban industrial society.* Unpublished doctoral dissertation, University of California, Los Angeles.

van den Broucke, S., de Soete, G., & Böhrer, A. (1989). Free-response self-description as a predictor of success and failure in adolescent exchange students. *International Journal of Intercultural Relations, 13,* 73-91.

van der Poel, M. (1993). *Personal networks: A rational-choice explanation of their size and composition.* Berwyn, PA: Swets & Zeitlinger.

van Dijk, T. A. (1987). *Communicating racism: Ethnic prejudice in thought and talk.* Newbury Park, CA: Sage.

van Oudenhoven, J., & Eisses, A. (1998). Integration and assimilation of Moroccan immigrants in Israel and the Netherlands. *International Journal of Intercultural Relations, 22,* 293-307.

Vaz, P. (1985). Social adjustment and social relations of foreign students. *Dissertation Abstracts International, 45*(07), 2259A. (University Microfilms No. DA84-23838)

Vazquez, L., Garcia-Vazquez, E., Bauman, S., & Sierra, A. (1997). Skin color, acculturation, and community interest among Mexican American students: A research note. *Hispanic Journal of Behavioral Sciences, 19,* 377-386.

Vega, W., Kolody, B., & Valle, V. (1987). Migration and mental health: An empirical test of depression risk factors among immigrant Mexican women. *International Migration Review, 21,* 512-530.

Volkan, V. (1992). Ethnonationalistic rituals: An introduction. *Mind and Human Interaction, 3*(1), 3-19.

Volkan, V. (1993). Immigrants and refugees: A psychodynamic perspective. *Mind and Human Interaction, 4*(2), 63-69.

von Bertalanffy, L. (1968). *General system theory: Foundations, development, applications.* New York: George Braziller.

Wade, B., & Souter, P. (1992). *Continuing to think: The British Asian girl.* Clevedon, England: Multilingual Matters.

Walker, D. (1993, May). *The role of the mass media in the adaptation of Haitian immigrants in Miami.* Unpublished doctoral dissertation, Indiana University.

Walsh, J. E. (1973). The universal person. In J. E. Walsh, *Intercultural education in the community of man.* Honolulu: University of Hawaii Press.

Walton, S. (1990). Stress management training for overseas effectiveness. *International Journal of Intercultural Relations, 14,* 507-527.

Ward, C., & Kennedy, A. (1994). Acculturation strategies, psychological adjustment, and sociocultural competence during cross-cultural transitions. *International Journal of Intercultural Relations, 18,* 329-343.

Ward, C., Okura, Y., Kennedy, A., & Kojima, T. (1998). The U-curve on trial: A longitudinal study of psychological and sociocultural adjustment during cross-cultural transition. *International Journal of Intercultural Relations, 22,* 277-291.

Ward, C., & Searle, W. (1991). The impact of value discrepancies and cultural identity on psychological and sociocultural adjustment of sojourners. *International Journal of Intercultural Relations, 15,* 209-225.

Warren, R., & Kraly, E. (1985). *The elusive exodus: Emigration from the United States* (Population Trends and Public Policy No. 8). Washington, DC: Population Reference Bureau.

Waterman, A. (1992). Identity as an aspect of optimal psychological functioning. In G. R. Adams, T. P. Gullotta, & R. Montemayor (Eds.), *Adolescent identity formation* (pp. 50-72). Newbury Park, CA: Sage.

Watts, A. (1951). *The wisdom of insecurity.* New York: Vintage.

Watzlawick, P., Beavin, J. H., & Jackson, D. D. (1967). *Pragmatics of human communication: A study of interaction patterns, pathologies, and paradoxes.* New York: W. W. Norton.

Weick, K. E. (1969). *The social psychology of organizing.* Reading, MA: Addison-Wesley.

Weigel, R., & Howes, P. (1985). Conceptions of racial prejudice: Symbolic racism reconsidered. *Journal of Social Issues, 4*(3), 117-138.

Weimann, G. (1983). The strength of weak conversational ties in the flow of information and influence. *Social Networks, 5,* 245-267.

Weimann, G. (1989). Social networks and communication. In M. K. Asante & W. B. Gudykunst (Eds.), *Handbook of international and intercultural communication* (pp. 186-203). Newbury Park, CA: Sage.

Weinberg, A. (1973). Mental health aspects of voluntary migration. In C. Zwingmann & M. Pfister-Ammende (Eds.), *Uprooting and after . . .* (pp. 110-120). New York: Springer-Verlag.

Weinberg, H. (1987). *Levels of knowing and existence.* Englewood, NJ: Institute of General Semantics. (Original work published 1959)

Weinstock, S. (1964). Some factors that retard or accelerate the rate of acculturation. *Human Relations, 17,* 321-340.

Weller, S., & Romney, A. K. (1988). *Systematic data collection.* Newbury Park, CA: Sage.

Wellman, B. (1982). Studying personal communities. In P. Marsden & N. Lin (Eds.), *Social structure and network analysis* (pp. 61-80). Beverly Hills, CA: Sage.

Wellman, B. (1983). *Network analysis: From method and metaphor to theory and substance.* San Francisco: Jossey-Bass.

Wellman, B. (1992). Which types of ties and networks provide what kinds of social support? *Advances in Group Processes, 9,* 207-235.

Wellman, B., Yuk-lin, R., Tindall, D., & Nazer, N. (1997). A decade of network change: Turnover, persistence and stability in personal communities. *Social Networks, 19,* 27-50.

Wen, K. (1976). Theories of migration and mental health. *Social Science and Medicine, 10,* 297-306.

Westermeyer, J., Vang, T., & Neider, J. (1986). Migration and mental health among H'mong refugees. *Pacific/Asian American Mental Health Research Center Review, 5*(3-4), 25-29.

White, R. (1976). Strategies of adaptation: An attempt at systemic description. In R. Moos (Ed.), *Human adaptation: Coping with life crises* (pp. 17-32). Lexington, MA: D. C. Heath.

White, S. (1991). *The unity of the self.* Cambridge, MA: MIT Press.

Whitney, C. (1996, January 7). Europeans redefine what makes a citizen. *New York Times,* p. E6.

Whorf, B. (1952). *Collected papers on metalinguistics.* Washington, DC: U.S. Department of State, Foreign Service Institute.

Williams, C., & Westermeyer, J. (1986). Psychiatric problems among adolescent Southeast Asian refugees: A descriptive study. *Pacific/Asian American Mental Health Research Center Newsletter, 5*(3-4), 22-24.

Wilpert, C. (1984). International migration and ethnic minorities: New fields for post-war sociology in the Federal Republic of Germany. *Current Sociology, 32,* 305-325.

Wilson, A. H. (1993). A cross-national perspective on reentry of high school exchange students. *International Journal of Intercultural Relations, 17,* 465-492.

Winch, R., & Spanier, G. (1974). *Selected studies in marriage and the family* (4th ed.). New York: Holt, Rinehart & Winston.

Wiseman, R. L., & Koester, J. (Eds.). (1993). *Intercultural communication competence.* Newbury Park, CA: Sage.

Wolfinger, R. (1965). The development and persistence of ethnic voting. *American Political Science Review, 59,* 896-908.

Wong-Rieger, D. (1984). Testing a model of emotional and coping responses to problems in adaptation: Foreign students at a Canadian university. *International Journal of Intercultural Relations, 8,* 153-184.

Wong-Rieger, D. (1987). Comparative acculturation of Southeast Asian and Hispanic immigrants and sojourners. *Journal of Cross-Cultural Psychology, 18,* 345-362.

Wood, M. (1934). *The stranger: A study in social relationships.* New York: Columbia University Press.

Wood, P., & Sonleitner, N. (1996). The effect of childhood interracial contact on adult antiblack prejudice. *International Journal of Intercultural Relations, 20,* 1-17.

Worchel, S. (1979). Cooperation and the reduction of intergroup conflict: Some determining factors. In W. G. Austin & S. Worchel (Eds.), *The social psychology of intergroup relations* (pp. 262-273). Monterey, CA: Brooks/Cole.

Worchel, S. (1986). The role of cooperation in reducing intergroup conflict. In S. Worchel & W. G. Austin (Eds.), *Psychology of intergroup relations* (2nd ed., pp. 288-304). Chicago: Nelson-Hall.

Wrightsman, L. (1994). *Adult personality development: Vol. 1. Theories and concepts.* Thousand Oaks, CA: Sage.

Yang, H., & Sachdev, I. (1994, July). *Chinese communities in London and Taiwan: Vitality and language use.* Paper presented at the Fifth International Conference on Language and Social Psychology, Brisbane, Queensland.

Yang, K. (1981). Social orientation and individual modernity among Chinese students in Taiwan. *Journal of Social Psychology, 113,* 159-170.

Yang, S. (1988, June). *The role of mass media in immigrants' political socialization: A study of Korean immigrants in Northern California.* Unpublished doctoral dissertation, Stanford University.

Yin, R. K. (1994). *Case study research: Design and methods* (2nd ed.). Thousand Oaks, CA: Sage.

Ying, Y., & Liese, L. (1991). Emotional well-being of Taiwan students in the U.S.: An examination of pre- to post-arrival differential. *International Journal of Intercultural Relations, 15,* 345-366.

Yoshikawa, M. (1978). Some Japanese and American cultural characteristics. In M. Prosser (Ed.), *The cultural dialogue: An introduction to intercultural communication* (pp. 220-239). Boston: Houghton Mifflin.

Yoshikawa, M. (1986). Cross-cultural adaptation and perceptual development. In Y. Y. Kim & W. B. Gudykunst (Eds.), *Cross-cultural adaptation: Current approaches* (pp. 140-148). Beverly Hills, CA: Sage.

Young, R. (1995). Conversational styles in language proficiency interviews. *Language Learning, 45,* 3-42.

Yum, J. (1982). Communication diversity and information acquisition among Korean immigrants in Hawaii. *Human Communication Research, 8,* 154-169.

Yum, J. (1983). Social network patterns of five ethnic groups in Hawaii. In R. N. Bostrom (Ed.), *Communication yearbook 7* (pp. 574-591). Beverly Hills, CA: Sage.

Yum, J. (1984). Network analysis. In W. B. Gudykunst & Y. Y. Kim (Eds.), *Methods for intercultural communication research* (pp. 95-116). Beverly Hills, CA: Sage.

Yum, J. (1986). Locus of control and communication patterns of immigrants. In Y. Y. Kim (Ed.), *Interethnic communication: Current research* (pp. 191-211). Beverly Hills, CA: Sage.

Yum, J. (1988). Network theory in intercultural communication. In Y. Y. Kim & W. B. Gudykunst (Eds.), *Theories in intercultural communication* (pp. 239-258). Newbury Park, CA: Sage.

Zaharna, R. (1989). Self-shock: The double-binding challenge of identity. *International Journal of Intercultural Relations, 13,* 501-525.

Zajonc, R. (1952). Aggressive attitude of the "stranger" as a function of conformity pressures. *Human Relations, 5,* 205-216.

Zenner, W. (Ed.). (1991). *Persistence and flexibility: Anthropological perspectives on the American Jewish experience.* Albany: State University of New York Press.

Zimmermann, S. (1995). Perceptions of intercultural communication competence and international student adaptation to an American campus. *Communication Education, 44,* 321-335.

Zubrzycki, J. (1958). The role of the foreign-language press in migrant integration. *Population Studies, 12,* 73-82.

Zunz, O. (1977). The organization of the American city in the late nineteenth century. *Journal of Urban History, 3,* 443-466.

Zurcher, L., Jr. (1977). *The mutable self: A self-concept for social change.* Beverly Hills, CA: Sage.

Zweigenhaft, R. (1979-1980). American Jews: In or out of the upper class? *Insurgent Sociologist, 9,* 24-37.

Index

About the Author

Young Yun Kim was born and raised in Seoul, Korea. After receiving her B.A. degree from Seoul National University, she came to the United States in 1970 and completed her M.A. degree in 1972 at the University of Hawaii under the sponsorship of the East-West Center. She continued her graduate study at Northwestern University in Evanston, Illinois, where she received her Ph.D. degree in 1976. She began teaching at Governors State University in Illinois, and since 1988 she has been with the Department of Communication at the University of Oklahoma in Norman. Professor Kim teaches courses and directs doctoral theses in the area of intercultural, international, and interethnic/interracial communication. Her research has been aimed primarily at explaining the role of communication in the cross-cultural adaptation processes of immigrants, sojourners, and native-born ethnic minorities. She has conducted original research among Asians, Hispanics, and Native Americans in the United States, and her work has been published in such journals as *Human Communication Research* and *International Journal of Intercultural Relations* as well as in the *Communication Yearbook*. Professor Kim has authored or edited 10 books, including *Interethnic Communication* (1986), *Current Research in Interethnic Communication* (1988, with William B. Gudykunst), *Theories in Intercultural Communication* (1988, with William B. Gudykunst), *Communication and Cross-Cultural Adaptation* (1988), and *Communicating With Strangers* (1997, with William B. Gudykunst). She is an active member of the International Communication Association, the National Communication Association, the International Academy for Intercultural Research, and the International Association of Language and Social Psychology, and she serves on the editorial boards of *Communication Research* and *International Journal of Intercultural Relations*.